TIME OUT FOR WAR

TIME OUT FOR
WAR

Ed C. Cury

TIME OUT FOR WAR

BY ED C. CURY

Produced by Ratzlaff & Associates

Published by Rainbow Books/Betty Wright
2299 Riverside Drive/P.O. Box 1069
Moore Haven, FL 33471

Printed in the United States of America

Note: Some names have been
changed to protect privacy.

Ed Cury (left), motion picture and television star Jack Klugman, comedian Jay Lenno, and TV talk show host Merv Griffin, on *The Merv Griffin Show*.

DEDICATION

To my dear friend Jack Klugman. Jack not only encouraged me to write my story — he told a national television audience, while we were appearing together on the *Merv Griffin Show* that I was writing about my World War II adventures. I had no choice but to complete this book . . . Thanks, Jack!

PREFACE

Captain Ed Cury was a member of one of the most colorful crews in the U.S. Eighth Air Force during World War II. In civilian life, he had co-starred in the original radio show in Tulsa, Oklahoma, with Patti Page and sung with top name bands. A handsome, virile much-decorated officer with an athletic background, Cury had a dashing quality, an air of romance, which women attach to men engaged in the deadly and devastating game of combat.

In October 1943, Ed Cury arrived in the European Theatre of Operations at the beginning of increased, long-range bombing raids. His first assignment was with the 305th Bomb Group at Chelveston, commanded by Colonel (later General) Curtis LeMay.

Fired with eagerness and anxious to engage in combat even before his crew was qualified, Cury volunteered for special night missions in a stripped-down B-17 aircraft to drop chocolate bars wrapped in propaganda leaflets over enemy territory. Two of these night missions were flown with Major Bob Walker, one of the few combat flyers to complete twenty-five missions; any crew member who passed the ten mission mark in those uncertain days was looked upon as a supernatural human being.

Cury's propaganda missions did not count against the illusive twenty-five bombing mission mark which sent crews home on rotation. Nevertheless, he didn't regret making them.It was experience, and if he was to survive, any knowledge he acquired would be invaluable.

Shortly thereafter, Cury and his crew were transferred to the 401st Bomb Group Station 128 at Deenthorpe, England, and assigned to the 615th Bomb Squadron, commanded by Major (later Brigadier General) William T. Seawall, later chairman of the board of Pan American Airlines. The commanding officer of this famous bomb group was Colonel (later Brigadier General) Harold W. Bowman, now retired and living in Tequesta, Florida. The 401st became famous for achieving the second most accurate bombing record in Eighth Air Force history. The group was decorated with many presidential citations and awards for its outstanding ability in the face of great odds.

Indeed, Cury and his crew flew some of the deadliest and most hazardous missions of World War II. One such mission was Ludwigshaven, Germany, where they bombed the I. G. Farben-Industrie Chemical Gas Works. Cury also flew on the well-remembered Oschersleben and Schweinfurt raids as well as the Munich, Brunschweig, Stetin, Keil, Frankfurt, Augsburg, Leipzig and on the first of two Berlin raids, all fiercely defended targets. On the first long-range raid to Berlin, all men married or above the rank of captain had to volunteer, since this was considered a probable no-return mission. Cury's group, part of the 94th Combat Wing in the First Air Division, was assigned to heavy long-range missions.

After surviving the second Berlin raid and on the verge of completing his twenty-five missions, Cury was once again faced by mounting odds. Stepped-up activities approaching D-Day required each man to fly an additional five missions, a total of thirty missions. Since few men made it to the twenty-five mission mark, the additional five missions were akin to signing a death warrant.

On a mission at the end of April 1944, Cury and his crew bombed the newly discovered M262 plants where the first German jets were produced. A week earlier his group had been attacked by the first jets flown by the Luftwaffe.

A participant in the June 6, 1944, D-Day invasion, Cury and his crew flew two missions in one day for a credit of one mission. Here was a place in time Ed Cury was not likely to forget. But he had his pleasures too.

Cury organized a dance band in which he sang to entertain his fellow officers after hours and often guest-starred on the Armed Forces Network. The only other recreational activity on base was drinking and gambling which most combat crews relished; Ed Cury especially loved to play blackjack and poker.

On one stand-down Christmas holiday, Cury broke the crap game as well as the blackjack game. Then, with over $16,000 in winnings, he entered a pot of seven-card hi-lo stud, with the joker wild, poker game. His luck continued against six ranking staff officers, and in a final hand the betting went sky high with table stakes. Finally, the game narrowed to three men: Lt. Colonel (later Major General) Allison Brooks, another lieutenant colonel, and Cury.

Brooks declared hi, the lieutenant colonel declared lo, and Cury had a natural 6-4-3-2-Ace for lo, catching the wild joker on his last draw. So, Cury declared hi and lo, both ways, with a straight flush for hi and a perfect lo. And Cury won!

Lt. Colonel Brooks shook his head in disbelief. He sat there holding four kings, while Cury called his crew to help haul off the loot, 7000 English pounds or $28,000 U.S. He had begun the night with twenty-four pounds chipped in by his crew and a close buddy, Lt. Lou Dubnow. Both on base and off base, Cury was legendary.

After sharing the winnings from his famous card game with the men who had backed him, Cury and his crew were granted a well-deserved 48-hour pass to London by Major Bill Seawell. At the Grosvenor House Hotel, Cury and crew rented six adjoining rooms with a suite. A wild party ensued, even surviving a long and heavy bombing raid by the Luftwaffe.

Before going to London, Cury had promised Seawell he would round up female hostesses and entertainers for the 615th squadron party on base. A day late on his pass, Cury returned in a chartered double-decker English bus loaded with sixty-two girls, to all of whom he'd promised soap, lemons, cigarettes, nylons, candy and ten English pounds each. Needless to say, the squadron party was an enormous success, and the well-liked commanding officer, Colonel Bowman, overlooked another of Cury's wild escapades.

Unknown, though, to Cury, despite his love of fun, games and romance, he was not prepared for what was to happen to him in the do-or-die days ahead. This is the true story which follows, a remarkable adventure which protocol, national security and the moral attitudes of the times prevented Cury from writing until now.

The Publisher

- 1 -

It was 0600 hours, June 19, 1944 . . . after twenty-nine missions, and one more to go . . . The curtain was raised in the briefing room, revealing the target for today, Merignac, a large airfield just outside of Bordeaux, France, where the Germans had concentrated a new supply of reinforcement ME-109s to counter the increased air activity of the Eighth Air Force and an anticipated second invasion. A sigh of relief rippled through the room. A milk run . . . Thank God!

We took off at 0700 hours and had been in the air three hours and ten minutes. We were approaching our target. Then, someone screamed over the intercom, "Bandits, eleven o'clock high!"

Within a split second came more calls: "Bandits coming in, two o'clock level!"

Then: "Bandits, three o'clock high!"

And: "Bandits, head-on at twelve o'clock!"

We had been jumped by a group of ME-109s!

Anyone could've recognized those bastards with their pointed nose spinners, thin black fuselages and blinking orange lights in each wing. Those deadly 20-millimeter cannons were firing. Now they were closing in for the kill and all hell broke loose as the twelve 50-caliber machine guns on our B-17 began firing; it was like twelve thunderstorms wrapped into one!

Our formation closed, but it was too late for evasive action. We were on our bomb run. We were committed and there was no turning back. We held a steady course and prayed to God we were going to make it.

We had flown some very rough missions. But between the ME-109s swarming in the sky and the concentrated flak over the target, I got the uneasy feeling we were in trouble.

The first bastard to come in at eleven o'clock high put a couple of

11

shells into our wing and a direct hit in our number three engine. Immediately the engine burst into flames.

Someone screamed on the intercom, "Two hits in the waist section and one in the radio room!"

Now the plane shook like a stuck pig. The engine was feathered, and we tried to snuff out the fire and steady the aircraft as we reached the I.P.

At 23,000 feet the run from the initial point to the target was only about four minutes. But it seemed like an eternity at 150 mph as we tried to fight off those black bastards. We knew that as soon as we reached the flak area they'd turn off . . . Then all hell broke loose again as we made our run.

The flak was intensely heavy, moreso than anticipated. And the plane shuddered violently . . . Another burst under the same damned engine with two apparent hits in the fuselage and the underside of the rear section . . . That poor old B-17, 002, had about had it!

We dropped our bombs and started our 90-degree turn away from the target. But old 002 was losing altitude so rapidly we had to drop from the formation as the flak continued to burst all around us.

By now we were at 14,000 feet; 002 was on fire and shaking like hell while those goddamn flak guns kept firing on us to make sure we went down. It was here that Bill Trimble began calling on the intercom, "Mayday, Mayday!" This was final. We were going down. It was every man for himself.

I crawled from my seat and into the bomb bay. Parachutes were beginning to blossom outside. I couldn't believe it was really happening. I'd come so far. My luck had held so well. Now this!

The night before in London I had been with a sweet little English WAF I'd been dating. Tough luck . . . I had only laid her once . . . on my last night, probably the last night of my life.

We had just a few hours before she had to get back to her post and I had to catch the last train from Charing Cross. She had rolled over on top of me, kissing me all over, saying, "Honey, please. One more time." But I was worried about missing my train. Now here I was about to die and I hadn't taken advantage of every moment of happiness . . .

My brief interlude of day dreaming was interrupted by the plane flipping over on its back, which threw me right through the radio room and into the rear waist section, where I was slammed against the fuselage bulkhead. Somehow I managed to grab the base of the .50-caliber machine gun on the port side of the waist, but I was thrown hard against it, chest first. Blood gushed from my mouth and nose. I had to get out of that goddamn airplane in a hell of a hurry!

Forcing myself to the side waist door wasn't easy. Centrifugal force pulled me against the opposite side as I fought to gain the exit.

Finally, I got my feet out, hung on for a moment while I pulled down my goggles, and then I tumbled free of the aircraft.

Suddenly the silence was deafening as I floated away. The noise I had left behind had been overpowering. Now this eerie silence . . .

I turned on my back, discovering how easy it was to control the body in a sea of air, and there I watched poor old 002 become engulfed in flames as it turned end over end to meet a fiery finish, hit the ground and, plowing up trees and shrubbery, to explode into a million pieces. She was gone.

I'd bailed out at about 12,000 feet. Instinct and training told me to hold off pulling my ripcord until I was at least 3000 feet above the ground. I knew the Nazis were in a class by themselves; often they gunned down anyone hanging loose in a 'chute.

I held off until I could wait no longer. I pulled my ripcord. And what a jolt! My 'chute blossomed and suddenly I was feeling a bit more optimistic. If I got to the ground safely, I might have a chance. We were only 35 to 40 kilometers north of the target in the peninsula betweeen the Atlantic Ocean and the Gironde River that flows into Bordeaux; I might be able to head south and cross the Pyrenees Mountains into Spain. We had been well-briefed on how to evade and all I needed was some good luck.

Now the ground came up to meet me. My ears popped and I could hear again. My eyes searched the area below. Trucks were converging on crew members who had landed safely. I began to control my parachute so that I drifted toward a large tract of woods. Yes, that was it . . . my only chance was to get into those woods and hide there, since the peninsula was open and flat.

Prior to all our missions we were given escape kits containing maps made of rice, fly buttons which were magnetic compasses to be sewn on our pants, dexedrine tablets, halazone pills to purify water, money for the country we were bombing and language instructions with phrases necessary for evasion and escape. In France we were told to seek refuge or help from local "madams" who operated legitimate whorehouses or contact a Catholic priest. This always amused me; it was one hell of a combination!

Suddenly the ground was coming up toward me, faster and faster. Prior to this I had experienced a gentle flowing, swaying motion. Now, all of a sudden, wham! I hit the dirt hard.

I didn't pause to worry about it. I tumbled into my parachute as I had been trained. Within seconds I had rolled my parachute into a ball, unhooked my harness and started looking for a place to hide the damn thing. This was a ridiculous act since the Nazis had undoubtedly seen me floating to the ground.

The parachute hidden, I yanked out my .45 Army automatic, carried in a shoulder holster under my flying jacket, and threw a shell into the chamber. Then I released the safety. I was ready for anything. Or so I thought.

– 2 –

If I headed north I'd get trapped at the tip of the peninsula. So I took off in a southerly direction. As I started to run, blood gushed from my mouth. It was then that I realized that I had been wounded. I felt my left eye, then my cheek; it was cut open. Somewhere in the fray I recalled getting hit in the leg. But never mind. First things first.

I stumbled across a creek; a sudden wave of weakness swept over me. I paused, tore open my escape kit and swallowed two dexedrine tablets with a gulp of water from the creek. Next, I shed my heavy fur flying jacket. This time I didn't give a damn about hiding it. Then, I took off running full speed.

I don't know how long I ran. But I heard whistles, shots, cars and trucks in the distance. All the while, I kept picturing the Germans as super-human beings. As everyone knew, they were rugged, tall and blond, just as Hollywood depicted them.

I broke out of the woods at the edge of a clearing. A macadam road separated the clearing from a second large tract of woods. I hesitated, took a deep breath and began my run toward the woods on the other side of the road. Half-way across two German soldiers jumped from the woods about thirty yards to my right and yelled, "Halt!" in a typical German accent minus the "H."

Though my gun was in my hand and ready, I wasn't about to fire. My best bet was to reach those trees. Then, the bastards opened fire when I didn't obey their command; one of their shots clipped part of my heel to ricochet off the road and make a hell of a racket. But I kept going. I dived into the underbrush, only to pick myself up and run another fifty yards before stopping to get my bearings. There I glanced over my shoulder.

The two Krauts were coming down the path after me. Much to my surprise they were the raunchiest, mottliest two soldiers I'd ever seen. They wore the typical Kraut helmets but they were dressed in what were fatigues for them, all strapped and belted for combat. Neither of them weighed more than 150 pounds soaking wet, and as they approached I sensed they were as scared as I was. And, believe me, I was scared!

The closer they came the more I could see their hesitation and fright. I decided to try and get the drop on them. I caught the first one with a slug in the neck.

His gun flew flew up in the air, he gurgled and yelled, "*Mein Gott!*" then spun around, going down.

The other German panicked. He dropped his rifle and ran away.

I fired again and heard the slugs bury themselves in his body. My heart was pounding after having killed my first German soldier on the ground, but somehow it didn't bother me. I moved to turn them over, one at a time.

The German I'd shot in the neck was still twitching and making gurgling noises; his eyes were rolling. I reached down and unhooked a couple of his potato masher grenades; they might come in handy. Then, I ran like hell, realizing the folly of lingering there any longer.

While heading south I evaded two other patrols. I wasn't quite so jumpy or gung-ho as I had been with my first encounter. I needed to rest. I took time to hide in a drainage ditch, pulling leaves down over me for cover. Then, a search truck drove up within ten feet of where I was hidden.

About a dozen soldiers jumped out to comb the area. Two stayed by the truck, smoking and talking, of course, in German. I didn't understand a word they were saying, but I got the gist of it. They might not be supermen, but they were looking for me!

My heart pounded. And my right leg and left eye throbbed like hell. I debated the issue of giving myself up. I might bleed to death in this ditch. Then again, I might not. I didn't want to be a prisoner. I wanted to be free, escape. I held off.

Some of the German soldiers on patrol returned to the truck. They had caught one of our men. It looked like Ed Travert, our top turret gunner, and he was all bound up. The German soldiers picked him up and threw him on the truck, kicking and hitting him with their rifle butts.

My first instinct was to try to help him. But a dead hero wouldn't help either of us. Anyway, my first duty was to get the hell out somehow, return to England and fight another day.

I know that sounds corny as hell in this day and age, but most of us felt that way, and I'm one of the real corny ones who still gets a lump in his throat when he sees the stars and stripes flying and hears our national anthem.

Time passed, perhaps fifteen minutes; the rest of the German soldiers returned and boarded the truck. As the truck started to pull away I noticed a machine gun mount on the top of the truck.

15

Suddenly I realized how wise I had been. What a stupid-assed stunt it would have been to try and help Ed with one lousy .45 and a few potato masher grenades.

Now two cars drove up to intercept the truck. Here was my second surprise of the day. Both were Dodge cars, about 1940 vintage, and I wondered: Where in hell did they get them? In time I was to become the most disillusioned soldier in the world. Neutral countries like Spain and Portugal purchased equipment from the United States and this equipment found its way into German hands.

Up to now war had been an impersonal proposition. War was made up of air battles; and, yes, I had indirectly killed many people on the ground when we dropped our bombs. But in the moment reality caught up with me, the kind of reality that doesn't go away, and it was a very, very personal proposition. I held my breath and waited, listening to the thudding of my heart and the Germans talking.

Soon the Germans got their act together; the truck and the two Dodge cars departed. I decided it was best to do the same.

I brushed away my cover and got going, still in a southerly direction, as fast as my legs would carry me. I kept traveling, traveling south. Hours came and went. But I kept moving, though every snapping twig or sound made me jump.

Near dusk I broke into a clearing containing a cluster of three farm houses and a large barn. Two women walked toward a house, and I thought, hell, what've I got to lose; I've got to get help or I'm done for! I stumbled into the clearing and my first words were, "*Je suis Americain*."

The poor women almost jumped from their underwear. Terrified, they dropped what they were carrying and ran into the house, screaming, "*Vite, vite, beaucoup Boche, beaucoup Boche*," meaning, "Quick, quick, many Germans!"

Nevertheless, I went to the door and knocked. I knocked and knocked. They were in there, but they wouldn't come to the door. They just kept yelling something in French which I couldn't make out. I gathered, from the lack of reception, they wanted me to go away. Finally, figuring no help was to be found here, I turned away, saddened. These were our Allies.

Pausing, I glanced back over my shoulder for one last look, shaking my head in disbelief, and an old man in his seventies came from the house, carrying a double-barreled shotgun. At the sight of me, damned if the old bastard didn't blast in my direction with both barrels!

Fortunately I was too far for him to do harm. But I could feel the spent pellets as they hit me. With this, I cursed everyone from President Roosevelt on down. Anyone who had a hand in sending me to help these goddamn frogs!

Overwhelmed by the obvious, I began to run again, picking up a road away from the farm. About ten minutes later I heard motorcycles and looked up to see three old-fashioned motorcycles with sidecars, heading toward me along the road. I remember seeing these as a kid in Allentown, Pennsylvania; the police had used them. Now I was seeing them used by the enemy.

I dived into the bushes as the motorcycles passed. One of them contained a specialized officer with a black uniform. In the other sidecar sat "the sweet, old man" who had taken a blast at me with his shotgun. The old bastard was helping the Krauts look for me.

I was so mad I didn't care what happened now. I pulled the pin on a grenade and heaved it in their direction. It exploded with a hell of a bang, and I got my ass out of there, not waiting to see what happened.

I headed for a small rise. As I reached the top I looked back to see what had happened. The grenade had blown the two motorcycles apart, apparently killing both drivers and one of the passengers. I couldn't make out if the old man was dead or not. Oh, well, who gives a fuck! I decided; get yourself moving.

As I ran I smiled a bit to myself. That was the first grenade I had thrown. I was amazed at the power of the thing. Meanwhile: Hell, I felt like Superman!

This thought kept me going for another five or six kilometers, until I started to hurt and was almost crawling from fatigue. Then, I encountered another small farm house with a few buildings scattered around it. A man stood at the door of the house and temptation caught up with me . . . I hurt so bad . . . Maybe all the French weren't informers. Maybe . . . I took another chance. I walked right up to the man and said brazenly, "*Je suis Americain.* I need help."

"Quick," he said. "Come with me. Soldiers are all over the place looking for you parachutists!"

I had hit the jackpot at last. He even spoke English with some facility. Wonderful!

"Hurry now," he said, urging me along.

I followed him to one of the buildings, a storage room of sorts, and into the back. Potatoes were piled there, a good five or six feet high.

His wife came from the house, followed by another woman. Without a word the women grabbed shovels and started shoveling potatoes off to the side of the room.

Now the man said, "Do you have to go to the bathroom? Are you hungry or thirsty?"

"Hungry and thirsty," I managed. I wanted to go to the bathroom badly, but I was too embarrassed to admit it in front of the women.

He retrieved a bottle of wine from a nook in the building, handed it to me, and spoke to one of the women in French. She went off. Then, he joined the other woman in shoveling potatoes.

In a few moments the first woman returned with a piece of ham, a large hunk of cheese and another bottle of wine.

While I ate the ham and cheese, and drank the wine, the three of them shoveled potatoes. It was all beyond me. But I was enjoying the French cuisine, and I was prepared to accept any and all help which they might offer.

Finally, they got down to the bottom of the potato pile. Quickly they threw down a tarpaulin and a burlap bag. The man told me to lie on top of it.

I felt stupid, but I did what he asked; and with that, they threw another tarpaulin over me, saying to keep quiet no matter what happened.

Back to shoveling they went, only this time they shoveled the potatoes atop me. The weight of the potatoes grew heavier and heavier. I wiggled myself a fairly good air space. I was even able to finish off the last of the cheese and sip some wine from the bottle.

At long last the decision was made for me on the bathroom front. I couldn't hold off any longer. It wasn't the greatest experience of my life, not with about two tons of potatoes weighing me down. But there it was, and I could smell myself in the worst way. I began to worry. If the Germans came, would they smell my awful stench?

Outside life went on, the kind of life I dreaded. I heard cars and motorcyles, followed by much commotion and excitement. The Germans were there, and clearly, they were searching the buildings and questioning the Frenchman. Then, I heard the dreaded sound of the door to the building in which I was hidden being opened. Footsteps crossed the stone floor. They stopped at the potato pile. Conversation ensued. Finally, a German gave a command. Shots were fired into the pile of potatoes.

What a lousy way to die! I thought, bracing myself for the end as shells pounded into the potatoes, hitting the stone floor, then richocheting back into the potatoes. At long last, the burst of fire ended. I had survived; and I wilted with relief . . . Then, it happened again. Another burst. The good Lord must've been watching over me. Once again I went unscathed, though my ears rang from the shooting. Almost any minute I expected it to begin again. It didn't. They left the room.

It had been hot under all those potatoes, but now I broke into a cold sweat and began to shake violently. All this crap about being a hero was so much bullshit. I was as scared as anyone could possibly be and not die of heart failure!

After a while I sipped the rest of the wine and tried to get a handle on myself. It wasn't easy with that load of crap in my pants. But I was grateful. Grateful to be alive.

Time passed. The potatoes began to move. They were shoveling. As they drew closer, I thought about my pants. How could I face anyone in this condition? Oh, shit!

The tarp was pulled away. I tried to get up, but I couldn't move.

Nothing worked but my arms and my head a bit.

The man came over and offered me a shot of what I thought was water from a plain bottle.

I took one great gulp and nearly choked. It was white cognac; and it was devastating. Though I waved him away, he insisted I take a couple of more swallows. I braced myself and forced it down. He was right. I began to feel better.

The woman, apparently his wife, massaged my legs and shoulders. When the feeling returned, they helped me to my feet, and then, the wife must've guessed what had happened to me, or smelled it. She went out and returned with an old towel, soaked it in water, and told me to drop my pants.

Like a good boy, I did. She cleaned me up. Believe me, this was humiliation at its worst!

Now the man said, "Do you have to go to the bathroom again?"

This time I answered, "Yes," firmly.

They helped me walk to an outhouse in back of the building where I did my thing to avoid further such disasters.

Upon my return the man said, "I've contacted someone in the F.F.I."

That was the French Forces of the Interior, a small organization, and not so well organized as the larger group, the F.T.P.F. — the Communist Party Underground Group. But it was part of the French Underground. "Good," I said.

"Help should come later, by evening."

It was now early morning. I had a long wait, and I didn't want to contemplate another day under the potatoes. I guess it showed.

"Don't worry," he said with a smile. "We have another hiding place for you. More comfortable."

He and his wife led me about 400 yards from the building into a small ravine with a large concrete drain pipe. "Crawl into the drain pipe," he said. "This will be your hiding place."

His wife passed me a small cloth bag. "Food and wine," she said.

"I could use a drink of water . . . "

"It's not fit to drink," the man said. "Anyway, water is only for fish and frogs to swim in. If you're thirsty, drink the wine." He covered the drain pipe opening with leaves, branches and twigs for camouflage.

Crazy, but I craved water, now that I couldn't get it. I would have given a month's pay for one cold glass of water, but it was not to be.

They departed, and I settled in, swallowing another dexedrine tablet. My wounds were bothering me, and it was better to have my temples pound than experience the pain. Eventually, I crawled to the edge of the pipe and peeked out, swallowing gulps of fresh air. This was so much better than being trapped under the potatoes, I couldn't resist it. Anyway, I figured they weren't taking any chances, so neither was I. I pressed my luck no further, for now.

– 3 –

Dusk arrived early. I glanced at my luminous dial watch. It was exactly 1800 hours. Then, I heard noises. My French friend had returned with two other men. Both of these men were armed to the teeth. Each carried one of our Thompson sub-machine guns along with English service pistols and grenade belts. Neither of the men spoke good English. But the man who had befriended me, hidden me from the Germans, said, "These men are members of the F.F.I. They will take you to join some of your comrades. They have located four of the men from your aircraft, and they are well."

Encouraged and hopeful, I was ready to leave. But my friend cautioned me, "You must follow these men, and no matter what happens, keep going in the general direction they are going. You will have to cross through German lines, pass within a few hundred yards of a German station. Now we prepare for the farewell."

His name, he said, was Louis. He was genuinely glad I had made it this far. He kissed me first on one cheek, then, the other. Now nothing would do but that I go by the farm house on my way out; his wife and sister-in-law wanted to say goodbye.

His wife had prepared a dish which appeared to be scrambled eggs, peas and onions. "You must eat," Louis' wife said. "It may be the only hot food you will get for some time." She poured the whole panfull on one plate, gave me a piece of bread, and ordered me to eat.

The three of them stood watching, urging me on. I put all the food away in minutes, washed it down with three full glasses of a delicious French white wine which they told me was *St.-Croix-du-Mont*. It was a rare white wine they had hidden in their backyard when the Germans had first occupied France. Regardless, I hadn't tasted better food or wine. I couldn't have gotten a finer meal in the grandest of restaurants.

Stuffed and feeling better, I said my goodbyes. Then, I took off with the two men who had arrived to pick me up.

We evaded two patrols — close calls — but these guys were real pros. They knew just when to move and how not to make a sound. They made me take off my shoes, as they did themselves two or three times. I thought to myself, These fellows know all the tricks! After all, it was night and we traveled only with the light of the moon.

They were nice looking chaps, Robere and "Jean le Boucher," the latter meaning, "Jean the Butcher." Where Jean had picked up the last part of his name went unexplained, but my admiration for them grew as the night wore on.

It was almost dawn when we arrived at a large open meadow with foot-high grass growing in it. Now we had to crawl on all fours as we headed for trees about 100 yards away. It seemed to take hours. My hands bled, my pants tore and my knees became raw as hell. But I made it.

On the other side of the meadow, we rested, and Robere blew three short whistles. Three short whistles were returned from the top of a tree less than ten feet away.

I looked up, and there was this guy in a tree, an automatic rifle pointed at us!

Still we waited, until Robere gave another whistle. At this point, four men came out and joined us, all happy that I had been found. They led us to an old abandoned farm house where a joyful reunion was in order.

There I found my closest buddy and skipper, Bill Trimble, as well as Joe Allard, Paul Gordon and Ed Macy. Immediately we set to exchanging experiences. Then, I said, "What happened to the other fellows?"

Swantz, who had panicked, had been the first to bail out; apparently he had gotten away. The other men were either captured or dead. Evidently, we were the only ones remaining. As it turned out, Swantz was never captured; he made his way to Bordeaux and onward to Toulouse, getting help from the French Underground and escaping over the Pyrenees to safety.

Louis and his wife were right when they'd told me it might be some time before I had another hot meal. There was nothing here, except wine to drink. However, I was able to get water.

An old well was in the middle of the yard. Finally, I talked one of the Frenchmen into letting me bring up a bucket of it. But he cautioned me to cut it with half wine since most of the water in France was contaminated.

I did exactly as he directed, and it wasn't bad. But when he wasn't looking, I took one big swallow of pure water, and you won't believe how good it tasted. Then, I drew another bucket and poured the water all over myself.

About forty men inhabited the abandoned farm house, and I understood this was the hard core group of the French Forces of the Interior. These were men who had fled or escaped the Germans. They had chosen to fight the Germans in any way they could. Now they were helping to save Americans. All were patriotic Frenchmen.

"What can we do for you?" they begged.

Although only a few spoke English, they wanted to be of help.

Robere brought me a clean towel, soap, a razor, and shaving soap. I don't know why in hell I wanted to shave, but it seemed like a good idea at the time.

An old beat up galvanized tub appeared; I cleaned it out and filled it with water. I bathed, shaved and freshened up as much as possible, feeling more like a human being than a hunted man.

The French bandaged my face as best they could and patched up my leg. Within a day or two, they said, a doctor would look at it, when we arrived at the main camp.

Afterwards we all sat around on the shady side of the barn. A feeling of tiredness caught up with me. Was it safe to sleep? Yes, it would be safe for me to take a nap. I stretched out on the ground and was asleep in seconds. Late in the afternoon I awoke.

Bill said, "You slept like the dead. I tried to wake you up a couple of times, and all you did was grunt and push me away!"

I could believe him. I had been the only guy to take a catnap on the way back from bombing Berlin!

Robere appeared with two machine guns. "Choose one," he said.

I picked up a folding stock .30-caliber type, manufactured by Americam Armament of Connecticut. Just touching it made me feel closer to home.

In talking to Robere I learned he was from North Africa. He had been a policeman in Algiers and later was taken prisoner by the Germans and sent to Germany to do slave labor. He had escaped and here he was.

Another of the men who befriended me was a fairly big guy named Pasqual. He was a former Italian officer, a captain who had deserted and taken up with a girl he met in an elaborate brothel which Mussolini had built in North Africa. Somehow I never found out how he had made his way to Algiers before World War II began and joined the Free French Forces. He too had been taken prisoner and escaped with Robere. I enjoyed his many tales of fighting in Ethiopia and Libya, and all his love affairs. He was a most interesting fellow.

Robere and Pasqual spent hours teaching me French. It was amazing how fast I picked it up, now that I really needed it.

Another friendly chap was a 17-year-old kid, one they called, "Bouchere." His father and two brothers had been killed by the Germans; he had such a terrible hatred for them that whenever he killed a German he always used a knife. Bouchere was forever sharpening his long pig-sticker knife, when he wasn't playing a sad French tune on his harmonica!

After the first few days in camp we met the leader of the F.F.I. Group, Colonel Charles Cometti. He arrived with other Maquis. He went by the name of "Colonel Charlie".

When I shook the man's hand I experienced an immediate dislike and distrust of him. His handshake was limp. His left hand had three missing fingers. Meanwhile, he couldn't look you in the eyes when he spoke to you.

Colonel Charlie came and went as he pleased. During our stay at the farm house he was there three or four times. He drove a car that wasn't run by charcoal burners as others were.

The second day one of the men brought in two buckets of mussels, the tiny variety. We sat around opening mussels and eating what little meat there was inside of them. They tasted lousy. But we were starved.

Our only other food was on approximately the fourth day. One of the men stole a cow from a neighboring farm. They brought the cow in, spread its hind legs and tied a board across them. Then, they tied a rope to the board and hauled it up over a branch till the cow's head hung about a foot from the ground. Finally, they slit the cow's throat as neatly as could be. The cow didn't make a sound!

After the blood drained, the cow was skinned. Bouchere and another chap ripped it open, disemboweling it and cutting off all the choice parts. Next they took several chunks of beef and placed them in the tub I had used to wash myself, adding water and wine along with salt, potatoes and what appeared to be turnips. This was cooked over an open fire for three or four hours. Surprisingly, it tasted damn good, and the cow took care of our hunger for a while.

I wondered how long this could go on. Then, we were told we'd be moving to the main camp within a few days. The new camp was off the peninsula and into the mainland, about 45 kilometers from where we were. We would leave camp in parties of three or four, Robere said; we mustn't arouse suspicion. In this manner we'd have a better chance of slipping through German lines.

The second week we had another pleasant reunion. They brought in Malden and Zemke, our navigator. Both Malden and Zemke had been picked up by Frenchmen farther south and had been hidden while the Germans intensified their search to the north.

By now we had gotten to know most of the fellows pretty well. Our French was improving, the lines of communication were opening. I felt much more at ease and took to going out to an old abandoned truck, a 1930 vintage Chevrolet.

The truck was stripped. Weeds grew around it. But here was a cool, shady spot, and often I went there by myself, or Bill Trimble would go with me and we'd chew the fat. We discussed how we were going to get out of there. We were tired of sleeping on the ground, living like animals.

In an attempt to improve our sleeping conditions Bill and I cut ferns from around the truck and brought them back to the old barn. We piled the ferns up in the shape of a bed. Then, we threw blankets over them and placed rocks around the edges of the blanket. Now we had a nice soft cushion on which to sleep. Meanwhile, I made the same kind of bed out by the abandoned truck to ease my recreational hours.

Colonel Charlie arrived then and said we would be leaving in a few days. Other members of the F.F.I. would be arriving at that time. He began to bug me about my A-2 leather flying jacket which I had always worn under my heated jacket, the one I'd discarded right after being shot down.

I made a deal with him. If he'd give me his black wool jacket, I'd give him my A-2 flying jacket. I figured I had a better chance without a jacket that carried my name, rank and insignia on it.

Although sentries were posted around the perimeter of the farm, we were allowed to wander anywhere within this area. Bill and I talked about the possibilities of getting to Toulouse and crossing the Pyrenees Mountains, even if we had to do it by ourselves. Some of these people were a bit weird; we didn't quite trust them to get us through.

Meanwhile, the routine continued much the same. We rose in the morning, lay around in the sun, ate whatever we could scrounge or was brought in and prayed that somehow we could get out of there. We had a habit of going to bed early since we didn't dare have a fire at night, nor were we allowed to smoke.

One particular night was muggy and hot. "It's stuffy in here," I complained to Bill. Though the barn had holes in the roof, this didn't seem to help. "I'm going to sleep in the old truck. Want to go along?"

Bill was out like a light by the time I finished my complaint. So I went off alone, picking up a cloth bag which held some grenades, my gun, and the .30-caliber machine gun. I don't know what prompted me to do this but I had that uneasy feeling which says something is about to happen.

Once at the truck in the open air and on my fern mattress, I dropped off to sleep. I don't know how long I'd been sleeping, when I jerked awake. I lay there listening.

I thought I heard the sound of a twin-engined aircraft. The sky was dark, but as I searched it intently a Luftwaffe twin-engined light bomber appeared overhead. Something dropped from the plane and the sky lit up like a Christmas tree. Flares were being dropped all over the place. Then, two other planes came over, dropping anti-personnel bombs. Three fighter planes followed and began strafing the farm. All hell broke loose . . . The men were screaming, shooting and firing in every direction. It was pandemonium!

Through the racket I heard the sound of trucks closing in. A trap had been set, a well coordinated trap!

Instinctively, I rolled under the truck to protect myself from shrapnel and the shooting. As I rolled out from under the other side of the truck I sprang to my feet and ran toward the barn to see if Bill and the others were all right.

As I came to an open space two trucks drove up. German troops began pouring from the trucks. These were followed by two weapon carriers full of Krauts. I fought my way back to the truck, dived under it and crawled out the other side where the bushes were higher. In the doing, I picked up the bag of grenades.

Now I crawled through the fields away from the farm. There was no more fighting back. From the commotion that reached my ears it seemed to me that everyone had been captured or killed. Later I learned that only two had escaped.

I was one of the two.

– 4 –

Soaking wet from the morning dew, I was torn and badly scratched from crawling through a field of prickly bushes. But still I pressed on.

Reaching an irrigation ditch, I tumbled into it, then began running again. Twice I was surprised by German soldiers. It seemed they had executed a well-planned operation, surrounding the entire area prior to the strike. I suspected Colonel Charlie. Later it turned out my hunch was right. He was a double agent, working for the Gestapo. Charles Cometti was tried and executed as a traitor after the war. (See newspaper clipping in center section.)

Though I kept crawling, running, hiding, I didn't know where to turn. Finally, I remembered the farm house where the Frenchman Louis had befriended me. I don't know how I did it, but I made it back to that farm!

Louis said, "I heard what happened. The Germans are everywhere. I can't take a chance on hiding you. The Germans were here less than thirty minutes ago. Your best bet is to head south to an abandoned old winery."

"How far?" I asked.

"Five kilometers." Then he gave me directions and said he would try to contact someone from another underground group, adding, "It may be a day or two before you hear from anyone. Keep under cover."

"I will," I promised.

Even in the excitement he asked, "Are you hungry or thirsty?"

I was.

He ran into the house and came out with several bottles of wine, some cheese and a loaf of bread in a bag. "Make this last as long as you can. Remember, it may be a day or two before you hear from anyone."

I couldn't blame Louis for not wanting to hide me on his farm. If he were caught harboring or aiding me the penalty was death for him and his entire family.

Thanking him and waving goodbye, I took off, following his directions as best I could, keeping away from roads and trails. At length I came upon a fairly decent path through the woods. I kept on this path until I came upon a small crossroad with a sign that gave directions to St. Laurent de Medoc. This told me I wasn't too far from the old winery. But I didn't want to cross the road and expose myself.

I tried to detour around. I couldn't. It was that simple. I would have to cross the road. I paused to catch my breath, deciding the only way to do it was to run like hell, crossing the road into the brush on the other side. One quick dash, I told myself.

Without hesitation, I was off and all hell broke loose on my left. Less than 100 yards away was a truck with a machine gun and crew. They had opened fire on me. Luckily, I reached the other side without getting hit.

I could hear the truck turning around to come back up the road toward me; orders were given. And ahead of me the brush was thinning out. So I doubled back, running parallel to the road in an area which was heavily covered with brush. The brush ended less than thirty yards off the road. I called it quits right here. Digging into the brush, I stayed there, not moving a muscle, my throat dry, my heart pounding away in my ears. I expected to be found almost any minute.

At this point, for some crazy reason, I pulled the pin from one of the grenades and held the release down with my thumb. I knew there was a delay on the release; if I had to let go of it I would at least have a head start.

Meanwhile, the Germans had split into two groups. Four of the men were coming towards me . . . It was now or never.

When they were less than fifty feet away I heaved the grenade, at the same time firing the small machine gun. Two of them dropped before the grenade went off. And when the grenade exploded it wiped out the other two. That done, I panicked!

I ran into the road instead of back for the trail, passing the truck which was unattended. My last remaining grenade I heaved at the truck, thinking they'd not have a truck in which to chase me.

The grenade exploded, blowing the truck over and setting it on fire. What a bonfire! But I'd been stupid. Now they'd be on my ass for sure.

I put on speed, heading down the road until I came to another small crossroad with a sign: Pauliac. I was traveling north again. I turned south towards the old winery, doubling back on my own tracks, turning into the woods again, until I found the trail I'd followed previously. After another kilometer or two I almost ran into a patrol. But I jumped off to the side of the trail, next to a very large tree. I thought I might have a better chance in the tree than on the trail. Up I climbed, about twelve feet off the ground, to straddle a large limb where I had a good view of the trail.

Sure enough, four soldiers from the truck were doubling back, having decided, no doubt, that I'd gotten away or gone in the other direction.

Now they were beneath me. I held my breath, thinking: Please don't look up! This was when I realized how stupid the Germans were. Their helmets came down over the back of the neck; they couldn't look up as long as they wore those damn helmets. Then, the wind went out of me. They stopped beneath me, one of the soldiers putting his rifle down. He had to take a crap, and he removed his jacket and harness to do so.

The other Germans lit up cigarettes, taking a breather, talking. After about ten minutes, one of the German noncoms gave an order; they picked up their gear and went back along the trail in the direction of the road. I laughed to myself, thinking: What a surprise! Your damn truck is on fire!

I sat in the tree for another five minutes, wanting to be sure the Germans were well along the trail. Then I slid down the tree. As my feet touched the ground I was off and running in a southerly direction. I didn't slow down until I reached the old winery.

Carefully I looked about the place before crossing the open ground around the winery. Satisfied that it was clear, I took a chance.

One of the old buildings had quite a bit of equipment in it along with a large, round, concrete tub which looked like something they might have used to mash grapes. There was also a spring in the room with a step down to concrete slabs. I peered into it, and there was clear, cool, refreshing water. Someone had dug down and built a well which held the spring water. Another level had an overflow which ran outside the building. It was wonderful!

I submerged my face in the water, easing the pain of my wounds. Beautiful! I grabbed a hunk of moss from the edge of the reservoir, soaking it in water, then, using it as a swab for my wounds. I don't know how long I stayed there, but I was grateful for this moment of respite and the cool, clear water.

There were three buildings in all. Only two of them had roofs. I couldn't understand why there were so many abandoned farms and wineries. I didn't know it then, but I was in the most famous of all wine regions. I later ran across an old sign which read: Castlemau de Medoc.

In the fray I had not lost my sack of wine, cheese and bread which had been strapped over my shoulder. As I calmed down hunger pains caught up with me. Sitting by the spring, I tore off a piece of bread and broke off a hunk of cheese which I washed down with the red Bordeaux wine. A feeling of confidence in myself and my ability to survive returned to me.

A strong breeze came from the west, the direction of the ocean, and it began to cool off rapidly. I was glad I'd made the trade for Colonel Charlie's warm jacket. Now all I needed was some sleep. But my better judgment told me not to bunk in any of the buildings. Finally, I found a sheltered spot about 100 yards from the winery in fairly dense woods.

I gathered up some ferns, softened the ground a bit, and settled in. I had barely closed my eyes when a weapon's carrier truck and two motorcycles drove up.

The truck had a searchlight and a mounted machine gun. It carried about seven or eight men. Soon they were out of the truck, searching the buildings. Moments later, convinced no one was there, they took off again. Mentally, I patted myself on the back for making the right decision one more time.

That night, as I lay there looking up at the sky, I thought about the unbelievable: what had happened to me. I remembered my buddies too, worried about them, wondering what had happened to them. I was lonely . . . in a strange land. Then my mind wandered home to Allentown, Pennsylvania, to my parents, my sister, my brothers. If they had been notified about me I prayed they had been told I was missing in action rather than killed in action. Later I was to find out my parents had received a cold, impersonal telegram from the War Department, stating their son was missing in action in enemy territory. The telegram was signed: "Ulio, the Adjutant General."

Thinking back over my life and my escape, I began to get a very cocky feeling. Call it arrogance, I don't mind. Whatever, I knew, knew for a fact, I would find my way out. I had restored my confidence and my faith in God. I could see this thing through and my faith would keep me going.

With this thought firmly in mind I dozed off and slept soundly until the bright sun shining in my eyes awakened me with a start. Something nearby had moved. Cautiously, I glanced around. It was a squirrel.

The squirrel was pecking at my food bag which lay near to me. I smiled, admiring the squirrel, thinking: What a beautiful tame creature of God!

At peace with the Lord, the squirrel had only one worry: to find something to eat. And here I was, a human being, hunted like an animal of prey.

I jumped up and tore my bed apart. I hid the ferns and rocks so that no one could imagine anyone had slept there. Then I circled the entire perimeter of the winery. It was safe, I felt, to go into the main building with the wonderful spring.

Inside the building, I dipped my head in the spring and washed myself off. I followed with a couple of swallows of water. To hell with contamination! It had to do me some good; my body needed liquids, and I was damned tired of drinking wine.

In the days ahead I found that everyone in France drank wine. Even little children were given half 'n half — half wine, half water. Seldom were they given milk although there were plenty of dairy cows. I don't know if this is good or bad. But for myself I know that I had little milk as a child, because we couldn't afford it. The only time I got milk was at breakfast when my mother served us half milk and half coffee with a roll or bagel to dip into the mixture. It was odd how my mind kept drifting back to little details of my life: the good food my mother had cooked, the many places we hung out, my buddies Lou Dubnow, Phil Parkinson, Lee Iacocca and the other kids I ran with, the girls I had gone with, all the pre-war memories . . .

Meanwhile, here I was in France, and I had yet to see a pretty French girl, the kind I had seen in movies, read about in stories or heard of by word of mouth. Never mind. I had more pressing matters at hand.

I thought about Louis' instructions to *cache* here and keep out of sight until someone from the French Underground contacted me. After washing up in the spring and eating the last of the cheese and bread, being very careful not to leave any telltale signs of my presence, I returned to the place where I had slept. It was a good vantage point. I could look out on the only road coming into the winery and on the foot trail I had followed.

Since I had so little to occupy my mind, except to watch the trail and the road, I took to brooding over my plight. Why in the hell did it have to be me? Then, I thought of my buddies. They could be in worse shape than I was. They were. They had all been captured, taken to Angouleme prison and from there transferred to Germany.

Along toward the end of that day I decided on another "dip in my pool." I paused, listening. Something was coming. This time it was an open touring car, a 1936 or 1938 Chrysler Motors product, mounted with a RDF (Radio Direction Finder). Two S.S. officers sat in the front seat along with a driver; three S.S. soldiers sat in back.

These guys were all young, well-built, wearing battle fatigues and combat equipment. But these babies had on their peaked caps. They looked like a different breed from the earlier Germans I'd encountered. And they were. They were the crack S.S. Wafen soldiers, and they acted the part as they carried out orders.

The touring car had driven directly to the building with the spring in it. I hoped that the spot where I had washed up had dried, and there were no telltale marks to give me away.

The Germans couldn't have been in there for more than two or three minutes. Then, they ran to each of the other buildings. Unlike the previous patrol these bastards split up and covered the area's whole perimeter.

Fortunately, I was well hidden, yet close enough to see their faces. They were grim, determined, real cold fish. I toyed with the idea of opening up on them with my machine gun. I even found myself leveling the .30-caliber machine gun right at them. I wanted to squeeze the trigger in the worst way, a stupid thought. If I didn't get them all, there'd be no place to hide. Still, I had come to hate them in a very personal fashion. I wanted to do it. I poised, ready to play my hand.

They rallied at the touring car, joking and laughing now, satisfied no one was around. They climbed into their vehicle and zoomed off down the bumpy old road.

Much later that day I heard noises coming along the trail. I watched cautiously as three Frenchmen strode into the open clearing. The manner in which they looked around told me they were "Maquis". They were more careful than those I'd met earlier. One stayed on the trail and the other two circled the area prior to going into the buildings one by one.

I stayed where I was, though. I wanted to be sure as hell they were friendly before exposing myself. Finally, the tallest of the three called out, "Eduarde, Eduarde!" I knew damn well they couldn't know my name unless Louis had told them. I waited another minute or two. Taking a good grip on my machine gun, I walked toward them.

They leveled their guns on me, the tallest, speaking fairly good English, saying, 'You are Eduarde, the escaped flyer, are you not?"

"Yes . . . " Then there was the usual, the kissing and hugging.

One thing I was learning: Frenchmen loved to hug and kiss. It was okay by me. I couldn't have been happier at seeing these Maquis.

They introduced themselves. The English-speaking fellow was Armand. The other two were Michel and Maurice. They appeared to be much sharper than the other Maquis, more intelligent in many ways.

I hadn't realized it but I was limping as I came toward them. Armand said, "Your leg. What is the matter?" I pulled up my trouser leg and showed him the angry wound.

He whistled softly, saying, *"Merde!"* a French curse word.

"That bad, huh?"

He nodded. The wound was swollen and beginning to fester. They would take care of it as best they could, right then and there.

We entered the building with the spring. Armand took out a knife, scraping away the scab on my leg and squeezing it. He seemed to know what he was doing. Painful as it was, I was ready for any help I could get. As he squeezed, the pus oozed from my leg, but he kept on squeezing until it was only blood. Then, he tore off a piece of his shirt tail and soaked it with water, washing away the blood. He called to Michel to bring a bottle of cognac they carried with them.

He poured the cognac slowly over the wound.

I wanted to scream. The goddamn stuff was more than 100 proof. It burned like hell. But it did feel better.

That done, Armand instructed Michel to go out and get "piger leaves." Michel returned with about half a dozen little round leaves. At home, as kids, we had called them "tiger pig leaves." Armand washed the leaves off and placed them atop my wound. Then he took the wet rag and wrapped it around my leg.

About half a bottle of cognac was left. Armand said, "Take a couple of big swallows. You will need it," adding: "The Boche are everywhere." He was going to try to get me to Lesparre where I could get medical attention and a place to hide. "We know we take chances, but there is nothing else to do. We must get you out of this area. A $5000 reward in gold is being given for your hide."

"That much?" I was astounded that I'd become so important.

He nodded. "We must take good care. Many Frenchmen are playing with the Boche. They would just as soon see you in German hands."

I told him about my first encounter with the old Frenchman who had trained his shotgun on me.

He shrugged and laughed. "We get turned in about once a week. Please join the club." Now he gave his attention to our departure.

I had my bag which contained my gun, machine gun and a bottle of wine.

"Hang on to it," Armand said. "You might need it all. Do you feel well enough to leave?"

My leg felt much improved, but I hated going in broad daylight. Still, they seemed to know best.

We had walked a couple of kilometers when we came to a road. A German patrol was covering it. We had to go back, running parallel to the road, to cross in another area where we didn't think we'd be seen.

Armand instructed Michel to cross the road first, then Maurice, then me. "I will cover. Just in case."

These babies used military tactics similar to our own ground infantry; I couldn't help but admire them.

Somehow we arrived outside Lesparre. I looked down the road and there was the town. But first . . . We would circle the town and go clear to the other side to some friends.

Circle we did, and another three kilometers beyond the town we came upon a farm house. Armand went directly to the door and called out. The door was opened and we received a friendly reception from a big strapping fellow with blond hair. His wife was an attractive petite brunette.

In broken English the fellow told me, I am *le Belgique*," meaning he was called "The Belgian." He'd been living in France since he'd married a French woman. They owned a good size dairy farm. When we had arrived I'd noticed a large barn and the black and white cows.

Now he introduced me to his family and friends. There was his wife, his daughter of fourteen, and his sister-in-law who was in her early thirties.

The sister-in-law was an attractive woman. When we were introduced she took my hand, held it and looked straight into my eyes, as if saying, "I'd like to go to bed with you." Her verbal response was: "Please call me, Lucien."

The family had been expecting us and had cooked a special dinner. We had soup, three or four vegetables with the main course of *lapin*, or rabbit. I had never eaten rabbit before. But they had fried it with onions, and it was delicious. In my condition, anything would have tasted good!

Throughout the meal they apologized because dinner was only three courses. Usually they had a six-to-eight course dinner in normal times, leisurely meals always. But under the circumstances they couldn't keep me in the house too long. German activity in the area was great.

We had just finished dinner when Armand thought he heard something amiss outside. He went to the door and opened it. There was one of their farm boys, a kid about fifteen. He entered the house. Armand said, "What are you doing here?"

It seemed the boy had been dismissed from work earlier and he had seen Germans down the road. The Germans were going from farm to farm, searching for me.

Armand decided we should stay out of sight, away from the farm house. But Belgique insisted we stay in a second barn, a hundred yards from the main house where he stored hay and corn for the cows. Finally, it was agreed that I needed a good night's sleep. So, I was to sleep in that barn while Armand and his two buddies stayed in the main barn. If the Germans came, Armand and his buddies could be passed off as visiting relatives since they had identity cards. Meanwhile, with all the commotion, I'd be alerted and have a chance to escape. Next came the instructions on what I should do if the Germans came, and where I should head and hide.

Belgique's sister-in-law insisted on packing a small lunch for me. I was so full of dinner I couldn't have cared less. She promised to bring it to me later; she thought I might get hungry again. Then, she went on to tell me I was typically American, just like those she had seen in pre-war cinemas. All this because I answered, "Okay!"

Down at the second barn Armand instructed me to hide in the upper loft, loaded with hay. A couple of old burlap bags, a blanket and a pillow, were provided for comfort.

I fixed up my bed, went outside to relieve myself, and had just flipped the small wooden latch on the barn door when a soft knocking occurred, followed by a soft voice saying, "Lucien." She had brought me a little snack since we didn't have dessert with dinner. I had a feeling what she had in mind for "dessert."

She lit a small candle she'd brought with her. We climbed into the loft and she opened a pouch which had been wrapped in a dish towel, revealing pastry cakes and a bottle of cognac. Now she insisted I eat a few of the small cakes and take a drink of the cognac. It was pretty rough. But I followed instructions. Meanwhile, it was Armand's instructions that I keep the bottle of cognac and continue pouring it over the bandage on my sore leg.

I pulled up my pant leg, removed the bandage, and she poured the cognac.

I gritted my teeth to keep from yelling. Never mind, Lucien was prepared for anything. She had a piece of bed sheet and made a new bandage for my leg, wrapping the bandage carefully, then, again, pouring cognac on the bandage. The original sting had numbed the wound, and I was up to anything. So was Lucien.

She massaged my leg, running her fingers right up my trouser leg to the side of my thigh and rubbing ever so lightly.

Although I was a normal young man, sex had been the last thing on my mind since I bailed out of 002. But Mother Nature knew best.

She unbuttoned my fly and out popped the jack-in-the-box. Once more, never mind. I allowed her to proceed, getting in the mood, when the sound of motorcycles and trucks entered our reverie. No longer was I lost in the pleasures of sex.

I jumped up, banging my head on the rafters. The jack-in-the-box wasn't interested any more either. Quickly I re-arranged myself, buttoned my pants, and put on my shoes. Hurriedly, Lucien on my heels, I peered through a small window at the farm house.

Two motorcycles, a truck and a touring car, all with soldiers pouring out of them, were there to see. The Germans began pounding on the front door, shouting something.

Lucien translated: "Open up or we'll shoot the goddamn door in!"

Quickly, I said, *"Adieu,"* to Lucien and followed Armand's instructions. I grabbed the small pouch of remaining cakes and the bottle of cognac. Then I got out of there in a hurry, Lucien complaining, "Now how am I ever going to explain my presence here?" I couldn't worry about that and said as much.

I went through the window, over the back roof and dropped to the ground. Crouching low, I headed for the trees Armand had pointed out.

Behind me there was much yelling and screaming. I wanted to look back, perhaps see if I could help. But I knew there was no helping.

I was on the run . . . again.

– 5 –

Forty-five minutes later I arrived at the place Armand had described to me in his instructions, the site of another old abandoned winery.

I circled the area and then picked a place to stretch out fifty yards from the winery buildings. Less than an hour passed and there was Armand and Michel, relating a grim story.

The young farm hand had told the Germans that an American was being hidden at the farm, hoping to be rewarded the $5000 in gold. The Germans had dragged the Belgian, his wife and daughter outside while they searched the house, the kid insisting I was there. Finally, Armand had told Maurice to walk right up to the farm house and tell the Germans, "I am the guest. I was here for dinner. The kid is mistaken."

Well, Maurice did, the Krauts grabbed him, said everyone was lying and shot the Belgian, his wife, daughter, and Maurice.

I shook my head in despair. "And Lucien?" I asked, remembering our brief loving moment.

Lucien had been very lucky. If she had stayed in the farm house, she would have been killed too.

The shooting had boiled down to such a simplistic matter. The Germans had counted the dishes that had been washed and placed in the sink. When all the guests couldn't be accounted for, the Germans had known the truth and shot them all in cold blood.

I couldn't believe these bastards. My hatred for the Nazis was growing ever bigger. I made up my mind. The next Kraut I ran into, chance or no chance, I'd blow his goddamn head off!

Armand said, "Even as we speak, my comrades are looking for the boy who turned us in. They will get him, you know."

The only thing I knew: Nobody was safe!

"Come, my friend," he said quietly. "We must go."

We headed down a trail through the woods, traveling until the sun rose, when we reached another of their hiding places in the woods. We would stay there until joined by others.

We found a good place to sleep. Both Armand and Michel were very calm, though I knew they hurt within over the loss of their friends. But it didn't show. Me? Well, I was about done in by shock and horror.

At noon the next day we were joined by another Maquis. Immediately, he reported that they had located the boy turned traitor. His name was Richarde. They were waiting for dark to grab him and expected to make an example of him, though they were afraid, in doing this, that others would be tempted to turn us in. Whatever, we stayed out of sight that day. About three hours after the sun set, we heard a commotion . . . I looked up. It was the kid, Richarde. He was blindfolded and his hands were tied. They had brought him to Armand and me.

They removed his blindfold so that he could see us. Then the bastard started spouting off at me in French: "Just wait! The Germans will get you. You'll get what's coming to you!"

Armand slapped the little bastard across the mouth, drawing blood. Then they gagged him and hauled him over to a small stump where they tied him up.

"You will now witness a little ceremony," said Armand.

They conducted a trial, then and there — even to the point of taking notes on the so-called trial. I couldn't understand everything being said, but Armand translated enough for me to know that the kid had been informed of his crime and the punishment for what he had done during war-time was immediate death.

The trial didn't last long. Soon they were leading the kid over to a tree where they tied both his hands around the trunk. That done, they removed the kid's blindfold, but not the gag. The kid's eyes were the size of silver dollars.

Michel was given the honor of shooting the kid first, since he had lost his friend, Maurice. With a British service pistol equipped with a silencer, Michel did the honors. Then, each of them took turns firing a shot into the kid.

I couldn't believe what was happening. But it was very light, the moon bright. The thud of bullets hitting the kid's body was evidence of the truth.

The first two shots landed in the kid's shoulder and neck. I could hear his gurgling as he tried to scream. The next man's turn came; he stood three feet away from the kid and placed a shot in the back of his head. The kid slumped to the ground.

I guess we Americans are a little soft. I turned away, feeling it was somehow my fault.

Michel's second turn came around. He would give the kid

the *coup de grace.*

Thank God, I thought. I turned back to witness the end, and I don't know why.

Michel shot twice. Square into the top of the kid's head.

It was over.

Now they made notes of the execution: the time, the date, etc. I was informed that my name was being recorded as a witness. If this event came up after the war (*apres-la guerre* — I was to hear that phrase often), I would be called upon to recount the facts as they occurred. Armand handed me the paper for my signature. I signed. Then, he said, "We better get the hell out of here!"

We moved at a rapid pace. We had to arrive at our destination before daybreak or we were dead ducks. We had heard the Germans had brought in additional patrols, including another 200 to 300 men from Bordeaux with trained killer dogs. Only Armand, Michel and I moved on to the Gironde, determined to get off the peninsula.

From my recollection of the map and briefing on my last mission, I knew the Gironde was a large river, running out to the ocean from Bordeaux, a main channel for ships coming into the Port of Bordeaux. The opening at the estuary was three or four miles, but I had no idea how wide it would be at the point we would cross. Armand thought it was about two kilometers. The danger would involve German boats patroling the river. The Germans had also mined the river to keep submarines from entering. There had been rumors that the Allies might open a second front through the Gironde area so the Germans had doubled their patrol and coverage of the mouth of the Gironde. "But do not worry," he said. "That is about all."

I kept talking in whispered tones to Armand as we traveled. I guess it was a morale booster. Perhaps he felt the same way. We kept up a running conversation.

"It will take possibly a good two hours to cross the river," Armand said. "We don't dare use a boat. But perhaps we can find a log to hang onto."

"Yes," I said. That sounded pretty much okay to me.

"Eduarde, can you swim? I forgot to ask!"

"I'm a very good swimmer," I replied.

"Then you'll have no trouble swimming two or three kilometers," he said good-naturedly. "The cool water will do us good . . . "

"I could stand a bath."

He laughed. Then he sobered, saying, "I hope your leg wound isn't bleeding any more. We get sharks in the river occasionally. Blood, I have read, draws sharks."

I liked the son of a bitch, but he didn't have to say that. It stuck in my mind, and I kept thinking: That's all I need now, a shark attacking me while I'm trying to swim a goddamn river!

We reached the river at about two o'clock in the morning. Armand might have thought it was two kilometers across at best, but it looked more like a good three to me. Meanwhile, he hadn't been kidding about the German activity in the vicinity.

We moved along the bank for about 200 yards until we came upon a sandy stretch with a couple of short logs. Here I received a shock. Armand couldn't swim!

"You can't swim?"

"No. Nobody in France swims . . ."

"Nobody?"

"Maybe five percent of the population. That's why I need the log. I have to have something to hold onto while I kick my feet."

The crazy bastard!

"Anyway," said Armand, "since you are such a good swimmer, Eduarde, I have more confidence. I know you will help me since I am helping you."

Such fortitude!

While this conversation was taking place at least four German patrol boats passed. Still, we couldn't wait for a lull in activity. After we crossed it was another four kilometers or more to our hiding place. We took the plunge, so to speak.

Though it was summer the night was cool, and we walked into ice cold water. Talk about a shock!

Armand and Michel followed, Armand having tied his belt around the two logs which were about four feet long. I was worried about him, and by moonlight I could see the fear in his face. "Look," I said, "I'll swim along beside you."

"Ha! I am more afraid of crossing the Gironde than I am of the Germans!"

Our teeth stopped chattering as we became accustomed to the cold. We moved ahead in rather good order. The moon was behind us. After spending so much time in the dark, the eyes grow more sightful at night. With the moonlight I could see a hundred yards or so.

Twice we came upon floating mines. In fact, I brushed up against the chains which linked the mines together. They were about 24 inches in diameter with the usual prongs.

"Don't worry about brushing up against them," Armand whispered. "It takes a heavy hit to set them off."

So, about half way out, we rested ourselves on one of the chains since Michel was growing weary. Still, Michel wasn't much encouraged. "Look," I said, "hang onto the log with Armand. Maybe that will help."

He did, and we swam on, me beside them, shepherding them across the Gironde.

I was surprised at how my strength held up. I swam ahead of them to check for mines and boats; then, I swam back. I don't know what made me so goddamn cocky, but I felt like I could swim across the Gironde and back!

At home I swam the Lehigh River dozens of times, both ways, but the Lehigh was only about half a mile wide. Tonight was different. Tonight I could do anything, it seemed.

Twice we stopped and hung low in the water when we saw patrol ships passing. They were the size of our torpedo boats. The second patrol ship we encountered had a search-light mounted on its bow. It swept the area where we were. We didn't make a move until the light passed on. But thirty minutes later, on its return, it wasn't so easy. The search-light settled on top of us. "Duck," I gasped. We submerged our heads into the ice cold water and the searchlight moved on.

To my surprise, Armand was weathering the swim well. I had to admire him.

His response: "By the time I get across I'll know how to swim!"

"Let go of the log and try it!"

"*Merde alors!*" he said, cursing. "I am holding this log like a baby to its mother's breast, and I won't let go of this son of a bitch until we reach the other side. In fact, Eduarde, I wouldn't even let go if the Germans were to come upon us!"

The bantering helped our morale. But it was scary at that. We were at the mercy of the Germans, for sure, if discovered. I eyed the shore; it still seemed damn far away. And I knew why.

The tide was going out, carrying us towards a wider area of the river as well as nearer to the ocean. I had no idea how far the ocean might be, but I sensed we were much closer than we had been in the beginning since the water was growing progressively rougher. I kept thinking about those sharks Armand mentioned.

Finally, the tide turned. The current began carrying us closer to the other side. Soon the shore was less than 100 yards away. "Kick harder," I said. "We don't have far to go." Then, I had second thoughts. "But don't splash too much. The moonlight will reflect this kind of activity." We kept kicking, but ever so softly. Finally, our feet touched bottom. We had made it, and nobody was happier than Armand as his toes dug into the mucky bottom.

Cautiously, we pushed towards the shore. Lights were visible about a hundred yards away to the south, but they were going away from us. We edged closer to the bank and climbed from the water. Then we pulled the logs up after us.

We had taken off our shoes and socks, and tied them to the logs along with our guns. Quickly we slipped on the socks and shoes, grabbed the guns and struck out for the main railroad line from Paris to Bordeaux. The railroad was very active, especially since the invasion. The Germans used it constantly and most of the activity was at night for troop trains, supplies and munitions. It was the only way they could keep our Air Force from shooting up the trains. Even then, according to Armand, the Germans painted the tops of the trains white with a green cross. Here he had shrugged and smiled.

"But you are not being fooled. I have seen your planes strafe the trains marked like this and blow up the engine!"

We traveled in an easterly direction, and we had only gone a short distance when we crossed our first road. It was a decent highway. Though night, there was plenty of activity on it with at least a dozen trucks, their headlights blacked out, showing tiny slits of light on the road. I wondered how they could travel so fast with so little light. Then I remembered the cab drivers in London. They were accustomed to it.

We waited for a clear shot at the highway, then sprinted across. Our luck seemed to be holding. "Another half kilometer and we will be at the railroad tracks," said Armand.

Fifty feet from the railroad the tracks shimmered in the moonlight. Then Armand whispered, "Wait."

Two soldiers were walking the lines. Both were smoking and their glowing cigarettes made an erratic pattern. Nonetheless, we edged nearer.

It was here that we received the first real scare of this journey. Armand stopped cold, saying, "Eduarde, Michel, don't move."

"What?" I whispered.

"We are in a mine area," he replied calmly.

Frozen in my steps, I looked down cautiously. Wires ran parallel to the railroad tracks. We didn't dare move until we made sure where we were stepping. Suddenly, I saw a small sign about five feet away: ACHTUNG MINEN, German for "Attention Mines."

Finally Armand said, "We back off, walk parallel to the area until we find an open spot."

We backed off, turned left and headed north. Every step was cautious. Thank God, there was a moon. The wires stood out plainly.

About 300 yards down the railroad track we came upon a pathway that crossed the tracks. "Wait," Armand said. "It could be a trap. The Germans often mark phony mine fields." Now he considered and concluded that our best bet was for one of us to go first, the other to follow about thirty feet behind.

It sounded cold blooded, but we had no choice.

"That way," he added, "if we hit a mine, at least two of us will make it."

Since I was the cause of all the bother I offered to go first.

"No, we are helping you and you are more important to the war than we are. We will go first."

Armand stepped out carefully, Michel following at thirty feet. I followed about twenty feet behind Michel. I felt guilty being at the back but I could understand their reasoning — why they were doing this.

With a sigh of relief, we gained the other side of the railroad tracks only to run upon another mine area. Armand walked along the stones for 300 feet. He turned off to the right into what seemed to be an open area. By now the first faint signs of light were in the east. "We must hurry, no matter what chances we take," he said.

I was cold and shivering in my wet clothes, more than happy to move along at a brisker pace. In fact, the wound in my leg felt better. Perhaps the sea water had something to do with that. So, we picked up our pace, running and walking, running and walking, until the sun came up; then we really moved 'em on out.

The sun did feel good, and my clothing began to dry. We came upon a small dirt road. Armand whispered back to me, "Eduarde, we are almost there."

The dirt road was just wide enough for a small car and we came upon a beautiful farm house and buildings which reminded me of Pennsylvania.

The main building was painted white and trimmed in black — almost Colonial American — with a tiled roof, unlike most of the thatched and wood roofs I had seen in France. Armand stopped and called out. Two men stepped into the road, one on either side. Then, directly behind us, three other men stepped from the woods and followed us for about fifty feet. We had arrived.

We were welcomed with open arms. Apparently this was the F.T.P.F. of the French Resistance, the larger, more organized group. The farmer and owner of the property came out to greet us. He was pleased we had arrived, and he spoke fairly good English.

"So this is the American I've heard so much about, the one who has caused all this trouble! Welcome, my young American friend, welcome to our home. Partake of our humble hospitality." His face told me he meant every word he said. Then he called to his wife.

She came bustling out; she could have passed for a typical farm woman anywhere: short, round, with a kind, happy face. At the sight of me she burst out crying, throwing her arms around me. "Welcome to our home, my American friend. We are the Ournays, Robere and Anne."

I might have been a long lost son returning from the war. Indeed, they had a son exactly my age; he had been killed in the war and they were intent on doing everything possible to liberate France. But first . . .

I must clean up while Madame made breakfast. I was so hungry. After all the energy I had burned crossing the Gironde I could've eaten a cow.

The farm house was more modern than any I had been in. There were spiggots in the kitchen with running hot and cold water. They even had a bathroom with a tub. Madame Ournay led me back to the bathroom and said, "Make yourself at home. You'll feel better after a hot bath and dry clothes."

I hesitated. After what had happened to the last French family to befriend me, well . . .

Robere had followed us to the bathroom. "Why do you hesitate?"

I told him briefly what had happened.

"Do not worry. We have men down the road for three kilometers. If anything happens, they will fire shots to warn us or send a runner. Go ahead with your bath. Why, I bet this is the first hot bath you have had!"

I smiled. Despite all the time in the water I must've smelled to high heaven.

Madame Ornay brought fresh towels and a washcloth made of sisal which was sewn into a rag fitted like a mitt. I looked around in disbelief. Everything was spic and span.

"Well," said Madame Ournay, "take off your clothes. I will just run your bath." She turned on the tap and the tub began to fill. She was a typical mother.

Still, I couldn't bring myself to remove my clothes.

She sensed my embarrassment, laughing. "I will wait until you get into the tub, then I will come back and help you wash."

This was a new experience for me. But what the hell! The moment she stepped from the room I shucked my damp clothing and hurried into the tub. Oh, it felt good.

Madame Ournay returned, as if on command. She lathered up the wash mitt with what looked like a large cake of lye soap. Then she scrubbed my back and my head, muttering in French something about how dirty my head was.

My leg was throbbing like mad in the hot water. Well, if I had to complain, this was the woman to whom I should complain. "My leg, it hurts," I managed under her vigorous scrubbing.

"The hot water will do your leg good. We have already sent for a doctor. He will be here later today. You are safe here, son. Now stand up."

Dutifully, I stood up. She scrubbed me all over, from stem to stern, talking all the way, as if we had a special rapport, and we did. "You look just like my son. When were you born?"

"I was born in 1921 . . .

Tears came to her eyes. "Our son was born in March . . . 1921."

"So was I," I managed.

We looked at one another in disbelief over this coincidence. Then she went back to scrubbing, and I do mean scrubbing. The sisal wash rag felt like sandpaper on my skin.

When she finished, she ran off the dirty water and made me stay in the tub as she refilled it with hot water. "Now," she said, "you soak in the clean hot water. I will get something to put on your leg and face, for the time being. The doctor will arrive later. Do not worry."

This woman was like my mother. She was so comfortable, so sweet, so thoughtful.

I soaked in the tub for another twenty minutes. Then I dried myself off, unplugging all that good clean hot water. It seemed a pity.

All the time I'd been sitting there alone I'd been considering the small mirror over the sink. Now I took a look at myself. I looked horrible. The sight even scared me!

Although my hair was curly, it was matted and tangled. I had a heavy growth of beard. But that wasn't the worst. The wound on my nose and left eye truly frightened me. In effect, I looked like a hunted, haunted animal, only in this case, I was a hunted, haunted soldier, trying to escape with his life to fight another day.

A large comb lay on the shelf next to the cabinet. I started to comb my hair but Madame Ournay returned. She carried a cup with shaving soap in it, a brush and, of all things, a German straight razor. It was stamped: "Solingen Steel." I remembered my father shaved with a straight razor just like this, and it was made in Germany. I guessed the Germans had their mark on every goddamn thing.

Although I had never used a straight razor, I was determined. My beard had been well soaked in the bath, so I lathered up and let it set for a few minutes. Finally, I tried my hand. I cut myself somewhat, but I got rid of the beard.

I washed my face in hot water. This stopped the bleeding, and I applied cold water. Madame Ournay bustled in, bringing me a large bottle of toilet water, saying, "Put this on your face. It will make you feel better."

She was right, except now I smelled like a French whore. So what! I even doused my hair with the toilet water, hoping to get out the tangles, and it worked.

Now I looked into the mirror and, sure enough, it was Ed Cury. My nostrils picked up the scent of one of the most beautiful aromas in the world: ham and eggs frying. I wanted to rush right out, but I didn't have any clothing. Madame had taken away my clothes while I bathed. I panicked: What if they'd taken my clothes and were waiting for the Germans to come? I stepped to the door and opened it slightly. I heaved a sigh of relief. They were all there, sitting around the table, joking and laughing. Armand was drinking coffee, real coffee. I could smell it. "Armand," I said.

"Oh, Eduarde, come join us for coffee and breakfast."

"My clothes . . . "

Madame Ournay threw back her head and laughed. She was washing my clothes. She got up, went into another room, and returned with a robe about double my size. I had weighed 188 pounds when I was shot down. Only God knew how much I weighed now. For sure, I was much thinner. I wrapped the robe tightly around me and strode into the kitchen. They all burst out laughing, clapping, cheering. "You look like an American!" they proclaimed. I was glad they felt this way; they were true French allies.

Already Madame Ournay had placed hot plates and food on the table. "Eduarde, this is special for you. We have cooked it just like we know the Americans do it in the cinema!"

Right there, in front of me, were six eggs, sunnyside up, on one plate. On another plate were three slices of ham, each about half an inch thick, and several pieces of French sausage. A long oval plate held two small loaves of French bread which had been cut open; large chunks of butter oozed from the bread.

My stomach growled; and I drooled. I tried to behave like a gentleman but they insisted I begin. God, this was heaven! I began to eat as if it were my first meal, or my last; take your pick.

Madame Ournay and her husband were wonderful people. Nothing was too good for me. Madame insisted I have another platter of eggs and more ham and, so help me, I ate that too.

Madame threw up her hands and said, "Wonderful! He is a marvelous eater!" Two big onions, sliced, were placed before me. "Eat those too. They will keep you from catching a cold after being in the water so long."

The onions disappeared down my gullet along with everything else. Then I faced the inevitable bottle of cognac. A half glass was poured for each of us. Armand rose to give the toast. "I wish to make a toast to our American comrade who has endured all of this with good humor and good faith. May we win the war together. *Viva la France!*"

We all took a slug of the cognac, including Madame Ournay. I couldn't help but marvel at her as she downed that half glass of cognac with nonchalance.

Again the glasses were filled. This time: "To my American friend and to the liberation of France!"

After many toasts Madam Ournay insisted we all get some sleep. "Eduarde," she said, "when you awaken, your clothes will be clean, dry, and mended!"

They would have it no other way. I should sleep in their bedroom, and what a beautiful surprise! Fresh sheets adorned an old French bed with a thick feather mattress. Reassured, clean, stomach full, I knew I was safe. Climbing into bed, I went out like the light.

I didn't awaken until a hand touched my shoulder. There were the Ournays like a benevolent mother and father, standing beside the bed. I must get up. It was four o'clock, she said. I had slept through lunch and dinner would soon be ready.

Food? I was so stuffed with breakfast I couldn't move.

"Oh, but you must." Madame Ournay had prepared a huge dinner. A surprise guest was arriving, and I would feel better once I got out of bed. But first . . .

Madame Ournay bustled off to return with a big round cake, a French pastry, and a large pitcher of cold milk. Here was a little snack to hold me until dinner. I couldn't believe these people!

In the luxury of my clean bed I drank the milk, the best I ever tasted, and I wasn't a milk lover. But this milk was fresh from the cow that very morning and had been cooling in the spring house. The pastry, it goes without saying, was delicious too and hot from the oven.

Having watched over my "little pre-dinner snack," Madame then brought in my clothes. They were scrubbed clean and mended. She had done her best, despite the condition of my clothes. She apologized for not doing better. She was like a doting mother.

As I dressed I wondered: If I'd been in the Ournays' shoes, would I have taken someone into my house as I had appeared on their doorstep and endangered my family? These people were truly wonderful, generous, hospitable, loving human beings.

The surprise dinner guest was their daughter Madelaine. She had bicycled a mere sixty kilometers from Bordeaux. She shrugged, laughing. "Sometimes I do it twice a week. Even my grandmother — she is 68 years old — often bicycles with me."

I was awed. Madelaine was not only personable, she was stunning.

In her twenties, she had coal black hair that matched her eyes and her complexion was as smooth and soft as a newly-grown peach. The curves were all in the right place, while her full bosom looked as if it was fighting to get out!

I tried to be a real officer and a gentleman. In other words, I tried not to stare and hang onto her every word. It wasn't easy. Each time our eyes met, it was electric, and I felt uneasy.

The Ournays suggested we get some fresh air. "A little walk," said Madame, "to hone the appetite." She smiled fondly on us. "It is safe. Don't worry. Just stay on the farm. It is all fenced. Robere's Maquis group patrols everywhere. They know everything, from Bordeaux to the farm."

Madelaine spoke fairly good English. I was amazed at how many people in this family were bilingual and said as much.

"Oh," said Madelaine, "we must study English or German in school." Madelaine had had four years of English in high school plus two years in college. She had studied to be a teacher, and this is what she did in Bordeaux.

As we walked about the farm she had many questions.

"What about your family? What are they like? Where are you from? What is it like there?"

In these violent and turbulent times it was as if Madelaine and I had dropped onto an oasis. It was sundown, the birds sang, and a soft breeze rustled the leaves of the trees.

Finally, "Where do you go from here?" she asked.

I didn't know.

"I heard them speaking of Bordeaux, of trying to get you to Toulouse, then across the Pyrenees into Spain, as they do many Allied flyers." She paused in thought. "I hope you don't leave too soon. This is Friday, you know, and I can stay at the farm until Sunday late afternoon."

No, I hadn't known it was Friday. I had lost all track of days. But I was heartened by the prospects of a weekend with Madelaine.

"Are you married?" she asked now.

"Not me!" I grinned down at her.

"Have you ever been married?" she teased.

"No."

"Have you ever been in love then?"

"Nope. Not me!"

Then, I'll be darned, she asked: "Will you marry me?"

Laughing, I responded in a flippant manner. "Are you kidding?" But I was stopped cold. She was serious. Really serious.

"No, I am not kidding. All of my life I've dreamed of meeting an American and marrying him, then moving to America. You see, I saw a movie, just before the war, with Errol Flynn. Errol Flynn in Hollywood. I would love to marry an American like you and move to Hollywood."

Like most French, all of her ideas of America were formulated from American movies: beautiful homes with swimming pools; and everyone had more money than they could spend. To them, America was a land of milk and honey; millionaires living the high life.

Since she was so very serious I tried not to disillusion her. "You have given me a great compliment, Madelaine. But I have an obligation to my country, to help end the war, and until our countries are victorious, I can't get married." I thought this might let me off the hook graciously while making it easier on her.

We continued walking. Then, Madelaine stopped. She looked up at me, placed her small hands on my arms and said, "Eduarde, since you will not marry me now, can you at least give me a baby . . . to remember you by? Then I know you will come back after the war and be my husband." She lifted her tempting lips to mine and pulled me down to her. I couldn't believe this was happening. I wasn't one to pass up a good piece of ass, but, by god, this was too much. I respected her parents and what they were doing for me; I wasn't about to wrong them in any way. They had given me friendship and hospitality, while laying their lives on the line for me. Yet, I wanted to hold her close, make love to her. Still and all, I was determined not to violate a trust.

I moved away, but she pursued me, kissing me with fervor and passion. And, aw hell, what was the use. I couldn't control myself. I had often heard the expression, "A stiff prick has no conscience," and now I knew it to be true!

She dropped her hands down around my backside and drew herself tightly to me in a rotating motion. I couldn't stand it. But my mind flashed back to Lucien, the farmer's sister-in-law, and what could happen if the goddamn Krauts found us.

Madelaine sensed my hesitation, whispering softly, "Eduarde, what is wrong?"

I wanted to say, "I'm afraid." I didn't get the chance.

She rushed on to say up front that their war had been long; they had suffered indignities and privation and death. She felt we were entitled to a moment of happiness. Although she had faith in her country and the Allies, she had no idea what might happen; and she wanted to make love to me so badly she couldn't stand it any longer.

Had I been made of stone, I might have resisted this impassioned plea. But since I was an officer and a gentleman, how could I refuse?

We moved a few yards off the road and into a small stand of pines. I pulled her down gently on a soft bed of pine needles. Here was a beautifully cozy spot with enough privacy; it seemed the perfect place to make love.

We were both kneeling on the ground, her arms entwined around me as she kissed me passionately. Then she broke away and whispered softly, "Eduarde, *mon cheri* undress me."

I reached around, fumbling for the buttons on her dress. My fingers were clumsy and I was shaking. I accomplished nothing.

She laughed and said, "Let me do it."

Madelaine stood up, reached around, unbuttoning the back of her dress and shrugging her shoulders until the dress dropped to the ground. Her beautiful firm breasts billowed over the top of her brassiere.

I waited, breathless with anticipation.

She unhooked the brassiere; it too dropped away. The breasts jutted out like the twin engine nacelles on a P-38 fighter plane. Her skin was like liquid satin but her nipples were dark brown, swollen with passion. I couldn't take my eyes from her.

Now she teasingly brought her hands down to her panties, rolling them downward very slowly until they too dropped at her feet. In one elegant gesture she kicked away the panties while stepping out of her platform shoes. Then:

"Eduarde, what are you waiting for? Please take off your clothing."

I pulled off my shirt. She came to me, pushing her firm young breasts against my chest. I was done for. I unbuttoned my belt and pants, let them fall to the ground, and stepped out of them. Then, I dropped down on top of her, spreading her legs as she fell backwards, pulling me to her.

We were locked in a passionate embrace, my mouth on hers. I tried to break loose to kiss her beautiful breasts, but she said, "*Vite, vite, mon cheri*, kiss me!" She reached down, guiding me to her *boite*.

As I entered her, she yelled in what I thought was pain, but whimpered into a sigh as she drew her legs up high, her motions delightful.

I tried to brace myself, so I wouldn't hurt her. But, hell, the way she was moving around, I just hung on for dear life.

"*Encore, encore, encore!*" she cried. "More, more."

I was trying to hold back. But it had been a long time for me. Her passionate responses didn't help my situation much. I tried to stop momentarily. But, hell, no! She came off the ground; she wasn't about to let me go. Within seconds she could feel me swelling inside of her. She wasn't naive. She knew what was happening. Then, she was screaming, "*Oui, oui, maintenant, maintenant, maintenant!* Yes I am coming too!"

My god, I hoped no one could hear us. Anyway, I couldn't hold back, no matter how hard I tried. She started moving and grinding in every way possible, her legs locked tightly around me. Once again, she screamed.

I clamped my mouth over hers, hoping to stop her passionate screams. I might as well have tried to stop a moving train! I saw stars, the moon and Mars . . . Hell, I didn't care where I was — France, Germany, America — this was it, by god. I exploded inside her and kept coming, until we lay gasping for breath. But she wouldn't let go of me; her tight little pussy kept throbbing and twitching.

I rolled over on my back; she rolled with me. I was still inside of her and we stayed that way without moving, without talking. Finally, we parted, lying side by side, her small hand on my chest, her fingertips playing with my hair. Finally, I got up and started to dress. But she stopped me, sitting upright and untying my shoes. I sat down and tried to reason with her. We must get back. But she wasn't listening.

She took off my shoes and socks, reached over and pulled my trousers and shorts clear. Then, she pushed me backwards, climbing on top of me, those beautiful breasts lightly brushing first my face, then my chest, all the way down. Her lips and tongue were tender and searching this time; and she was teasing, tantalizing me, taking me into her mouth and sucking ever so gently.

She had such expertise for one so young and sweet. I just stretched out and enjoyed myself, my cock swelling, vibrant and alive again. Then, suddenly, she stopped. She straddled me. She was on top of me.

At first she didn't move. Finally, though, her mouth was on mine, our tongues entwined, and slowly she began to move in a gentle figure eight, increasing the tempo gradually, until she sat up, leaning back and placing her hands on my ankles.

I watched with interest and pleasure as she turned her head side to side, now moaning softly French words I couldn't understand. Her face was filled with pure ecstasy.

I pushed up, lifting us from the ground. I was proudly holding back, and now she began to move faster, not saying a word though her mouth was open, until she flung back her head. Then, I felt her throbbing and her warmness running down between my legs and this time in English, she said:

"Now, my darling, now! Come with me, now, please!"

I exploded within her as we both uttered wild animalistic sounds of passion.

Madelaine fell asleep in my arms. I looked up, and it was cooler now, the sun going down. I was content too, but far from relaxed. I thought about Madelaine's folks, and I awakened Madelaine.

"What is wrong, *mon cheri*? Don't move. I could stay like this forever."

Common sense took over. "I think we should get dressed and go back to the house." I stood up, reached down and pulled her up.

We stood looking at one another, slightly embarrassed.

She smiled and said, "You have made me so wet. I need something to wipe myself."

I handed her my G.I. khaki shorts to use. When she handed them back to me, they were wet. I buried the shorts beneath the pine needles; the odor of our passion would have been a dead giveaway of what we had done, as if we could've hidden our feelings.

That done, we dressed carefully, walking back to the farm house, hand in hand, Madelaine glancing up at me every now and then with a very satisfied and possessive look on her face. I thought of the possible complications that could follow. But *c'est la guerre!*

When we returned to the farm yard, we became an instant center of attention. Where had we gone? How was the walk? Did you enjoy yourselves?

Everyone had a sly, knowing look. I felt guilty as all hell, excused myself, and went immediately to the bathroom to wash up, thinking, Will she tell her parents? Or have they already guessed? If so, they had every right to turn me out, let the Nazis capture me. I deserved it, but I had a lot to learn about the French.

When I returned from the bathroom they were all sitting in the parlor talking. Armand said, "Eduarde, we must have a talk."

Oh, my god, I thought, this was it! He took my arm and led me to the far end of the parlor. He wanted to discuss how we would get to Bordeaux, how we would get in touch with the French Underground who would take me to Toulouse and across the Pyrenees. I sighed with relief. We were back to reality. There really was a war going on.

There were Basque guides who could take me across the mountains. They were accustomed to the difficult trails and knew how to evade the many German patrols at guard stations throughout the mountains. I wondered aloud, "Why will they do this?"

Armand laughed. "I will tell you why. They are not doing it for you or for us. They are doing it for the love of gold. As soon as any American or British flyer is delivered safely to the British consulate, they are paid the equivalent of $9000 in gold coins, and this is reason enough for them to risk it." But even at that they could not all be trusted.

Several months before, Armand had heard of a Royal Air Force flyer who had been shot down and evaded the Germans; when the French Underground took him to the Pyrenees, the Basque who was to guide him had turned him over to the Germans and collected a similar reward or more. "Once you get there," he cautioned, "this is the only danger. Some Basques, Andorrans, and Spaniards are pro-German. Even many Frenchmen in Vichy France feel the same way."

Here Armand reminded me of the many young French women who had become mistresses of German officers, living with them and gaining favors. Meanwhile, there were many merchants making money off the Germans; the Germans were smart, treating these businessmen well, paying them highly. The Germans understood they lived in a hostile environment where they needed any and all friends at whatever the price, and they hired whoever would work for them.

Since the stakes were so high, I couldn't imagine anyone wanting to serve the Germans, but we Americans were naive when it came to the cold, cruel realities of war. The French had been occupied time and again; and they, in too many instances, viewed the occupation as an inconvenience for a few years.

The most disconcerting aspect of talking with many Frenchmen was the question, "But what will happen to our colonies *apres-la guerre?*" meaning, once the war was over, what was going to happen to their North African colonies and French Indo-China. I couldn't understand this attitude when they were sitting there occupied by the Germans. They seemed to feel they couldn't survive without the colonies and told me that we must understand this, especially Winston Churchill and President Roosevelt.

Regardless, the plan for my escape entailed a great risk. Armand said we would take the train from Jonyac to Bordeaux. Hundreds of workers commuted on the trains daily to work in Bordeaux; these people worked for the Germans in the railroad yard, at the power plant, and on the docks.

"I think, though," Armand concluded, "we cannot wait until Monday. Saturday is a work day. I believe you can get by with one of our men's identity cards. He was killed. Though the photo doesn't look like you, the Germans seldom look closely at the photos." He shrugged that typical French shrug. "Most of the officials who check the trains are Vichy French police, forced to work for the Germans. They are still true French patriots at heart. They overlook many false cards."

In an effort to make everything appear as normal as possible, I should purchase the ticket myself for the train trip. It would look suspicious if Armand purchased it for me.

I agreed. All I wanted was to get out of France and back to my own people.

We rejoined the Ournays, then the doctor came. He looked at my wounds. He couldn't do anything about stitching my face. It would be a dead giveaway. The cuts had healed some. But he did sew the wound in my leg so it would heal. He apologized for having no sulfa powder.

Madame Ournay announced dinner. She had outdone herself again. My god, it looked like a banquet table. I asked how they managed so well. They grew food on the farm. What they didn't need, they traded for what they did need and sold the rest.

Madelaine didn't have too much to say, but I sensed she was hurt that we were planning to leave. I feared she would tell her parents about our affair. I could almost feel the shotgun in my back and hear the words, "Either marry my daughter or else!" As dinner progressed I made up my mind that if it came to that I'd go through with any kind of ceremony which might be held. Once I returned to England, nothing could be done about it.

After dinner we sat around the table talking and sipping cognac. When the talk wound down the Ournays suggested we go out back and sit under the grape arbor on their back porch. It was beautiful out there, a soft breeze blowing, a moon shining. In fact, it was so peaceful I had difficulty imagining anyone at war. They continued to ply me with questions. "How big is your swimming pool?" I didn't have a pool. Then: "How many cars do you have?" I made it very plain that I was just an ordinary kind of guy.

"Oh, you are too modest!" Madame proclaimed. "We have seen all the cinemas. We know you have a swimming pool. Armand has told us what an excellent swimmer you were in crossing the Gironde. Anyone who swims that well must have a swimming pool in which to learn."

I said, "Most Americans are lucky to have hot and cold running water, a bathroom, a job and an automobile."

They threw up their hands in laughter, saying, "All Americans are rich!"

At ten o'clock the decision was made that I should hit the sack. I must be well rested. Tomorrow would be *tres dangereux*. Had I known what lay ahead, I would have kept my ass right there on that little farm and maybe married Madelaine, if I had to.

Madame insisted we have a bedtime snack. Out came the wine, the brandy, the small French pastries and cakes. I sipped on a large glass of Napoleon brandy and purred like a kitten. The brandy was over fifty years old, brought out only on special occasions. And it was devastatingly smooth.

Now Madame said, "I will prepare your bed." Her husband had already disappeared with a mysterious wink. Shortly, she returned, saying, "Come along now."

I bid everyone, "*Bon nuit,*" and followed Madame back to that beautiful featherbed mattress. She had placed a pitcher of cold water, two glasses of milk and a small tray of little French cakes beside the bed. It was as if someone might be going to sleep with me since there were two glasses. "Why two glasses?" I asked.

She muffled a giggle and said, "You will see," bustling on her way.

I washed up, undressed and climbed into bed. Ah, I thought, what a way to fight a war! I was completely nude, since my shorts were buried under pine needles from my tryst with Madelaine. But that was part of the luxury. The sheets felt smooth and wonderfully enticing to my body. I rolled over, preparing to say my prayers, when a knock came at the door . . . and in swept the Ournays with their lovely little daughter all done up in a cute nightgown drawn tight around her neck. Wow!

The Ornays didn't mince words. Said Messr. Ournay, "Our daughter has fallen in love with you. But, since you cannot marry her and because you are a good and brave soldier who wishes to return to your country and fight, the one thing she desires above all else is to sleep with you and have your child."

Taken completely aback, I began to stammer and mumble like an idiot.

Madame reached over and placed a finger on my mouth. "Do not say a word. We understand. You are a good soldier, and we admire you for putting your country first. But now we want you to make our daughter happy." She pulled back the covers.

I rolled over to hide my nakedness. But they all just giggled, and Madelaine climbed into the sack with me.

The covers were pulled up around us: Madelaine and Eduarde there in bed together.

The Ournays smiled, lit a small candle by the bedside and took their departure, leaving Madelaine and I alone. I rolled away from her thinking this must be some kind of a trap. By U.S.A. standards this sort of thing just didn't happen.

Her little arms encircled me as she kissed the back of my head and neck. Then, she stopped and sat up in bed. What was she doing now? I turned back toward her.

By candlelight I watched as she removed the nightgown, her body was as lovely as ever. I wondered if I could perform again after our previous session. It was so soft . . . Then I'd just have to die trying.

The nightgown out of the way, an arm came around me and her other hand reached between my legs, touching me. "Eduarde," she whispered, "I can see you are *tres fatiguee*, since we had such a beautiful love affair earlier. Relax. I just want to sleep in your arms now."

And believe it or not, I was grateful!

We wrapped our arms around one another, her well-shaped leg in between mine, in a loving embrace. And this was how we slept the night away. Never have I slept better.

Messr. Ournay's voice awakened me, saying, "Eduarde . . . very softly.

"What's wrong?" Suddenly, I was wide awake and alert.

"It will soon be daylight. You and Armand must start early. It will take an hour to get to the village of Jonyac. You don't want to miss the early train to Bordeaux. There will not be another until late afternoon when there are not so many workers on the train. You will have less chance of being discovered by the Germans on the morning train."

Madelaine was sound asleep. I slipped from bed quietly as he drew the drapery back from the window, a little daylight showing. I lit the candle and went to the bathroom to wash up. I figured I might as well look my best; I wanted the Germans to think I was going to work in Bordeaux.

My identity card was for Louis Cataine. He was listed as a *mechanic bateau*, from the town of Begle near Bordeaux. His photo didn't resemble me at all. His face was much thinner; his nose was hawkish. But I hoped for the best.

I tried the straight razor again and won the battle. Then, I patted on toilet water as after shave lotion and laughed to myself. Hell, the Krauts wouldn't imagine an American officer trying to evade them would have toilet water on his face!

Now I glanced at the photo of Louis Cataine again. I brushed my hair as tight as could be. I was trying to match the straight hair in the photo. Then, I came from the bathroom and looked over at the bed.

Madelaine was awake and crying. I went to her and pulled her into my arms, kissing her softly.

"Au revoir, bonne chance, mon amour," she murmured. Goodbye and good luck, my love.

I'm not much on goodbyes. I kissed her again.

Madelaine whispered, "I'll be waiting for you."

I released her and turned away, going out into the hall and into the kitchen, smelling the aroma of breakfast.

Madame Ournay had prepared ham and eggs, rolls and strong black coffee. While the Ournays, Michel, Armand and I ate, Armand briefed me. In the village of Jonyac I was to take the 600 francs which they gave me and follow Armand to the railroad ticket window, push the money through the window and say only, "Bordeaux." My ticket in hand, I was to follow Armand to the platform, stay as close to him as possible, and when we boarded the train, sit beside Armand. Since I didn't speak French well, supposedly Armand would carry on a conversation with me. I was to mumble *non* or *oui* occasionally, nodding my head as if I understood every word being said. The trip to Bordeaux would take two hours since there were many stops. However, I was to remain as calm as possible.

"Do you have any personal identification on you?" Armand asked. "Anything that says you're an American soldier?"

"My dog tags. I sewed them in the lining of my pants behind my belt along with my crash bracelet. And my shoes, of course." I had exchanged most of my clothes with the Maquis earlier in the first camp.

They shook hands, talking in French excitedly.

"What is it?" I demanded, wondering what had gone wrong.

Messr. Ournay said, "The beret. You must have a beret. That is what's missing!" He left the room and returned with a black beret, showing me how to wear it, cocked to the side of the head and tilted slightly forward. Then, they all stood back and laughed.

"By god," said Armand, "you look like a real Frenchman now!"

"What about my face?" I asked.

Armand shrugged. "Not to worry. Many Frenchmen have been wounded from the air raids. Anyway, your cuts don't show too badly."

"Then, I look okay?"

"Very good!"

Once more I was reassured. But he added: "If we get through the train trip you have it made, since at the station - Leguarre - we have only a kilometer or so to a bakery in Bordeaux where we meet our contact."

Despite his caution about the train trip I felt very sure in my heart we would make it. I had confidence in all of them. They had treated me as one of their own and were obviously more than a little sincere in their efforts to see me escape and return to England.

Madame and Messr. Ournay embraced me now, tearful with kisses. As far as they were concerned they imagined I was already their son-in-law, so to speak. The gist of their farewell: "My son, we will be waiting for you and hope to have our grandchild for you when you return."

Michel wasn't going with us. I bid him a fond farewell too.

Now Armand threw his arms around me, kissing me on both cheeks. *"Bonne chance, mon camarade!"*

"Good luck to you, too!" I swatted him on the back, adding, "What about our weapons?"

"No guns, my friend. We would be dead as the proverbial baked duck. If anything happens, we will jump off the train. Which reminds me. We will get seats very near an exit. Come. We must go."

We walked into the courtyard. The day was bright and beautiful; the sun shown brightly. With a wave of our hands we set forth briskly. But as minutes passed, a funny gnawing uneasiness took hold of my stomach.

Goddamn it, I thought, there's my intuition at work again; and it was always bad news!

– 6 –

In the village of Jonyac I was amazed by the number of German soldiers and Vichy police at the station. Following Armand, I kept my face placid and looked neither to the right nor left, as if I might be accustomed to the scene. At the ticket window the line was short. I waited behind Armand, watching those ahead of us pushing their money through the window and saying, "Bordeaux."

Soon Armand was at the window. I was next. As Armand moved away, ticket in hand, I shoved my money through and said, "Bordeaux." The man stamped my ticket, handing it to me without any sweat. Relieved beyond belief, I went to stand on the platform with Armand.

Armand lit a cigarette and glanced at me. Then he handed me a cigarette, lighting it for me, though he knew I didn't smoke. I guessed he figured it would look more natural if we both were smoking.

I took the cigarette and puffed away casually, being careful not to inhale. I didn't want to start coughing and attract attention.

Several times German soldiers came by in pairs. They didn't give us a glance. So I relaxed a bit and looked around.

Two men dressed in civilian clothing were standing in a doorway about fifty feet from us. They were attired in trench coats and slouch hats although it was summer and warm. Instinctively I knew who they were: Gestapo!

Armand whispered, "Be careful. Don't look at them."

The French feared the Gestapo. Well, so did I. But it was hard to stifle a laugh. They could've been spotted by a blind man.

After about five or six minutes the train arrived. It looked brand new and much cleaner than any train I had seen back home. Surprised, I followed Armand onto the fourth car. He walked back through two more cars where he found two seats side by side. He beckoned for me to enter first.

I sat next to the window, half open, which gave me some feeling of assurance; I figured I could dive through the window, if necessary. Then, I glanced around as casually as possible, looking for exits. We were seated in the second row from the back.

The car soon filled with French workers; the whistle blew and the train moved out slowly. My intuition nagged at me. Nevertheless, the train made two stops without incident.

Every once in a while Armand talked to me. I nodded my head in response, saying either, "oui," or "non," depending on what he said. I decided I had a natural inclination for foreign languages since I was beginning to understand French somewhat.

As the train pulled away from the third station two Vichy police, accompanied by two German soldiers, came through the car checking *cartes de identites*. The Vichy police checked the cards while the German soldiers followed along mutely. As they neared, sweat popped out on my brow.

This was the severest test so far, and I had to pass it. I got a grip on myself and calmed down. But I felt naked as hell without a weapon, should I have to fight my way out.

The Vichy arrived at our seats. Armand handed them his identity card without looking up.

The other Vichy said to me, *"Demande le papier."*

I followed Armand's lead, handing over my card and not looking up. He grabbed the card, glanced at it and handed it back. Then, they moved to the last row and on to the next car.

Armand grabbed my forearm and squeezed, as if to say, "I told you so."

Inwardly, I wilted. Only briefly, though.

The train slowed for the next stop, and I'll be damned, it was a German camp with German officers lounging around a swimming pool as if they didn't have a care in the world!

God, I thought, if they only knew an American was watching them.

Armand leaned over and said, "Eduarde, another thirty minutes or so and we will be there. Then you will be safe."

He had spoken in English. Evidently he felt confident. I gained strength from his words.

During the next thirty minutes we didn't talk. Finally, the conductor came through the train, calling out, "Bordeaux . . . Bordeaux."

We were entering the marshalling yards and there were many tracks. I wondered how we'd missed bombing them, especially with all the trains there.

I counted at least four freight trains loaded with materials and equipment. A German troop train was just pulling out. I wished for an American raid then and there.

We disembarked, following the crowd of workers. Outside, many German soldiers, Vichy police and even civilian plainclothesmen were standing about. But everything went smoothly.

The terminal was the first I'd seen of civilian activity. Frankly, I was a little excited by what greeted my eyes. The station was beautiful. I couldn't help marveling at the architecture.

We passed through the large terminal, arriving at the far end, where we headed up a long row of stairs and into the streets. I must've been rushing right along because Armand cautioned me twice, "Take it easy." I was trying. But I wanted to get out of this place and into the city.

We made it to the main room and out into the open street. Armand turned right; I followed. Then, *it* caught my eye.

A black, four-door Mercedes was parked on the right side of the street and we had to pass it. It was too late to change directions. Armand whispered, "Keep walking. Do not be afraid."

As we walked by the Mercedes I noticed two soldiers in the front seat and two plainclothes bastards in the back. Gestapo! We kept walking. Then, I heard the car doors open behind us. I forced myself to look straight ahead, not backward. Boy, it was tough!

We were walking along a low wall that was part of the station. To the left was the busy street, cars and trucks everywhere, even with war and gas rationing. Armand was about six feet in front of me, walking calmly but briskly. I experienced that goddamn funny, fuzzy feeling in the back of my head again. Then, I heard it!

"Halt!" in that goddamn gutteral accent; the halt without the "H."

Armand muttered loud enough for me to hear, "Keep walking."

Again: "Halt!" This time I heard the unmistakable sound of a machine gun being cocked and a shell thrown into the chamber.

Armand yelled, "Run!" and we took off at full speed.

I was almost up to Armand when the first two short bursts came. I expected the bullets to go through me. Instead, I saw Armand's body move erratically. He ran out into the gutter and fell.

"Keep going, Eduarde," he yelled. "Keep going!"

I kept going, zigzagging as I ran, bullets flying all around me. I figured there were two guns firing at me. From the sound I guessed one was a pistol and the other, a machine gun. "Halt!" came the angry command behind me. Thanks, but no thanks. I was running for my life.

I darted to the right against the wall. Then, I cut out left across the street, dodging traffic. It seemed as if every vehicle on that street tried to help me. They stopped, let me go by and moved on. At one point I even ran headlong into the traffic. Finally, I was on the other side of the street.

A Frenchman stood next to a fruit stand. He yelled something which sounded like "Down ze ally, down ze alley."

Yes, there was an alley, and I ran down the narrow alley, many walls and fences on either side of it. I came to another alley that veered off to the right, and followed this route.

I could hear shouting behind me. Thank god, the firing had stopped. But I kept going full speed for perhaps ten minutes, then slowed down, regaining my confidence that I had shaken the Gestapo pursuers. Still, I moved on, wondering where I should go, who I could contact. All Armand had told me was "a baker in a bakery shop." He didn't know the name of the street himself, just where it was located.

I came upon a small street with many trees in full bloom. It was peaceful and quiet without traffic. I slowed to a walk, not wanting to attract attention or arouse suspicion. I walked for several blocks. Then came the unmistakable sound of police cars, "De-Da, De-Da." I figured I better get the hell off the street. I turned into the first alley.

I hurried onward until I came upon a high wall of stone; I ran parallel to it until I reached a small opening. It was the gateway into an old cemetery, and I was struck by a good idea. Why not hide here? I climbed over the locked gate and went along the wall.

Staying close to the walls where there was a good growth of shrubbery, I eventually found a spot where the shrubbery had grown heavily into a corner. My heart was pounding like mad and my leg hurt like hell. I had to rest. I crawled deep into the shrubbery and stayed there.

Outside the cemetery the commotion kept up. I could hear police cars and motorcycles. After a few hours it quieted down. So I began to think about finding that bakery shop. But how? After dark, I told myself. After dark.

I would've given anything for a glass of water. I pulled a couple of leaves from the shrubbery and chewed them. It didn't help. They were bitter as hell. I decided to forget my thirst although I knew there had to be water in the cemetery. I didn't dare leave my hiding place.

In time I came to a conclusion. To hell with the bakery! I had to get out of town. When the sun began to set that afternoon, I would head south with the sun to my right. My plan was to head for Toulouse or south to the mountains on my own. Only a few hundred kilometers were between me and my goal. I left my hiding place and climbed over the gate.

I slipped from the cemetery along the walk, the way I had come, and stepped into the alley, turning . . . My god! There they were!

Two motorcycles and soldiers were at the far end of the alley. I stopped and turned around. Soldiers and a car waited at the other end.

A soldier yelled, "Halt, *Amerikaner!*" and leveled his gun at me. They had me this time!

– 7 –

To the right of me was the wall surrounding the cemetery; the wall was too high to climb. On the other side of the alley was a six-foot-high wooden fence without an opening.

Tears welled in my eyes, not from fear but from anger. I was trapped like an animal — without a gun, without anything with which to fight back. Suddenly a shadow crossed my mind: How in the hell did they figure out where I was? But I didn't linger longer over the thought. What would they do to me? This seemed a good deal more pertinent.

One of the Germans yelled out something in German. I didn't understand but I knew what he meant. I threw my hands up over my head.

The car behind me had driven up within a few feet and stopped. I heard the doors open. Though I didn't want to, I turned and looked. It was the same Mercedes we had encountered outside the railroad station. The two plainclothesmen came out wearing their nice, fucking, tan raincoats and tan slouch hats, followed by the two uniformed S.S. Waffen officers.

The shorter of the Gestapo agents walked up to me and said in English, "Well, my American friend, we have finally caught up with you. You have given us a good chase, but this is the end of the line. What is your name?"

I was overcome by rage. "Go fuck yourself, you Kraut bastard!"

He turned around and said to his companion, *"Was is das fuchunt?"* and they laughed. Then he returned his attention to me. "You can cuss all you want, Yank, but we have you now, and you will be one sorry son of a bitch."

Two soldiers came toward me, one slipping a loop of wire around each wrist, drawing it tightly and wrapping one end around my waist a couple of times, then back around my arms again. I was trussed up like a pig.

They marched me back to the Mercedes and pushed me into the back seat. Then they all climbed in and off we went, two motorcycles in front, leading the way.

Except for me everyone was all smiles, laughing and joking. Perhaps this was a feather in their cap, catching me, and they weren't making any bones about it, the bastards!

The short, little Gestapo guy said to me finally, "Well, my American friend, what is your name? You know you've had it now. We've got you. There is nothing you can do about it. In fact, my American friend, we can shoot you down in cold blood now. We have caught you in civilian clothing. As far as we are concerned, you are no longer a soldier. Now, what is your name?"

I spit it out quickly: "Cury, E.C. 0670027, First Lieutenant."

The Mercedes drove on. I couldn't tell what direction we were going. But at that point, I was so goddamn disgusted and dazed it really didn't make much difference.

How stupid I had been! Why hadn't I stayed hidden in the cemetery? Why did I have to come out into the alley? Why hadn't I brought an easily hidden gun along?

Only the deadness that encompassed my arms and wrists took my mind off my failures. If I moved, the noose only grew tighter. I had to calm down, gain control of myself. My heart and temples were still pounding, and I had a sickening, sinking feeling in my stomach.

Finally, I decided: I should've surrendered in the beginning. I could've saved myself all kinds of hell. Then, my mind flashed back to my encounters with the two French mademoiselles. It all seemed so far away.

I glanced out the window. We were passing the railroad station. We continued down the main thoroughfare, turning off into a small side street. There the Mercedes came to a halt before the Vichy police headquarters. Everyone got out except me. They didn't give me time to do it on my own but dragged me from the car like a sack of potatoes. As I tried to stand the guard yanked, and I lost my balance, falling to the ground. Then, a sharp pain hit me in the back of my head. The motherfucker had kicked me. Again the pain struck; and again. I rolled over and pulled myself up with my legs. It wasn't easy. It hurt. But I stood taller than the little bastard who spoke English.

"How did you like a little taste of that, Yank?" he asked. "This is what you can expect from now on." With this, he backhanded me a beauty, tearing open the wound on the side of my nose.

Blood ran down my nose, across my lip and into my mouth.

He hit me a second time, enjoying himself just fine.

From that blow I gained a mouth full of blood. I spit it right in his face, a stupid thing to have done, but when you're young you're impetuous.

What followed was not a happy circumstance . . . I awakened, tied to a chair in what appeared to be an interrogation room, the back of my head throbbing with pain. One of the bastards had smashed me across the back of my head with a rifle butt. I wanted to reach up to feel if I was badly hurt but my arms were bound and tied to the chair.

The blood had caked around my mouth. I licked my lips and tried to spit away the blood. Except for one guard I was alone in the room. He stood there smirking at me, saying something in German which I couldn't understand. But the gist of it: I had gotten what was coming to me!

My head was spinning, and I had a hell of a ringing in my ears. Could I possibly have a concussion? It seemed likely. I couldn't keep my head up and I must've semi-passed out again; my head was falling to one side.

I don't know how long I sat there like that, but I came back to stark reality with a sharp pain in my head. I had been grabbed by the hair and jerked straight up; it was my little, short German who spoke English. He was accompanied by two officers, one of whom appeared to be a captain and the other a major. Now the questioning began.

Who are you? Why are you in civilian clothes? Were you helping the French Underground? Where are your comrades? Where are your headquarters? Where is the next invasion?

With each question I began the name, rank and serial number crap, and each time, pow! Right across the face. Finally, I mumbled, "The Geneva Convention."

They roared with laughter. "Geneva Convention? Geneva Convention?" said the little, short German. "Who do you Americans think you are with your Geneva Convention? We intend to make a mockery of you and the whole damn Geneva Convention. So far as we are concerned you have been captured as a spy and you're already dead. We don't even have to report you as captured. We will shoot you like the pig you are. Unless, of course, you talk. This will weigh heavily in your favor."

The captain wearing black leather gloves was the one who had hauled off and belted me repeatedly, always across my face, the temple, the forehead. After about the fifteenth or sixteenth time I could no longer feel the pain. My nose and eye were bleeding badly. Otherwise, everything was spinning, spinning, spinning, until I threw up, spitting blood, food and bitterness. If I had been free, I could've torn them apart with my bare hands!

Since I refused to talk the beating continued. Finally, I passed out to awaken in a small dirty cell, lying sideways on a wooden slab suspended by chains from the wall. The cell was seven or eight feet wide and about ten feet long. Except for the slab coming from the side wall, there was nothing inside the cell.

I made an effort to move. But all I could do was roll from side to side. I tried sitting up, but another slab suspended directly above prevented it. Never mind. My head throbbed wildly, but not so wildly that I was beyond thought.

I wondered if our government knew how the Germans treated prisoners. I remembered how well we treated Germans when they were captured, and the thought infuriated me.

Finally, after great effort, I managed to sit up, avoiding the cot above. Then I stood. God, it hurt! But I knew I must move around, try to sort things out, get a grip on myself.

A small grill, about a foot square, opened in the door; there was my short, little German friend saying, "Well, how is our guest? I hope you feel better." He muttered something in German, and I could hear the guard unlocking the cell door. He entered with two guards. "I'm glad you are up and around. I thought you were dead when they carried you down here. But, then again, you are a big strapping fellow and it would take a lot to kill you." Now he set out to charm his way into my heart with a smile. "Listen, my friend. I want you to know that I want to help you. I am doing my job, just as you are doing yours. If you cooperate it will go a lot easier with you." He motioned to the guards. "Schnell," he said, or something like that. And I was taken from the cell, around the corner and into a room which had a table, stools, four chairs and an electric stove with coffee heating on it. Now he really turned on the charm. "I'll bet your arms hurt, don't they?"

He had to be joking . . . the fucking bastard!

"Well," he continued, "we are going to have to take the wires off. I know they must hurt very much."

I said nothing. My hands were so numb I could barely move my fingers

The guard with an ugly face and a machine gun backed off into a corner and sat on a stool. The other guard took out a pair of pliers and snipped the wires that bound me.

God, what a relief! My arms fell to my sides. I tried to lift them to look at my wrists. But my arms were too numb. So, I attempted to make my fingers work, slowly at first, until I was able to bring my arms up. My wrists were covered with vicious black and blue marks from the wire, and much of the skin was rubbed off, leaving raw flesh. Finally, I forced my arms and hands up, despite the weakness, to feel the back of my head. My hair was matted and sticky with blood. There was even an indentation in my skull. I felt to see if my skull was cracked, but the cut seemed mostly flesh, swollen and infected.

"Do sit down," my little German captor said with a flourish. He indicated a chair. "My friend, I told you I was just doing my job. I love America and Americans. In fact, I attended school in the good old

U.S.A. I don't like war any more than you do. To tell you the truth, we are all fighting the wrong enemies. The U.S. and Germany should be allied together, fighting those goddamn English and the Russian Communists. It was, you know, the Jews who got you into the war; the Jews and Roosevelt. You're being played for a sucker by them, you and millions of other guys just like you, and it's sad. We Germans love Americans. Look at all the Germans who are in your country . . ."

He was right there. We did have many Germans in the Pennsylvania Dutch country where I'd grown up. But I didn't reply. I just kept looking at him.

"Look, my friend, I know you've had a rough time. I know you've been treated badly. Put yourself in our place. You were captured in civilian clothes, and you didn't give yourself up easily. We have been looking for you and your friends for the past few weeks. Now if you will cooperate, I will cooperate with you."

Still I said nothing.

He turned away and said something in German to a guard. The guard stepped over to the stove and poured a cup of coffee.

The little German said, "You must be hungry, my friend, and thirsty." He handed me the cup of coffee. "Just take it easy on that coffee for awhile, and I'll get you something to eat. I really meant it when I said I liked America and Americans. I hate to see what you're going through. If you will cooperate, I will show you how well we can treat you, and I will show you what true Germans are like."

Motherfucker! My mind snapped; I already knew what they were like. But I kept my mouth firmly closed.

"I'm going to get you medical attention. I know you are hurting. After you are fixed up you will feel better and realize we mean well. I know then you will cooperate."

The coffee was hot and bitter. The moment it hit my gums and teeth I wanted to scream. The inside of my mouth and cheeks were cut up, and hot coffee made it feel worse. But I needed the strength the coffee gave me. I kept sipping away, no matter how badly it hurt, until I finished the cup. Then I handed the empty cup back to him.

"Another?" my German friend asked.

I shook my head in the negative.

"Now, my fine American friend," he went on, "I'm going to take you for medical attention. I hope we don't have to wire you up again. You know you are helpless, especially in this place. It is heavily guarded. It is useless to try anything."

They led me from the room, through a long corridor and down the stairs into a dispensary with a white cross and something written in German on the door. Then, they took me into a second room where I was told to sit down. The big guard with the machine gun stayed right behind me along with two other guards. None of them took their eyes off me.

63

In a few moments a doctor and a nurse entered; they were French. I could understand much of what was said.

"This poor devil was given a severe beating," the doctor said. "Let's see what we can do." He examined the back of my head. The doctor muttered something to himself softly; it sounded like a curse word. Then he asked the nurse for scissors and cut away my hair. With a sponge soaked in a solution he dabbed at my head.

I asked him, "How bad is it?"

He didn't understand, but he said, *"Pas bon,"* to the nurse, meaning that it wasn't good.

The doctor and nurse treated me with care and kindness as they sutured the cut in the back of my head, the nurse saying, "It's going to hurt. But it has to be done."

Though it hurt like hell, I wasn't about to make a sound. I could see the smirk on the guards' faces, as though saying, "Go ahead, American. Show us how soft you are." Well, fuck 'em!

The stitching over, the doctor put down the curved needle and swabbed my head again. He applied a solution from a purple bottle to my head, saying something which sounded like, "That will be much better."

Next he examined the side of my nose and face, shaking his head all the way. Out came the needle, the thread, the antiseptic solution. I was chicken. I didn't want to look, so I turned my head, gritting my teeth as they worked away, keeping my eyes closed. Soon he was finished with that. He went on to the top of my eyelid, pushing inward. I felt a sharp pain. But evidently it wasn't bad enough, that spot beneath my right eyebrow, to stitch. Later, I discovered this was a piece of flak which had become embedded above my eye.

Now my German friend returned, all smiles. "See? Didn't I tell you we would care for you? These are good Frenchmen, Vichy French, who believe in the alliance between Germany and France. Someday Germany and France will be one nation, and we will be happy together, won't we?" he said, turning to the doctor.

The doctor smiled weakly, and the nurse came over with a large comb. She brushed my hair back carefully. They were trying to be kind and gentle, while not giving themselves away. I nodded my head in thanks, and I could see they understood.

Next the doctor examined the inside of my mouth. Nothing could be done. But he gave me a cup of solution and told me to rinse my mouth out three or four times with the solution and I would feel better. I did, and the nurse and doctor left the room.

"My friend," said the little German, "we will now go back to my office. We will sit down and have a long talk. Oh yes, you must be hungry . . ." He turned and said something to a guard. Then: "Come. I will have it sent to my office. You can eat while we talk."

Since I had no choice in the matter I followed him back down the corridor and up the stairs to one level above the dispensary. The big ugly guard with the machine gun came along with two other guards, keeping their distance and not speaking a word. Inside the little German's office I was told to sit down. Then it began again, the usual questions:

"Name, rank and serial number? Home town? Family? What group are you in?"

He must've asked a million questions. Again I told him only, "I am an officer in the United States Army Air Corps. My name is Cury, E.C., First Lieutenant, Serial Number 0670027."

He went along with that, saying, "I know you're trying to do your job as a good soldier. I can't help but admire you. But, my friend you are going to be taken to another interrogation station. You will not be treated well there. I have a personal interest in your case. I was the one who captured you . . ."

A commotion occurred at the door. Another guard entered with a short dumpy woman carrying a tray of food. She placed the tray on the table and removed the cover: soup, knockwurst, sauerkraut and mashed potatoes. It smelled damn good. German or not, I made up my mind to eat it. I was going to need all the strength I could muster.

Said my German friend, "Take your time. I will ask you questions. You can just nod your head yes or no. How's that?"

I didn't answer. I was trying to eat, but my mouth hurt badly.

"How's the soup?" he asked. "This food is directly from our officers' mess. It is the same food our officers eat. After all, we officers must be good to each other. Since we are both professionals, I will try to be nice to you and cooperate with you. I have a great admiration for Americans, you know."

Fuck him! I thought, and kept on eating, trying to eat some of the soup, then dug into the knockwurst, sauerkraut and potatoes. My mouth hurt like hell, but I kept eating. The only bit of food on the plate which I couldn't manage was a big piece of brown bread; it was just too hard.

While I ate, he asked, "Were you a West Point graduate?"

I shook my head, indicating I was not.

"Are you a professional soldier?"

I shook my head to the contrary.

"Were you a reserve officer?"

Again, a negative response from me.

Then, came the big ones: What bomb group were you with? Are you really a flyer or was your mission to come here and organize the Maquis to prepare for a second invasion? "Come on. We know all about it. The Allies are planning a second invasion in the Bordeaux peninsula sector. We know that." Here he shifted and leaned forward, as if in confidence. "I'll be honest with you. My superiors know of your plan and they intend to get this information from you one way or another. Believe me, if you cooperate with me, I will help you as much as possible and see it goes easy for you. Believe me, Cury, if you do not cooperate, they will shoot you immediately. Since you know the Geneva Convention so well, you know that if one is captured in civilian clothes, one is considered a spy, not covered by international law. So, come now. Be a good sport. Cooperate. What have you got to gain by being obstinate? You know damn well this whole war is being fought for the benefit of the Jews and the Wall Street brokers who are all Jews. Your whole country is controlled by Jews. You know that. The banks, newspapers, radio, Hollywood, Wall Street — everything! Why are you being a chump for them?" Here he paused and took a deep breath. "Remember one thing. We are going to win this war, and when we do, the U.S.A. will be a German colony. We will treat those who cooperate with us well, after we houseclean all the capitalists and Jews and return things to the hands of the good people."

The man had to be dreaming. There was no way they were winning the war, and I had heard about what these inhuman Nazi bastards had done to the Jews. Having grown up in Allentown, Pennsylvania, where almost every family was first generation American, I had grown up with the Jews, Irish, Slovaks, Syrians and Italians. There were Catholics, Protestants and Jews. But we didn't have any religious or racial prejudices. In truth, my best buddy, Lou Dubnow, a member of the Jewish faith, was closer to me than my own brother. These fucking Germans believed their bullshit propaganda. Still, I didn't say a word. I just let him talk.

He went back over the same old territory, both of us growing weary. I could see things might take a turn for the worse at any moment, so I decided to play him a bit. I gave him my name, rank and serial number. Then I said, "I was on a mission to bomb the Merignac air field outside of Bordeaux when I was shot down. I had nothing to do with any invasion or plans for any invasion. My job was to bomb the air field. That's it. So far as evading capture, that was my duty, no different from your own flyers."

He shook his head. "That can't be so."

"It's true," I said.

"It can't be," he responded.

"It is."

He leaned forward. "If it is so, then how did you know how to evade for so long and to do the things you did? We know you killed many of our men. You didn't learn to fight like that on the ground, being a flyer. We know that."

It was time for a well-turned lie. "Kill Germans?" I said. "Why, I never killed any Germans. I only evaded them. I was doing my job."

"That's not so!" He jerked a folder from a bunch of papers on his desk, as if he had the evidence in hand.

He's full of shit! I thought; but I was wrong.

He began by telling me about the first two soldiers I'd killed, or thought I had killed, since no one had lived to tell *them* about it. He related the incident of the old man who shot at me. Looking me squarely in the eyes, he said, "You blew up the trucks, killing some of the soldiers with grenades you had stolen."

Christ! I thought. I was really in trouble.

A guard entered, said something to him in German and he excused himself politely, "I'll be back."

The dinner plate held a smidgen of mashed potatoes with gravy and the hard bread. Buddy, I told myself, this could very well be your last meal. I picked up the bread and swabbed the plate of what remained of the mashed potatoes and gravy.

The guard in the corner looked at me for the first time, saying, "Ya, dot's goot!" following with something else in German which I didn't understand.

My plate clean, I sat uneasily, waiting for my interrogator.

Upon his return his face was long and serious. "Well, my friend, I told you it would soon be out of my hands. You have been ordered to be taken to Gestapo Headquarters for this sector. I know they will not be easy on you, like I have been. But there's nothing I can do. Whether or not you are a flyer or a saboteur, I don't know. But God help you!" Now he nodded to the guards.

They took over, slipping handcuffs on my wrists, pulling both my arms behind me. While it wasn't comfortable, it was a hell of a lot better than the wire.

When we walked into the day and the light hit my face and eyes, I took on new life. Fresh air! I looked at the sky, and it was a beautiful clear blue. The tops of the trees on the other side of the wall rustled softly. One didn't appreciate a beautiful sky and trees until the chips were down. And they were truly down.

– 8 –

Driving to Gestapo Headquarters, I grew despondent. I believed what had been told me about being caught in civilian clothes. The fact that I had dug my dog tags from the lining of my belt to prove a point had meant nothing, though they were now tied around my neck with a string.

In the courtyard there were two sedans and a weapon carrier parked. Drivers were in both cars and four soldiers and a driver were in the weapon carrier. Standing off to the side of the first car were two black uniformed S.S. Waffen officers and two plain-clothesmen, wearing the typical trench coats and slouch hats. These guys really played their parts to the hilt, I thought.

My guards led me over to an officer and handed him a folder. He, in turn, gave them a piece of paper, perhaps a release form for me. I was then placed in the lead car with two guards, the driver, and the S.S. Waffen officers, where the conversation got off to a flying start. One of these officers also spoke English.

"Well, Cury," he said. "You're a celebrity. We have heard about your exploits, and I give you credit. You gave them all quite a chase! Did you realize over 300 German troops were looking for you in the peninsula? I don't know how the hell you got out of there. But that was something!"

Ah, I thought, the old cozy-up approach. I remained silent.

"Who helped you?" he asked, as if this might be just conversation. "Who were the people? We know you could not have done it alone. We had every road blocked, every checkpoint blocked. It was impossible!"

I didn't acknowledge the impossibility of it all, since there I sat, not happily.

"You must have crossed the Gironde some way and you would

have had to have help to do it. Who helped you?"

To forestall any more such dialog I gave him my name, rank and serial number, and informed him, "This is all I have to say." But it didn't stop the constant chatter and questioning in our ride together.

Over the next few hours we paused for four road blocks and checkpoints, finally stopping to take a leak. While this went on they watched me like hawks. It was dark now and the stars were bright. The moon was to my right. We were heading north. To where? I had no idea.

Back in the car the questioning went on, especially about the second invasion — when it was going to hit and how had I planned it. The man must've been a fool. We didn't know until the morning of each mission where we would go; and he didn't know much about the U.S. Army Air Corps, especially those below the rank of major. I wasn't privy to any secrets.

At a motor depot they stopped to fill up with gas. I was allowed to stretch my legs, again under heavy guard. They had coffee and sandwiches, promising to allow me to have some food when we returned to the car, since that was the only time they were allowed to uncuff me.

Once again we headed north. After a few words, I reminded the officer of his promise to uncuff me.

"Oh, yes, I did promise." He handed the key to the guard sitting beside me. The handcuffs were removed. Then he opened a small pail and took out the coffee thermos and a sandwich for me.

The sandwich was meat, perhaps pork; it wasn't good. But I ate slowly, savoring every bite. The coffee had cream and sugar in it, not half bad. I was pleased to note that my mouth was feeling somewhat better.

No one spoke while I ate. But the guard and the officer in front didn't take their eyes from me. When I finished, the officer reached back for the empty cup. "There," he said with satisfaction. "We Germans are not as bad as your Hollywood makes us out to be. I understand you were a civilian before the war. I, too, was a civilian. In fact, I was a student at the University of Leipzig when the war broke out in the Sudetenland. But we have to stick with our country. I am a member of the Nazi Party. It is my country first. I guess you feel the same about America."

I nodded my head affirmatively.

At long last we arrived. It was pitch dark. We stopped at a small bridge; it appeared to be the entrance to an estate or chateau. There we were checked out by a guard in a hut. Then, as we progressed along the road, statuary in gardens was illuminated by the dim blackout lights of the car. Finally, we pulled up in front of what had to've been a castle at some point in time.

Here I was treated differently. They actually helped me from the car. In fact, one officer reached over and pulled down my jacket, buttoning the top two buttons. "We must make you look good," he said. "Now, if you are asked about your wounds, you are to say, 'This is what happened to me in evading capture.' Not one hand was laid on you. Do you understand this? It will make everything easier for you."

I half believed the bastard.

We entered and walked down a main corridor. The place was loaded with antiques, and ornate and expensive furnishings. There was even a massive Louis XV reception desk. It was all very elegant!

They checked in with the orderly at the desk and led me along a hall into a large room. Here the guard told the officer accompanying me that I had to be put away for the night, or something to that effect. I was then taken down long circular steps to what was the second basement and a hall with cells on either side. Only one guard held the fort here. He snapped to attention. I was settled into the last cell on the right and the light was turned on for me.

"This will be your cell while you are here; as long as you cooperate, you will be treated as an officer. I will see you in the morning. *Guttennicht!*"

The cell was furnished with a cot, mattress, blanket, a small toilet and washstand, but no mirror. I was anxious to see what my face looked like after the beating. Since this was an impossibility I opened the spigot on the washstand and, since there was no cup or glass, I bent over and got a mouthful of water. The water was cold and not half bad. I turned to see the guard watching me through the grill opening in the door. What the hell! I went to the toilet and much to my surprise there was a roll of toilet paper there. This had to be a high-class prison since even soap was provided.

I washed my hands and gently patted my face with water. I was afraid to apply the soap to my face lest it get into my wounds. But having my hands free again was pure luxury. I moved my hands and arms around, feeling good about myself. The guard must've thought I was loco.

The cell was a little cool. But I took off my clothes, except for my trousers. Then I crawled into the sack, pulling the blanket atop me, staring at the ceiling. The guard peered in again. Finally I spoke to him, saying, "Can you turn out the light?"

He replied, "*Nicht Ferchte.*" He didn't understand English.

I pointed to the light.

He shook his head.

I tried to reach up to the light, but it was too high. So I pulled the blanket over my head in an effort to get badly needed sleep which didn't come easily. It was a fitful time, waking occasionally in a cold sweat, my mind playing tricks with me:

Had I seen my parents for the last time? Will the Nazis execute me? If so, how will they do it? If I'd only kept my khaki G.I. shorts.

That would prove to them I was no spy. I half smiled, remembering how I'd used them.

Finally, I fell into oblivion. I was so tired. Even agonizing worry couldn't keep me from sleeping.

A banging at the door awakened me, the guard yelling, *"Raus, raus!"*

Since I could figure out what he meant, I got up, washed myself as well as I could and dressed carefully in anticipation of the day ahead. My wrists felt better but they were still marked and the skin broken from the wire. I sat on my bunk and wiggled my fingers, exercising them, until a commotion broke out in the hall.

Two guards entered, and they had breakfast. On a small metal tray was a large tin cup of coffee and a plate of what looked like farina or oatmeal, a large piece of sausage and a spoon. But there was no fork or knife. Nevertheless, I was being properly fed, or fattened up for the kill!

I took time eating, thinking with every bite, yes, this is my last meal. For a last meal it wasn't very good. but it was better than nothing. A tall S.S. officer entered. "Gutten tag," he greeted me. Then: "I shall teach you German. That means 'good day,' or as you Americans say, 'good morning'." He appeared to be in an amiable and sociable mood.

"Our German is very much like your language. In fact, the Germans and Americans are so closely related it's a pity we are fighting each other."

Funny, I thought; every German had the same old line. I wondered if they really felt that way or if it was just so much propaganda bullshit. Frankly, I was inclined toward the latter conclusion. I figured the Germans had no love for anyone but Germans. I had seen enough to make my blood boil. I kept my mouth shut.

"I hope you are feeling better. Today you are being interrogated by our colonel." Then he gave a few snappy orders in German; the two guards came in and slipped the cuffs on me again, damn it!

Out the cell we went and up the two tiers of stairs. Then, it was down the corridor to the colonel's office. And, boy, was this some kind of interrogation room!

A beautiful Oriental rug and a long Louis XV table with high back chairs covered in heavy thick velvet were the center piece. The walls were decorated with oil paintings and the draperies were elegant.

The two guards and the S.S. officer stayed with me. Then, in came the colonel with his aide, and the colonel was sharp!

I guessed his age to be about sixty-five. He was ramrod straight. From his bearing and decorations, obviously he was someone very special.

"Good morning, Leftenant Cury," he said with a sharp English accent. "I hope you slept well."

I snapped to attention without thinking.

"Ah, I am happy to see you American officers are respectful of rank. Thank you, *Leftenant* Cury."

He knew my name!

"Please be seated," he said, apologizing for not being able to remove the handcuffs. "But I'm sure you understand."

Then, of all the goddamn things, he apologized to me for his job. He was a Prussian officer, a graduate of the German military academy, a lifetime professional. The only reason he was doing this job, instead of fighting in the real war at the front, was because of his age; he was seventy-four years old. He had been wounded in the early fighting.

"Under the circumstances," he said politely, finally getting down to the nitty-gritty of our confrontation, "you can understand why we must assume you are a spy or a high ranking liaison officer parachuted in to set up and prepare for a second invasion, which is inevitable. We are certain it will take place in the Bordeaux sector, since the land is perfect for it. In fact, as a professional, I would have launched the original invasion there, instead of Normandy. The Allies have made a big mistake in landing at Normandy. Your general staff must have bats in their belfry to have made such a mistake. They will soon be pushed back into the sea and all your forces will be eliminated."

I wondered at the pure English accent more and more. Perhaps he had been schooled in England. Whatever, he loved to talk and I sat listening, not saying a word until the questions began. He really and truly believed I was a saboteur or liaison officer.

I told him I was a member of a B-17 air crew shot down on a mission to Merignac; I was only doing my duty by trying to evade capture. It went on for hours.

Finally, he said, "Cury, we have had a long session, and I know you must be quite hungry as I am . . ." He pushed a buzzer, summoning a guard into the room. Then, he gave curt orders in German.

About twenty minutes later, the guard returned carrying a large silver tray in ornate chased silver. Atop the tray was a large silver coffee pot with a sugar and creamer, two cups for coffee, and sandwiches.

The colonel looked at me. "Cury, I should not do this, but I will grant you the courtesy of an officer and gentleman, providing that we will not have trouble with you if we remove the handcuffs while you eat lunch. How about it, young man?"

I agreed readily with a nod. This guy was really something, an impressive officer and gentleman through and through. In fact, he offered me the coffee and a sandwich first.

We ate slowly, not talking. But his eyes never left me. Here I was being treated decently. If I had known what was in store for me, I might have eaten with less relish.

The coffee and sandwiches under our belt, the colonel apologized for no dessert, saying, "I must always watch my diet."

At this point I was once more handcuffed, as soon as the other guard came back into the room. The colonel had snapped a curt order and that was it.

One thing aroused my curiosity. Although I couldn't understand the orders in German, I could tell the orders were curt and filled with disdain. There was simply no banter between officers and enlisted men.

"Now, Cury," said the colonel, "we will continue." He leaned back and eyed me sternly. "I have been more than patient with you. But now I want to know the facts, the hard facts. If you will not give them to me voluntarily, there are other means. It is entirely up to you . . . " And he was off and running again, question after question for hours more.

When nothing new developed, the colonel threw up his hands and said, "Well, it is apparent I am getting nowhere with you, and, reluctantly, I will have to turn you over to the experts. As I told you, I am a Prussian officer and a gentleman, and I do not believe in such tactics. But you leave me no choice." He pushed the buzzer again and the same two guards came in. He barked out orders and nodded his head to me.

The two guards escorted me out, one on either side, along with the fellow who had stood in the corner with a machine gun. It was as if the guards knew something I didn't know. They handled me roughly, and I was dreading what lay ahead of me.

Down the two flights of stairs we went to the end of the corridor where we were met by a Gestapo officer and two men in gray jackets similar to what doctors wear. There I was taken into a room. My arms were loosened, slipped over the back of a chair and hand-cuffed again. A long black leather belt was placed around my waist and the back of the chair. Again, there were questions, questions, questions.

Who are you? What are you doing here? What are the plans for the second invasion?

I held up pretty well until one of the men stepped over to a small table and picked up a rubber hose about two feet long . . . Just like in the movies. I braced myself for the worst; and it was not long in coming.

Every time the Gestapo officer asked me a question and I shook my head, this bastard struck me with a rubber hose on the side of my head, grinning all the way, as he changed sides, hitting me first on one side of my head and then on the other. The blows were not hard enough to do real damage, but after a dozen or more I became almost numb. The only real pain was the tingling in my ears, since the hose didn't cause cuts or abrasions. But it was getting to me in more ways than one. Each time a blow was struck now, my head grew more and more numb, and the noise of the hose hitting my head grew louder.

After I don't know how long, the oberleutnant grew tired, gave an order in German, and the bastard stopped hitting me. I sagged as they unfastened my bonds and took me back to my cell, my legs wobbily, as if most of my coordination had gone by the boards. But the guards knew what to do. They grabbed me by the arms and practically carried me there, throwing me into the cell and slamming the door shut.

I tried to pull myself up to the cot and fell. So I lay on my stomach, hands cuffed behind me, since that was the only comfort I could find on the floor with a head and ears that hurt so badly I can't describe it.

Could this really be happening to me? Yes, it was!

My throat tightened and I began to choke. I couldn't help myself; tears filled my eyes. I turned my head away from the door. That damn guard was there. And at long last I fell into a semi-conscious state.

I awoke from this condition to two guards jerking me to my feet. They returned me to the interrogation room and the treatment was repeated for a couple of more hours.

The Gestapo officer asked the same questions and I shook my head. Then, the hose was applied, only this time the blows were harder. Finally, I gave in and let myself pass out.

I awoke face down on the cot in my cell. I had no inclination to move. It didn't matter. I passed out again.

A short time later I awoke with a desperate need. I had to go to the bathroom. I called out to the guard. His face appeared in the opening. He didn't understand or didn't want to understand.

Time went by. A guard came in, and I explained to him my problem. He unhooked my handcuffs and allowed me to "do my duty." Here he entered into a discussion with another guard leaving the handcuffs off. I stumbled to my cot where I cradled my head on my arm, taking the pressure off my ears. They were sore as hell, since any little touch caused a streak of pain through my head. With this relief, I fell into blessed sleep and awakened later, feeling some better.

Carefully, I sat on the edge of the cot, touching my ears. They didn't feel as bad as before. I massaged them gently, hoping that would encourage circulation. This didn't last long. The first *oberleutnant* came in with two guards; I was handcuffed and returned to the interrogation room.

The oberleutnant told me, "We have ways of making anyone talk. As much as we dislike using these methods you had better talk now."

I remained mute and sullen.

"We have drugs that can make anyone talk," he emphasized. "As a last resort we will use the hose treatment."

I thought I had already had the hose treatment.

He made me understand this hose treatment was different. "What we do is insert a hose into the rectum, turn on the water, causing great pressure. If continued, the pressure of water ruptures the bowels, causing a very painful death. A few weeks ago we did this to a leader of the French resistance. His internal organs exploded!" he finished with satisfaction.

Oh, dear God, I thought, help me.

Since I failed to respond, pro or con, he snapped out an order in German and the two gorillas in the jackets came in. One of them carried a hypodermic needle, a syringe and a vial with liquid in it the color of urine. I dreaded the needles more than anything. But I had no choice.

They strapped me back into the chair with my hands cuffed behind me. Then, a large rubber band was wrapped around my arm, followed by the sting of the needle burning. Almost immediately a hot flush swept over my body, and the room began to spin . . . I passed out.

– 9 –

When I awakened in my cell, lying face down on the cot, my arms free, I had no idea what had happened to me, except . . .

Thank God, I'm alive!

I had lost all track of time. I tried to get up, but I couldn't make it. So, I lay there on my cot, half dazed, passing out, coming awake, seemingly lost, except for the goddamn light burning overhead, my only point of reference.

Some time later, the bathroom beckoned again. I managed to sit up on the cot. I braced myself as best I could and managed to stand on my own two feet. I made it to the commode, but had to brace myself against the wall. I was just finishing my business when the cell door opened. Once more, the oberleutnant and the two guards arrived. They dragged me to the middle of the room. They hand-cuffed me again, not saying a word. Catching me by the arms, they escorted me from my cell.

This is it! I thought. This is it!

I was taken up two flights of stairs and outside into beautiful fresh air, a touch of heaven. Through blinking eyes, I couldn't resist asking what was happening.

"You are being sent to Germany. In fact, you are being taken to Munich." The oberleutnant smiled. "I wish I could be going with you."

The guards shoved me into the car and everyone climbed in after me. After an hour's ride, we pulled up to an air field without much activity. Darkness had descended and only a few lights were show-ing. Then, it dawned on me . . . No lights with the black out.

The car drove on down an apron, stopping at what might have been an operations shack. The oberleutnant got out and entered the shack. He came back to poke his head in the window and say, "Well, Cury, you will be leaving in a short while. The transport plane is due within minutes."

The unmistakable drone of a multi-engine aircraft approaching the airport, reached my ears. How could the plane land without runway lights? I searched the sky. An aircraft was on final approach, and the lights came up. The moment the aircraft touched down and started to taxi, out went the lights again.

The plane taxied up to where we were. It was a tri-motor, a large transport. Two cars and a truck arrived. Soldiers jumped from the truck and began removing items from it. The engines on the plane died, and the doors were opened. Two high-ranking officers stepped out, followed by crew members. Five officers boarded, while bags and cartons from the truck were loaded. Now it was my turn.

I was taken into the plane and placed in one of the back bucket seats. My handcuffs were loosened. It didn't last. One hand was cuffed to the side of the fuselage. I glanced around. The inside of the plane was similar to our DC-3. A guard sat next to me. Then the plane taxied down the runway, lifting off.

In the air, an officer who had boarded the plane turned back to me and said in English, "You are an American, aren't you?" His English was broken but fairly good.

I nodded my head.

"I could tell you were, even in your French civilian clothes. Are you a saboteur?"

I didn't reply. Then the guard spoke to the officer in German.

The officer laughed and said to me, "You must be special, to take you back to Germany." He opened a fancy cigarette case, extracted two cigarettes, lighted both and offered a cigarette to me.

I thanked him, saying, "I don't smoke . . . "

"But I thought all Americans smoked. Are you sure you are an American?" The other officers turned to look at me, their eyes running over me carefully, as if in speculation.

During the two-hour flight to another air field, where no one left the plane, but two more officers boarded with bags that evidently contained mail, there was no more conversation. The flight continued for another few hours. Looking out the small porthole I could see the sun rising. We were heading in a northeasterly direction. Finally, the pilot cut back on the power, the flaps were lowered and we were landing. I craned my neck to see what lay below, but the guard pushed my head away.

The plane landed, taxied and came to a stop. The fuselage door opened and everyone disembarked, except the guard and me. Then, the pilot and co-pilot came back, looking at me curiously, but passed onward.

When all the cargo had been taken off, two officers boarded. I was released from the fuselage and my hands were cuffed together again. I was given orders to disembark in German, though it took some doing to understand what they wanted me to do.

As I stepped down from the aircraft, I turned to get a better look at the plane. The guard jerked my head around. Evidently, they didn't want me to look at anything.

I was taken to a truck. The two officers, the guard and I climbed into the back of the truck, and away we went, a canvas covering the rear of the truck, so that all sights were hidden from my eyes. Only once did I catch sight of anything. As the truck pulled away from a stop, I glanced through the open flap and caught a glimpse of a sign: Munchen. Munich!

The truck rumbled on for another hour. I guessed I was being taken to a conventional prison camp, and my hopes soared slightly. I kept going over the same old ground: Had the injection worked? And if it did, what had I told the Germans?

Suddenly, a light went on in my brain. Hell, there wasn't much I could've told them, except for our group code name, "Sylvester," and that wouldn't have meant much to them one way or the other . . . Finally, the truck came to a halt.

Both flaps were pulled back; we were entering a large compound surrounded by a high fence with patrol guards. The truck moved on past a guard tower with a machine gun mounted on top, several buildings, then, stopped at a large dark building. Two guards appeared at the back of the truck, dropped the back gate, and we jumped to the ground. I was taken inside the building to a large reception office; the guard uncuffed me and an oberleutnant entered the room. He was tall, blond and in his mid-thirties.

"Good morning," he said. "How are you, Cury?" He beckoned me to a table where we sat down. He noticed my dog tags and reached across, looking at them. "I see you are from the Lehigh Valley."

My home address was Allentown, Pennsylvania, and it was on my dog tags. I wondered how in hell he knew that Allentown was in the Lehigh Valley.

He read my face, laughing. "We are like old neighbors. I lived in the Lehigh Valley for five years."

I couldn't help myself: "Why, you fucking traitor!"

Calmly, he looked back at me. "No, I am not a traitor. I am a German. I graduated from the university and studied metallurgy. Long before the war I was sent to Bethlehem by my company to learn their methods, and I was there for five years. When the war broke out, I was called to active duty." He rambled on about all the places he knew in Allentown and Bethlehem — Joe Kinnys, a favorite hang-out for the younger set in Bethlehem, the Mannerchoir Club and other German clubs in the area: Algameir, Liederkranz and the Saegerbund Club.

I knew all of these places. My area of Pennsylvania was predominately Pennsylvania German. I had always found the German Americans friendly and honest hard workers. To say I was taken aback by this German, whom I might have met on some occasion and not realized it, is putting it mildly. I didn't linger over it long, though. The questions began.

"Look, Cury, we know more about you than you know about yourself." He opened a folder, told me where my father worked, my sister worked, how many brothers I had . . . He also told me I must have been on one of my last missions.

How in the hell did he know?

Then he said, "I see you have received the Distinguished Flying Cross twice, five or six Air Medals, ah, and even the Purple Heart. I know they award one Air Medal for five missions. Since you are a bomber crew member, you must have flown over twenty-five missions."

I listened, dumbfounded. Why, the bastard even knew what I did before the war. He was telling me now! The surprise was clearly visible, I'm sure.

"Look, we know much more. If you wonder how I have this information, let me tell you. We have friends of Germany all over the world, people who cut clippings on servicemen from newspapers. These clippings are sent to Brazil where they are microfilmed before being sent on to the Fatherland. We keep them on file for just such an occasion as this. There are records that tell us where you graduated from, what flying schools you attended. You see, all the Germans in the United States are waiting until we take over, and I can assure you we will. Yes, we will soon win this war. Just you wait and see."

I couldn't resist getting in my two-bits. "I wouldn't hold my breath if I were you."

With a half smile he said, "Your country is in for a big surprise," and he was off and running, parroting the same old propaganda bullshit about fighting for Roosevelt, the Jews and Wall Street. Finally, he ended by saying, "Yes, the Germans and Americans should not be fighting each other. They should be allied in the fight against Russia. It is a shame, we are so much alike. We are both clean, industrial nations, and our people are intelligent, hard workers — not like the French and Italians — all lazy, cowardly slobs."

All was not going well with Germany's friend, Italy, it seemed. I raised my eyebrows in thought as he rambled on, waiting for him to wind down. At long last, it happened.

"Well," he said, "your problems are over. You will be processed and assigned to an *Oftlafflug* for the remainder of the war."

Two guards came and took me along a corridor to a dispensary where I was examined by a German doctor. The oberleutnant said, "We will work on your face. Perhaps we can do a better job for you. You are being assigned to a hospital for now. If you behave yourself, everything will be taken care of."

After this examination, I was led to another room. My clothes were removed and I was given a thorough check-up by a medical attendant who spoke to the doctor in German. My German friend from Lehigh Valley translated. "You have picked up a bad case of scabies. The wound in your leg is festering and will be treated. You look hungry to me."

Now that he mentioned it, I agreed, "You're right, I am hungry."

With that, I dressed, and he had two guards take me to another small building. It was the mess hall. I could smell the food before we entered.

It was good to hear the chatter of other soldiers. These were English soldiers, orderlies of some sort. A couple of them came over and said, "Welcome, Yank. We're glad to see you." I wondered if other Americans were here, but I had no chance to inquire. I was hustled along to the end of a table, where I was seated with two guards and the oberleutnant. Shortly, a tray of food was brought for each of us. There was coffee, ersatz bread and a large bowl of stew. It smelled good, and I was so damned hungry. I would've eaten an elephant.

After the meal, the guards and the oberleutnant took me to the far end of the compound to the hospital. Two doctors, one German, one English, greeted me.

The English doctor said, "How were you captured, Yank?"

I hesitated. While the fellow had every appearance of an Englishman, I was wary.

"Don't worry, ole chap, I'm a prisoner too. A doctor. I was captured in North Africa. Been a prisoner for over a year." He cut my trouser leg and examined the wound. The Englishman spoke fluent German. He discussed my leg with the German doctor. Then, they examined my face. "Well," the Englishman said, "the leg isn't too bad. But we're going to cut and resew the wounds on the side of your nose and the side of your eye. We'll take care of your leg right away, though." He set to work, scraping away the scab on the leg, swabbing it with a solution. Then, he shaved my leg around the wound and swabbed it again, finally dusting the wound with sulfa powder. "That should take care of it. I hope so, anyway. Sulfa is in short supply in Germany. They don't like us using it on prisoners." He bandaged my leg, adding, "Hope to see you in a day or so, ole chap."

I was returned to the truck. We rumbled back to the other side of the compound to the detention center. Inside, I was locked up in an enclosure with another prisoner, supposedly an R.A.F. British flyer.

He shook my hand. "James Martin, Spitfire pilot, Royal Air Force." Then, he started asking me questions.

When were you shot down? Where did you hang out in London? Where were you stationed?

He seemed to be the genuine article. But I didn't trust him, careful of my every answer.

Finally, he said, "I was shot down several months ago. I was assigned to a prison camp. But I tried to escape, was picked up and brought here."

His accent and the uniform, all of it was authentic. But by now I had run into so many German officers who spoke English with a perfect English accent that I wasn't ready to trust the first person I met. I especially remembered the perfect English accent of the colonel back in France; he could've passed for an English nobleman.

I stretched out on one of the four cots in the detention cell. "I'm bushed," I told him.

He nodded, as if in understanding.

I drifted off to sleep.

When I opened my eyes, I heard my pal, the English R.A.F. pilot, speaking to a German oberleutnant in German. They were whispering. I was right. This guy was no English flyer. He was a phony, probably a Gestapo agent educated in England.

I stayed where I was, pretending sleep, listening to them talk, understanding nothing. As I listened I tried to rationalize it all. Many Englishmen spoke German and French, since their countries were so close together. Nevertheless, I decided to watch my step. The conversation ceased, but I continued to pretend sleep for another half hour. Then, I let out a long sigh and awakened.

"Well, my Yank friend," my cell mate boomed out. "You must've been tired. You were out like you'd been run over by a bloody truck."

"Haven't had any sleep for two nights," I replied, coming alive.

He stepped over to my cot. "You must have been dreaming. You moaned and turned in your sleep."

In truth, I had been day dreaming. I was at the Grosvenor House ballroom in London which had been converted into a gigantic officers' mess and bar. I was remembering an incident with my buddy, Fred Swantz; this had given me an idea.

"Come now, what were you dreaming, my Yankee friend?" asked my cell mate.

"An incident which happened with our co-pilot at Willow Run . . ."

"Willow Run? What is that?"

That was the name we had dubbed the transient officers' mess at the Grosvenor ballroom; it fed thousands of men daily in assembly line order. The officers' mess was the size of a football field and hard to forget.

As one entered the place, a tremendous lobby and foyer, which opened into a large mezzanine surrounding the ballroom, swallowed one up. Two stairways on either end led down into the ballroom with its floor of marble. It was like a palace, tremendous crystal chandeliers hanging all over the place.

"You remember Willow Run — the nickname we gave to the Grosvenor ballroom," I prompted.

"Oh yes, ole chap, it just slipped my mind."

The fucking bastard was lying, but I thought to let him go all the way. I launched into a story about Swantz.

We had gone to the Grosvenor ballroom for dinner. The place was jammed. So we went into the bar and had a few drinks, one shilling or 20 cents per drink. I had three drinks and Swantz put away about six. Still, the line was long to go down into the ballroom where dinner was served cafeteria style. We decided to have a few more drinks. Standing next to us was a paddlefoot colonel, i.e., an officer who didn't wear wings. He was a real dude, up to and including a pin-point waxed moustache and a swagger stick, regulation for most high-ranking British Army officers, but some of *our* brass had begun imitating them.

The colonel admired his moustache in the mirror behind the bar. Then, he admired his profile. The place was so crowded, we couldn't help but bump him once in a while, at which point the chicken colonel let us know we were to realize that he was a full colonel and was entitled to the respect of junior officers. Meanwhile, he didn't think much of combat flying officers. To avoid a final confrontation with the bastard, we went off to the elaborate men's room.

With two lines leading to the urinals, Freddy got in one line and I in the other. Here I noticed the chicken-shit colonel was two places in front of Freddy. As the lines moved up, men split off to the vacant urinals. Except for the bird colonel, it was a gorgeous place.

The room was done up in carrarra marble, except, about four feet up, the walls were mirrored. Fancy crystal candelabras were everywhere. It was, in a word, much better than home!

When it was my turn to go to an open urinal to my left, I noticed Freddy went to the right with the bird colonel who was in the urinal in front of him. I couldn't help myself. I stared into the mirror. The chicken colonel admired his profile, swagger stick under his arm, while he held his pecker with the other. Then, his face grimaced with the weirdest expression and he let out a fearsome howl.

Freddy, directly behind him, being half lushed, had taken out his cock to piss, and being unable to control himself, had pissed all over the back of the bird colonel.

"Lieutenant," screamed the enraged colonel, "you are pissing all over me!" and then he yelled for the M.P.s

Freddy just kept on pissing; there seemed to be no end to it.

The colonel jumped to one side; his pink trousers — really a delicate gray pink, but affectionately called officer's pinks — were soaking wet in the back.

Most of the officers in the men's room were lieutenants like us. The laughter turned into a roar. It was a riot!

I grabbed Freddy by the arm and pulled him out of there, battling lines all the way. Then, I rushed him through the mezzanine to the cloakroom, and quickly gave the girl the checks for our hats and short coats. We could still hear the colonel yelling for M.P.s The girl handed over our coats and caps. We bolted for the door. The colonel was demanding our arrest now, and called the two M.P.s stationed outside the entrance.

We stepped to the side and ducked behind a couple of officers as the M.P.s rushed into the foyer. Then, we dashed out into the black out, heading up towards Marble Arch as fast as our legs would carry us.

Freddy, half looped, kept mumbling, "Hell, I didn't do anything. What's the son of a bitch moaning about?"

As I told this to my so-called R.A.F friend, purposely I omitted the description of the walls in the men's room and only remarked about the mirrors and candelabras, while casually mentioning the beautiful wallpaper. "I have never seen wallpaper like that. It almost looked like embossed silk." The trap was set.

"Oh, yes," he replied. "We use a lot of that wallpaper in England. It is flock cloth."

That clinched it. There was no wallpaper in the men's room, only marble and mirroring. If I ever saw Freddy again, I'd have to tell him this story. Meanwhile, my better judgment told me to play it cool and let this imposter ramble on, though I wanted to kill the fucking spy right then and there.

He continued to ask questions, to which I had some pretty crazy answers. I lied through my teeth. He was gullible enough to believe me.

When he asked for a code name of some sort, I replied with a Walt Disney character: Pluto, Mickey Mouse, Minnie Mouse, Donald Duck . . . The dumb fucker couldn't have been English; the English knew about these characters.

Now came the question: "Have you heard about a second invasion?"

I was ready for him. "I've heard that rumor too, only it really isn't a rumor. My information comes from a brigadier general from our wing. We rode to London on the same train; we shared a compartment on the two-hour ride."

"Yes?" The bastard swallowed it hook, line and sinker. Generals didn't ride on trains. They had their own staff cars with chauffeurs.

"What general said that?" he wanted to know.

To make this work I had to use the name of a real live general. "General Julius Lacey." Lacey was a brigadier general in our wing headquarters. "The general said the Normandy invasion had gone off so well they were planning a second invasion in Holland."

"In Holland?" His eyebrows arched. "But that seems like a very dumb place. What about the water and dikes?"

"That's the secret. They're bringing large super-sized pontoon boats from the States. The general told me these were due in during July. The invasion is scheduled for early September."

He couldn't conceal his excitement. The questions started anew. I threw the bullshit to him. I even came up with the landing point:

Nijmegen, a checkpoint we used on bombing raids in crossing the Dutch coast.

"Well, it seems rather improbable," my so-called friend said, though he obviously believed every word I said.

"Yeah, you're thinking like the general said the Germans would think. Cross 'em up. Anyway, the general said that most high-ranking German officers are either political appointments, lunatics or imbeciles. Very depraved. Like Hitler himself."

The rage in his eyes was a sight to see. But he had played the part of the R.A.F. officer, so he had to keep his mouth shut.

Now I frosted the cake. "The general had heard from top secret British Intelligence that Hitler has syphilis and his brain is damaged badly. He's become . . . mentally incompetent!"

I thought the poor son of a bitch was going to croak. He tried a feeble joke. "That is funny." But it was like watching your mother-in-law go over a cliff in your brand new Cadillac; it was killing the poor bastard!

Having done my duty, nailed him to the wall, I dropped into my cot and stretched out, supposedly falling into a sound sleep.

He paced the floor, occasionally going to the cell bars and trying to peer down the corridor. Eventually, after about twenty minutes, a guard came by. The so-called R.A.F. friend must've given him some kind of signal. The guard went trotting off to return with a hauptman and an oberleutnant. We were informed:

"You will both be taken for further questioning."

My R.A.F. buddy was led in one direction, and I was led in another. I smiled all the way. I figured my remark about Hitler had done it. I couldn't wait to see *their* faces.

- 10 -

I was handcuffed, loaded on a small truck by two guards and driven back to the hospital. What goes on here? I wondered.

Nothing. At least for three days, while they attended to my medical problems. On the fourth day, though, my Lehigh Valley oberleutnant came into my cell, a big smile on his face, saying "Congratulations, Cury. I have good news for you."

Inwardly I cringed. He wasn't designed for good news.

"You are being sent to a permanent *oftlaflug*. You will spend the rest of the war there which will be all over very soon." He smirked. "To show you my good feelings, I have brought you a present."

Well, I'll be damned and go to hell; he carried a covered casserole.

He whisked off the top of the casserole. Inside was the wonderful aroma of sauerkraut and pork. "You know, I live on the base. My wife cooked it especially for you." He snapped his fingers at the guards, and two plates, forks, knives, cloth napkins, hot rolls and real butter appeared.

While we ate — I wasn't about to turn him down — he ran the usual bullshit by me about how Germans loved Americans. As I enjoyed the food I glanced up once or twice, and, yes, he really believed it.

"When will I be leaving?" I asked casually.

"Your papers are being drawn this morning."

"Where am I going?"

He just smiled at me, as if I might really be his friend.

Weird; really weird.

A German S.S. captain entered here. The oberleutnant jumped to his feet, giving his customary Heil Hitler salute, the captain returning it, as if they were members of a comic opera. I smiled and concentrated on the food his wife had cooked. It was real home

85

cooking! The oberleutnant ate with his fork in his left hand and his knife in his right hand, never changing. When he picked up his food, he used the knife and fork at the same time. The French families with whom I had stayed operated their utensils in the same fashion. For some reason, I thought it was important to remember this little facet of life. Well only time would tell . . .

My Lehigh Valley friend extended his hand to me.

"*Auf–weidersein,* my good friend. I hope we meet again. Perhaps in the Lehigh Valley." He couldn't pronounce the "V" well. "When we take over the United States I will be one of the officers sent there since I speak English. I can assure you I will look up up."

When you're twenty-three years old and full of it, restraint is not a long suit. "That'll be the fucking day! If you want to make some fast money, bet all you have that the war will be over for Germany within a year." As it turned out, it was over ten months later. "Meanwhile, I appreciate your efforts and the food. But as an American officer, I can't help feeling otherwise."

He nodded sadly. "It is a shame. You're intelligent. If you were in the German Luftwaffe you would be at least a major or higher."

"Please send a letter stating those remarks to the Eighth Air Force Command!"

He laughed good-naturedly. "God be with you;" and he said this almost wistfully, his hand still extended.

Hell, I was an officer and a gentleman. I shook his hand. "Good luck to you too. God be with you and your good wife. Thank her for the fine dinner."

'Lehigh Valley' departed with a wave, and I sat down to wait.

I couldn't believe I was really going to a permanent prisoner of war camp. Perhaps 'Lehigh Valley' knew something I didn't know.

Early the next morning with only the oberleutnant and one soldier, I was taken out into an open courtyard. I wasn't handcuffed, and it was welcome change.

In the courtyard were two large convoy trucks. The only difference between these trucks and our own was a squared-off hood. Then, I noted the heavy duty steel wire grill gates on the backs of the trucks. Several soldiers stood nearby, and as we approached the trucks, the gates closed.

I was led to the second truck; there were soldiers locked inside. Then, I heard a welcoming sound. "Hey, there, Yank! Join the club. You're holding up the show!"

A sergeant in charge of this group yelled, "Keep quiet or I'll come in there and shut you up!"

"Fuck you, you bloody Kraut," was the response.

These were R.A.F. prisoners. Instinctively, I knew they were the real thing. One was an R.A.F. lieutenant and the other three were enlisted noncoms. Then, I felt a touch on my shoulder.

It was the oberleutnant,his hand extended. "Good luck, American. I really mean it. I know you had a terribly rough time, but you must understand our situation. To tell you the truth, there is still some doubt about you. My superiors think you are not what you seem. Believe me, you are damn lucky to get away from here and be taken to one of our *stalaglufts*."

My better nature got the best of me. I mumbled a quick, "Thank you," and shook his hand.

The sergeant in charge ordered me into the truck in broken English. The wire gate on the back of the second truck was opened. The R.A.F. flyers reached down and pulled me up. We must've sounded like a bunch of old hens having a reunion. The gate slammed behind me.

The lieutenant's name was Richard Parkinson. The minute I grasped his strong handshake and looked into his eyes, I knew I liked him. His eyes had that steady, cold, cocky look of a typical fighter pilot; he confirmed my feelings. He was a Spitfire pilot who had been shot down, badly wounded. He had been hospitalized for some time.

The other three were crew members from a Wellington bomber which had gone down on a night mission. They had also been in the hospital. The radio operator, a tall, thin, red-headed, freckle-faced kid couldn't have been more than twenty; the other two were gunners.

They all asked me a million and one questions. I let loose and told them I had been shot down in a B-17, captured and brought to this place. Now I didn't know where in hell I was being taken.

I had been mistaken in believing they were all British. The lieutenant informed me he was an Aussie and damn proud of it. But he had that typical, crazy British accent, and I felt right at home with him as well as the others.

There were benches on each side of the truck. The lieutenant sat with me. I had one thing to say for the R.A.F. They always wore their uniforms with their short jackets on combat missions, their flight caps inside their jackets, heavy duty flying jackets on top. If they were shot down, they looked more than presentable. And one thing I had learned, the Krauts did respect uniforms and rank.

The truck hadn't moved. I glanced at Parkinson and said, "Wonder what's holding us up?"

He shook his head. A little conference was going on outside.

I edged toward the back of the truck. The oberleutnant was handing over a clipboard to the sergeant. At last, it looked like we were about to move on. Then, the sergeant barked out an order. Two men headed for the front of our truck, the sergeant going toward the front truck along with another soldier. These were Wehrmacht soldiers; they were a bit more classy than the ones I'd seen, all spic and span, and armed to the teeth. Why, their shoes were even shined. Then, bingo!

I heard the sound I hadn't heard since being shot down; and it was very welcome: air raid sirens!

Everybody started running in all directions. I could see one large air raid shelter, a special triangular mound of dirt piled up with sand bag bunkers in front. I yelled, "The planes have got to be ours! They've got to be ours!" I crouched on the floor, straining to look out at the sky.

It was a beautiful day, what flyers call CAVU, "Clear Altitude Visibility Unlimited." Now here were B-17s strung out in formation, their white contrails fanning out behind them. Obviously they weren't interested in this base; they were headed on down the road. Why in hell was everyone running around like mad? Then, all hell broke loose.

German "88" flak guns opened up in their towers. The noise was deafening: the guns firing, the sirens blowing, the horns screaming intermittently.

"Sons of bitches, they've left us here in the truck to get bombed!" I knew we weren't the target, but I said it anyway.

I counted the first group to come over. They were flying squadrons of twelve, four squadrons to a group. I counted six groups and wished for binoculars, yelling all the time, "Give 'em hell! Give 'em hell!" My R.A.F. buddies were yelling with me. God, what a morale booster!

The planes passed from sight, but the flak guns kept firing for another five or ten minutes. Then, the sirens died away and finally the all-clear was sounded. I envied those guys in the B-17s; they'd be going home at the end of the day, at least most of them!

The Germans came from their shelters. Two of them opened the back of our truck and climbed in. They slammed the gates behind them, pointed their machine guns at us, and shouted something. It wasn't hard to figure out what they wanted. We moved to the far end of the truck away from them. In the doing, both of them charged their guns, putting a shell into the chamber. Obviously, one false move and we were done for; the air raid didn't set well with them.

One of the soldiers was a big, heavy-set fellow, a good 210-15 pounds. His round, pimply face was marked by acne. He didn't look mean. I smiled at him.

The other soldier backed himself against the grill gate and kept his eyes on us. He had a long straight pointed nose that told me his finger itched to pull the trigger.

The truck started up. I turned around and said to Richard, "Dick, I say there ole chap, do you mind me calling you 'Dick'?"

"Yes, I do," he laughed. "My parents called me Dickie and it bugs me. Call me Parkie or Richard, if you will."

"Okay, Richard, do you think these bastards speak English?"

"You can't tell what the bloody bastards can do."

"Well, let's watch the expression on their faces and see if they understand anything we say." The others nodded, grinning. In the direction of the big guy, I said, "Hey, fatso, your mother is a no-good, fucking whore. She sucks cocks!"

"Yah," he said, nodding soberly.

I repeated it again, adding, "Yah, goot?"

"*Yah, das ist gut.*"

Now I tried it on Hook Nose. "You're a no-good, motherfucking son of a bitch, and your mother has syphilis."

I smiled throughout my recital.

They both smiled in return, one saying, "*Nicht ferschte, nicht ferschte.*"

I turned to Richard and said, "Well, that's one in our favor. We can talk freely." Nevertheless, we spoke in hushed tones.

We talked about my capture since the marks of the stitches on my face were still obvious. Was I captured by the Wehrmacht or Luftwaffe? When I replied, "Neither. The Gestapo," they all let out a low whistle.

Richard shook his head. "You don't have to say much more, Ed."

"That's the truth . . ."

"How do you feel about going to a prison camp?"

"Like shit. It was my last mission. I feel cheated. I would do anything to get the hell out . . ."

"You mean escape?"

"That's right. Escape. And right now."

"But . . ."

"I've been sizing up those two bastards. If we could get their guns, we'd have a chance."

"You've got to be kidding!"

"I'm not kidding."

"But what about the others in the cab of the truck, and the other truck?"

"I think we could do it."

"I knew you Americans were a crazy lot, but so are Aussies," Richard said. "I'll tell you what, ole chap. If you have any ideas, I'm with you 100 percent."

"We should grab Pimple Face first." I paused in thought. "Do you know where we're going?"

He had no idea. They'd lost all track of time and place in the hospital. But we were north of Munich, probably 70 or 80 kilometers. That was it. The only other thing we knew is that we were moving by truck along a two-lane, concrete highway, heading north.

Richard and I went on discussing the possibilities, while the other three guys slept. Then, I needed to take a leak. I hadn't gone since early morning. Three cups of coffee and a glass of water were begging to be released. I stood up in the truck, bracing myself against the cross section with my hands. I pointed to my fly, yelling, "Hey, fuck face!"

Pimple Face laughed. Hook Nose just stared.

I pointed at my fly, repeating, "Piss, piss, piss."

Pimple Face pointed to the grill work at the back of the truck.

There were braces across the top of the truck which held the canvas cover in place and these crossed every two feet. I used them for leverage as I moved to the end of the truck.

Hook Nose slid down on the bench as I came to the grill. He was directly behind me and he placed the machine gun right on my back while Pimple Face kept his eyes on the other guys.

I pushed myself tight against the mesh grill and pissed through the mesh, all the while looking around the area through which we traveled.

Richard called out, "Hey, Ed, be damn careful. He has that machine gun against your back."

"I know, Richard," I called back. "I can feel it."

Hook Nose yelled something here. Obviously, he wanted us to keep quiet.

I slipped my pecker back into my pants. But I couldn't button the fly without two hands. I turned and started the balancing act back to my seat, bracing myself from rib to rib. My buddies clapped their hands and yelled, "Good show, Yank, good show!" They were all laughing. Even Pimple Face joined them in laughing.

As I had edged back to my seat, Hook Nose slid past me and back against the mesh gate, taking no chances. I should've pissed all over his seat, I thought.

When I sat down, Roger, the sergeant, said, "I say there, leftenant, did you know your bloody fly was open?"

We all laughed again, and I buttoned up.

While I'd been at the grill, I'd taken a good look at the latch. It was a simple pull-down latch with a slide bolt that worked on both sides. A lock hung on the outside, but it was banging loose, locked only on our side. I told Richard about it. Both of us were surprised that no one had locked the mesh gates on the outside.

– 11 –

I had dozed off, and I thought I was dreaming when I heard a screaming noise above. But, no, it was the unmistakable sound of fighters coming in to strafe.

Fear filled the faces of our guards. Both turned their heads to look from the back of the truck.

This could be our chance, I thought.

Then, Hook Nose spun around, yelled something in German, and began waving his machine gun up and down at us.

Richard yelled, "He wants us to get on the floor."

We did.

The planes made their first pass, .50-calibers spewing death. At any other time I would have welcomed them. But there was a very good chance we might be killed by our own people since they had no idea who or what might be traveling in the trucks.

Suddenly, the truck began to lurch from side to side. I dived flat, near the rear of the truck bed, hoping to see out. I couldn't see the planes, but I knew that beautiful whine of Allison engines in P-51s and the noise of their air scoops.

The truck lurched violently now. I reached out and wrapped my arm around the base of the bench bolted to the truck side. The whining drew nearer, the machine guns chewing up the road and the truck. My god, they were loud!

It was terrifying as all hell. Then, a terrific explosion was followed by the sound of a crashing truck. I yelled out to the guys, "I think the other truck got it."

One of the sergeants yelled, "Oh, my god, my friends were in the truck ahead of us."

The P-51s were climbing again, swinging around to make a 360-degree turn for another run on us, the whine of the engines telling

91

more than I cared to know. Then, our truck lurched wildly, and the guards came tumbling down.

"Now, Richard!" I yelled. "This is our chance!"

But hell, we couldn't move either. We were being thrown from side to side, until a final, crazy, mad lunge, and the truck slammed into something very solid.

I covered my head as my body was propelled toward the front of the truck then came to a halt with a horrible jolt. The twisting of metal and the breaking glass sounded in my ears. My feet plowed into someone beneath me. Something heavy and hard lay on top of me; it was Hook Nose.

I pushed him aside and pulled my legs from under one of the sergeants. A grotesque pile of humanity faced me. I would have been in the same position if I hadn't thrown myself with my head toward the back of the truck. Then I realized the only sound I could hear was the hissing steam from the radiator. And I smelled smoke. I yelled for Richard. There he was, pulling himself from that mess of bodies. I grabbed his hand and yanked him free.

My first thought was to look for the machine gun. We rolled Pimple Face over. His helmet had been torn off by the impact and his head had smashed against the bulkhead; he was dead. But the gun was under his arm.

I grabbed it, along with an extra clip attached to his belt. Then, I turned him over again and took his pistol from its holster.

Hook Nose, twisted grotesquely in the corner of the truck, was evidently still alive; he was moaning. Richard grabbed his gun, saying, "Let's get the other guys and get the hell out of here!"

I said, "Let's check the other truck first and the guys in front, or we'll blow this whole deal!"

The impact had torn one gate from the side of the truck. We crawled out easily. "Check the cab first," I yelled.

Richard and I separated, Richard going to one side of the truck, me going to the other side. The truck had crashed into a large boulder by the road. The boulder had smashed through the windshield, killing both men in front.

"The other truck," I yelled. We climbed the bank of the road, seeing black smoke pouring upward. The other truck was a ball of fire. But now we had another worry.

Two planes were heading for us. Running down the road, I started waving, thinking they might see us.

Richard yelled, "You're crazy. Get off the road!"

We dived over the bank, rolling down soft grass. Machine gun shells hit the concrete as the two planes zoomed in. Then, I heard a horrible explosion. "Oh, my god!"

Richard and I went tearing up the bank and ran across the road. It was too late; our truck was going up in flames, shells having hit the gas tank, blowing the thing sky high.

The planes had passed. Engines were climbing again; and I heard a German voice cry out.

Richard and I spun around, peering down the bank. It was the sergeant who had been in the lead truck. He had been thrown from the cab into the grass, and he was trying to get up, though badly wounded; and I'll be damned, the son of a bitch had a pistol in his hand and was trying to fire on us. He never had a chance. Both Richard and I opened fire at the same time, cutting him in half.

Now we turned our attention to our truck. The flames were so hot we couldn't get close. I yelled to see if anyone else had escaped. There was no reply. "Let's get the hell out of here," I told Richard.

The P-51s were returning again. The sound of .50-caliber shells strafing was all around us. We found shelter behind a big boulder. "Let's stay here, in case they make another pass." And they did; those babies wanted to be sure they destroyed everything.

Although my heart was heavy for the three R.A.F. boys in our truck, I couldn't help but feel pride and joy at the P-51s. They were a sight to be seen, doing their duty.

Finally, Richard said wearily, grief-stricken over friends lost, "What'll we do now, ole chap?"

"Let's get the hell out of here as fast as we can!"

Armed with the two machine guns we had acquired, we felt confident, running in the direction from which we had come, which was south, and paralleling the highway, though keeping away from it.

We climbed a steep bank, over a fence and into a meadow with cows in it. Cows had to be stupid. With all the fire and shooting, they were grazing as peacefully as if nothing had happened. I envied them.

We didn't do much talking as we ran. It was only after we had crossed the meadow and started up a steep hill that Richard said, "I'll be a fucking son of a bitch!"

"What now?"

"I dropped the gun clip. It must've come off when we scrambled up the bank."

There was no use going back for it. We were too damn far away. I was sure with all the noise and confusion, people from farms nearby had descended on the scene. We agreed to keep running, up the hill. Here Richard had to stop to rest.

"I thought you Aussies were real tough cookies," I joked.

"We are. But where I come from it's all flat country. Hell, I lived in the outback. I've never gone up a hill before."

The hill was really a small mountain. It had taken about forty-five minutes to climb it, and it was a good look-out. I found an advantage point on top of a rock and cautiously climbed to its pinnacle.

Richard yelled up to me, "You better be careful. Someone might see us from the road."

He was sure as hell right. Though we were a good way up, people were down in the road in what looked like an old farm truck. I reported this to Richard.

"Of all the lousy, bloody luck!"

"No," I said. "It might be a break for us. With the fire and explosion they may think we were all killed or burned."

"I hope so;" and he followed me as I struck out along a ridge.

Below was open farmland. I felt our best bet was to walk along the ridge. We moved as swiftly as possible, pausing now and then for a brief break, then moving on. Occasionally the ridge ran close to the road, then back away from it again.

We had been running well over an hour when we decided to take a good rest. We found a vantage point where we could look down on the road and settled in. But briefly, of course. It was bound to happen . . .

A German armored car passed along the road with a motorcycle escort. They were heading north toward the spot where we'd been hit. Richard and I exchanged glances and began running as if the devil himself was on our tail. Hell, if they got me now, I'd really be in for it; I still wore civilian clothes. Richard, at least, had some semblance of a uniform and insignia. As for the rest . . . Could we really get out of Germany? I could only pray real hard.

We were at least 100 miles north or northeast of Munich; and it was probably another 200 miles or more beyond that to the French border. It seemed an impossible feat. Once, when we had run out of breath and were taking a brief rest, I wondered if we shouldn't just go down and stand by the side of the road. Give ourselves up. Richard had mentioned this idea when he started to drag. For damn sure we'd probably be better off in a regular prison camp. Then, I weighed all the consequences. BULLSHIT! With or without Richard, I wanted out. I'd come this far and I wasn't about to give up.

We paused at a high point to look down on the road where it crossed a large bridge. I remembered our crossing this bridge in the truck, remembered that special racket a truck makes when the tires hit a different surface. In fact, I had looked out and seen the girders through the grill.

The bridge was an old-fashioned steel and wood bridge, crossing a fairly good sized stream. We were at least eight to ten miles away from where the trucks had met their end. As we rested there, considering our route, two more trucks, very similar to the ones we'd been in, rumbled by, crossing the bridge with one hell of a racket. Then I heard it! Dogs!

The dogs were barking and yapping. Perhaps the trucks were hauling dogs to the scene of the wreck. "Do you hear that?" I asked Richard.

His face was very serious. "How soon do you think they'll be on our tail?"

"It'll take them at least another twenty to thirty minutes to get there, probably another ten or fifteen minutes, figuring what in the hell happened. No matter how you look at it, we have at least a two to three hour start on them." I sought to reassure him. "Don't worry about it, Richard. We'll get the hell out of here, I guarantee you."

We took off, though Richard didn't seem very reassured. "I know one thing," I said as we ran, "if we can hold out until dark, we've got a good chance, and especially if we have a place where we can cross a stream or water of some sort." It was a hell of a shame the stream below didn't cross our path; it ran parallel to the road, and we couldn't take a chance on the road.

By now the sun was going down. Although it had been very warm, the wind was beginning to whistle through the trees, cooling the day. My throat was parched, and I knew Richard's was no different. But neither of us had mentioned being hungry or thirsty. I encouraged myself by remembering how hungry I had been the first day of my previous evasion, but how much better it got after that, to the point where it didn't bother me.

The mountain sloped downward now, and the small path we'd been following widened. "I don't like the looks of this," I said. "It means only one thing. We're coming to a well-traveled area."

Ten minutes later, I was proven right. Power lines followed the path into an open section. We didn't dare continue. We had to take cover in the trees. It was a hell of a lot harder; we kept getting hit in the face by the bushes. Of course, in the doing, we were leaving a telltale trail. I'd done enough hiking and camping as a kid to know a blind man could pick up the trail we'd left behind. But we had little choice.

We continued until we came upon a wide open space of several hundred yards. There the mountain sloped downward again. As we drew nearer, we discovered another problem. A small dirt road crossed our path. On the other side was open farm land. Again, no choice. But first . . .

I signaled Richard to stop. We had to reconnoiter to be positive no one was around. We were near a large tree. I wished for a coin so that we could flip to see who climbed the tree. Richard smiled and said, "You're doing all the worrying. It's only fair I do it. Besides, I'm lighter than you." He shinnied up the tree, and that Aussie could really climb. I was amazed at his agility.

At about twenty-five feet off the ground, he yelled down to me, "I can really get a good look-see from here, Ed. It's clear in both directions. I don't see a bloody thing one way or the other."

As Richard came down the tree I considered the country through which we were passing. It was beautiful, everything in summer full bloom, neat and geometric. Those damn Germans were something else again!

Richard had placed his machine gun at the foot of the tree. On the ground again, he started off without it.

I said, "Don't forget the gun."

"What's the use? I don't have a clip for it."

"If you leave it, I guarantee they'll know we've been here."

Richard nodded, picked up the gun, and we were on our way again.

At the road, where hard stones protruded from the bed, I suggested we try to step on the stones and not leave any marks. We crossed gingerly, going through the open fields and into the trees again. Within the woods we found another path leading up a hill, and we followed it. We seemed to've gotten our second wind. It wasn't nearly as tough as before.

We reached the crest of the hill and continued, heading south. After some time we came to another drop off. At the bottom of the hill was a big lake, heavily wooded along its shores. As we descended, I noticed trees growing in the middle of the lake as if from an island. Still closer, we saw that swamp followed the outline of the trees all around the lake, which seemed to be a few miles long and about a mile wide.

We came to a point where the grass turned to marshland. I knew we didn't dare walk there. Our footprints would be easy to follow. "Let's back off and try to go around the right side. Maybe we can find a place where we can step into the water without leaving marks."

"Why?" asked Richard.

"Well, if they've got dogs on us and we walk in water, we'll shake 'em."

"How in hell do you know all this?" he demanded. "I thought you were a city boy."

"I am. But I remember seeing stuff like this in the movies. Maybe it's so."

We kept to the perimeter of the lake until we came upon a wide stream which drained into the lake. Here was a real break.

The creek wasn't very deep, but very rocky and running swiftly. "We'll go into the stream," I told Richard, "and instead of heading into the lake, we'll go back upstream a few hundred yards and then come out and retrace our steps.

Richard followed along without saying a word, though it was obvious he had doubts about my sanity.

The water was damn cold. Icy, in fact. But never mind. The water came up to our knees in places, but we kept away from the rocks which jutted from the surface. Finally, I found the perfect place. We left the stream, going up a slight bank. I told Richard, "Leave as many footprints as possible going up the bank into the open field."

Resigned to the care of what I imagined he thought was a lunatic, we made our way into the open field for fifty yards or so. Then, I said, "We'll retrace our steps going backwards."

"You bloody Americans have got to be crazy! I'm with you, and I'll do whatever you do. But it's crazy!"

I just grinned and began moving backwards toward the stream, being careful to step into my own prints. Richard followed suit. Then, we waded back down the stream and into the lake.

"Now what do we do?" Richard said wearily.

I remembered looking down from the hill onto the swampy area and a half-submerged island. From this point we could see the island trees in the distance. "Our best bet," I told Richard, "is to go out there."

"We'd be trapped, if they came."

"If they do, we'll be caught one way or the other. But I really feel they'll think we crossed that field. We left all the marks . . ."

"Okay, I'm with you, Yank."

The two machine guns had leather straps on them. We slung them over our shoulders and waded into deep water. As the water came up to our necks, I said to Richard, "I hope you can swim."

"I bloody well can."

We swam for it, using the side stroke I suggested. Though the sun had gone down, I wanted as little splashing as possible. I was afraid someone might hear us. Then, Richard began to lag behind. "Are you okay?"

"Keep going. I'm with you."

The island appeared to be only a few hundred yards away. Man, was I wrong. We kept going and going and going. Fortunately, the lake grew more shallow and at last we were able to wade, though I cautioned Richard to stay down in the water. Only about half an hour had passed, but it seemed much longer. Now for the real surprise . . .

True enough, this had once been an island, but it wasn't any more. The island was a good two feet beneath the water. Evidently, heavy rains accounted for the swiftness of the creek.

"What are we going to do now?" Richard said dismally.

"It's perfect," I told him. "With the brush and the trees, it's a perfect place to hide."

I didn't hear enthusiastic applause, but we searched for a dry spot. Eventually, we crawled up onto a fallen rotten tree; other smaller trees had grown up around it. We even found a limb on which to hang our guns, and it was fairly comfortable there, straddling the tree.

At length I went off to reconnoiter at the end of the small island. From there I could see it was one hell of a long way to the end of the lake. Never mind. This was perfect; cold and wet as we were, we couldn't've been in better shape for the end of a long hard day on the run.

Back in the tree with Richard I found an unhappy companion. He grumbled endlessly. But when it got down to the bottom line, he was with me.

The only aspect of our situation which disturbed me was the glimpse we caught of a couple of snakes wiggling away in the water. Thank goodness, they were scared of us. We both agreed we could do without snakes. Germans were bad enough.

In the end, we found a few dead limbs which we placed across our rotten log as a kind of makeshift rack. There we could get fairly comfortable without tumbling off.

The moon came up, and we decided that one of us should keep watch while the other snoozed. We'd take turns. Beneath the bright moonlight, we could see rather well, since our eyes were growing accustomed to the darkness.

During the night we kept our voices low since sound quite obviously carried well across water. We heard owls hooting and once a tomcat crying. "As long as we hear the tomcat," I whispered to Richard, "we know that no dogs are around."

I had no more uttered these words than our peaceful silence was disturbed by the gutteral voices of Germans and dogs yapping and barking. Lights appeared several hundred yards away. Evidently they'd come to the creek we'd waded, and I wondered if our trick would work. We sat still, listening, anticipating. The noise grew fainter, going away from us. Mentally, I began patting myself on the back.

Richard said, "By god, Yank, you're a regular Errol Flynn. I think they're doing just what you said they'd do."

My fame as Errol Flynn was short-lived. The Germans returned to the lake. They had several large lights, much bigger than flashlights. I counted at least a dozen lights. Then the damned lights began splitting off in two directions. I whispered to Richard. "They're going around the lake!" Now we could hear water slushing as they waded the swamp.

The dogs had a sharp bark. The only thing they could be were goddamn bloody dobermans, the kind they'd used at the first prison compound in which I'd found myself. The thought sent a cold chill through me. I'm a real dog lover, but I hated those bastards. We departed our roost for the water, laying low . . .

The barking seemed to get farther away, only to grow nearer again. The slushing and barking came from both ends of the lake, and it wasn't easy to follow what was happening. We stayed in suspense for hours as they searched for us, and we were grateful when that very bright moon began to settle in the west. While dawn couldn't be far away, at least we'd have the cover of darkness for a while.

Chills ran through me as the sounds converged on the far east side of the lake, lights flashing out across the water. While their lights were too far away to reach us, they seemed to be seeking so thoroughly that I imagined they'd catch up with us at any moment.

Finally, the lights disappeared and the sounds faded. Only the occasional hoot of an owl or the croak of a frog broke the stillness of the night. To make the time pass more swiftly we spoke in whispers, not moving from the water, speaking of crazy things, like what we did before the war, where we had been stationed in England, our trips to London. Funny how all flyers do the same things. Richard and I might have done it all together: the same girls, same bars, same hotels. We decided the English were beautiful, staunch, brave and polite, warm and kind to GIs, but England was one miserable, damp place. At long last, the sun peeked over the horizon. As it rose, the heat felt wonderful. Richard and I took a chance and crawled up on our log, pulling small limbs and leaves toward us as we hid in our makeshift place.

As full daylight was upon us I noticed my hands. They were shrivelled and absolutely white. They might have been old wrinkled prunes. I showed them to Richard. He glanced at his hands and they were no different.

"As soon as we get to shore," Richard muttered quietly, "I'm going to take off my shoes and socks to dry my feet."

"It's going to be some time before we get to shore," I cautioned him. "We're not budging for a while."

"Aw, you've got to be joking."

"Nope. I'm serious," and I was. Since we'd gotten through the night without discovery, the Germans were bound to believe we were farther away. I felt our safest bet was to stay where we were, and I said as much.

Richard stared at me in disbelief. Finally, he came around with a faint smile. "You've been bloody right so far, and by golly, I'm with you, Yank!"

We settled down, stretching out head to head on our makeshift rack beneath the sun. God, it felt good!

"Perhaps, Yank, we ought to take off our clothes and dry out."

"What's the use? If they come around again, we'd only have to duck in the water."

In time, though, the sun did dry us off somewhat, but suddenly that was the least of our worries. We were hungry, damn hungry. So, we talked about our favorite foods. I recalled the hot dogs with onions, mustard and chili sauce from Yocco's in Allentown, Pennsylvania. It was owned by Lee Iacocca's uncle. Then, I moved on to hamburgers. Richard had never eaten a hamburger or hot dog; they didn't have them in Australia. We were so hungry we both decided we could even go for those tiny little tea sandwiches done up with watercress and small pieces of fish served at tea dances in London.

The subject exhausted momentarily, I bent over and washed my face, taking a couple of good gulps of water to rinse my mouth, while using my finger to brush my teeth. Richard thought I was crazy, but, hell, it felt good. Convinced by my review of this event, Richard tried it himself and had to agree. But he had another problem. "Hell, I've got to take a crap!"

"Then, you'll have to get in the water."

"I don't want to get wet again. Maybe I could do it on the log, huh?"

"No way. You'll stink up our bed."

He slipped into the water.

"Could you possibly move off a ways?" I asked politely.

"Bloody sanitary, you Yanks!" he said, moving away about ten yards or so.

I couldn't help laughing. There he was squatting in the water, while bubbles surfaced from below. The look on his face was a riot.

Richard had no more than climbed aboard our nesting place than I felt the call of nature, the power of suggestion, no doubt. I slipped over the side, and there on a log, was a nice fat frog, sunning himself. He glistened green and bronze, and his eyes bulged with wonder at me. I was infringing on his territory. I moved away.

When I came aboard the log again, I mentioned the frog to Richard. We held a war conference over that frog, making up our minds to capture the son of a bitch dead or alive. We were just that hungry!

The frog sat eight feet away from our log. We figured if we didn't nail him right off the bat, the frog would head east where the water was deep and brush made for good cover. What we needed was a club or a limb, each of us converging with our weapon from either side. We broke off two short limbs from the dead tree trunk, careful not to make noise; we didn't want to scare off that frog. Then, we slipped into the water quietly. The frog just sat there staring with those great big eyes.

I was the frontal attack and Richard came from the rear. It seemed to be working as I drew within a few feet of him. The dumb bastard didn't move, just blinked his eyes a few times at me. Behind him, Richard raised his club slowly, awaiting the signal from me. I nodded my head. Then: POW!

Though Richard had clobbered him smack on the head, the damage extended to the frog's body. He was a hell of a mess and still twitching. I picked him up by his hind legs. Boy, was he big!

Back on our log, the big question: How the hell do we eat him?

We laid him out on the log and contemplated our dilemma. Finally, I did say, "Well, I'll eat only his legs. Everything else looks horrible!"

Richard recalled frog legs cooked with butter and lemon which he'd eaten in Darwin. With that thought firmly in mind, we got to work.

With the sharp end of one of our sticks, we held the frog's legs down and pulled them off, throwing the smashed body and head into the water. Then, we pulled the skin down off the legs. My eyes lit up. "Looks kinda like a small chicken before cooking."

"Frog legs are good," Richard allowed.

We washed the legs in water. That done, we decided to wait a while. There was no hope of cooking the legs. We needed to screw up our courage. Eventually, hunger got the best of us.

I picked up a leg and tried it. The frog leg seemed horrible at first, slimy and sticky. But the more I chewed, the better it got. I gulped the first bite. God, it was slimy. But I took another bite or two. I hated myself for doing it, but I didn't have a choice. I glanced over at Richard who was working away on his frog leg. "You look like you just ate shit!" I said.

"Bloody bad," he said. But he kept eating.

Our meal over, I dropped into the water. "I'm going for a drink of clean water." I didn't want to drink from the area where we were, so I moved toward the north end of the log, only to stop cold in my tracks. I heard the sound of dogs, and they seemed to be heading our way. I waded backwards to the log and shared the news with Richard. Swiftly, he joined me in the water. Only our heads were exposed now, and we had moved under the log.

"We gotta be real careful," I whispered. "They're bound to have binoculars."

In another ten minutes, a patrol of about six German soldiers and two dogs appeared on the west side of the lake. They were circling the perimeter, heading south, the sounds of the dogs diminishing, then growing louder again.

Richard murmured, "You were right, Ed. It's a good thing we didn't take off or we would've been caught. The bloody bastards know that we got away. They must've counted the bodies."

We stayed below our log the remainder of the day. When the sun dropped below the hills in the west, it must've been around four or five o'clock; and no longer did we hear the dogs. But we weren't taking any chances.

We boosted our morale by chattering away in whispered tones. We learned many aspects of one another's lives, trading off experiences as we went. Richard had gone through the same incident as I had with the phony R.A.F. flyer in his cell. Apparently it was an old Kraut trick; but at least he had been warned by British Intelligence, which was superior to ours. Then, we heard a light plane overhead. We looked up into the sky, straining our eyes through the trees. It was an observation plane similar to our L-IA.

The plane was flying very low. it was black with the familiar white Nazi markings. Here was our adversary, searching for us, flying back and forth across the lake. A lump rose in my throat, my heart beating like a trip hammer. I glanced at Richard; his face was filled with fear.

For five minutes or so the plane flew back and forth, covering a full 360 degrees. We didn't speak. We just watched, until power was applied and the plane began to climb away from the lake. Richard said, "Do you suppose they saw us?"

"We're pretty well covered," I said. "I think we ought to stay here the rest of the day and tonight, no matter how miserable and wet it is. Anyway, if no troops arrive in an hour or so, we'll know we weren't seen."

We sweated out every minute of the next hour, straining our eyes to catch any movement on shore. Dusk was upon us at last, and I felt a hell of a lot better.

The second night in the swamp was as bad as the first. Since we had spent the better part of the day in the water, we were soaking wet again. Neither of us got much sleep that night. We heard every night noise in captivity, all of which was ominous as hell. Meanwhile, we itched like crazy. It was as if something might be crawling all over us. Mosquitos and other bugs had done a job on us, but this was something new. At one point, Richard had to go to the bathroom. When he returned, he claimed he had felt something crawling in and around his pants. Who knows? It could've been anything; our imaginations were playing games with us.

Forever passed, and we welcomed the broken rays of rising sunlight through the trees. Our shivering bodies soaked up every bit of warmth, and when the sun rose fully, we stripped down to the waist, even removing our shoes and socks. We stayed that way until around noon, drying out, only to get wet again late that afternoon when we decided the time had come to get the hell out of there. I reasoned that if by chance we ran across anyone looking for us, we'd have a better chance getting away in the dusk.

– 12 –

We made the decision we would head up over the hill to the west of us for several miles, away from the lake and that goddamn highway, before turning due south. So, we set to work finding a couple of good sized logs and putting them together to carry my machine gun, our shoes and socks. We were deep-sixing Richard's machine gun in the water.

After a thirty-minute swim, pushing the logs before us, we approached a grassy, marshy shoreline. We knew we'd leave telltale marks there. So we swam on, slightly south along the shore, looking for a better place.

An unusually large tree was just ahead; and damned if the thing didn't have a long rope hanging from a high limb with a tire at the end. Some farm kids must've used it for a swing over the water. A wave of homesickness swept over me from home — those aimless, lazy summer days spent on the Lehigh River in Allentown as kids. Never mind. We used the swing to come ashore.

"What a bloody nice place for a picnic!" Richard said. "All we need is a basket of food . . ."

"Don't start it," I muttered. "I'm starving!" The only good aspect of our predicament: Though hungry we were somewhat rested from our enforced stay on the log and ready to go.

I checked the clip on the machine gun. Only nine shells remained, with one in the chamber. I had been a damn fool wasting ammo on that Nazi sergeant thrown from the burning truck; he'd been all but dead anyway.

Now I confided in Richard, "I have a fly button which is a magnetic compass."

Richard laughed. He did too.

I found a small piece of wood about the size of a pencil and bit off a sharp point to hold the fly button which I had torn off my pants. The button had a small notch in it. If placed on top of the point, the notch would spin and settle at due north. We checked our directions accordingly; I had been right. We had come out of the lake due west. Our directions confirmed, we put on our shoes and socks in a hurry and began running at full speed to get as far from the lake and road as possible in the shortest amount of time.

In about thirty minutes we were at the foot of the mountain where we found a narrow foot path which took us straight up. The climb was slow, but we kept a brisk pace. It was close to dark when we got to the top. Luckily, we found a wide path running north and south along the ridge; it reminded me of our old Appalachian trails in the Blue Mountains of Pennsylvania which I'd hiked so often.

Heading south, we came upon another path going down the other side of the mountain. Below were open valleys and farm lands to the west. In the distance was another range of hills and mountains. This would be our destination.

As the moon came out, we ran downhill, much easier going, and soon we were at the bottom. The path had widened and crossed a logging trail large enough to accommodate a wagon or small truck. We followed the road until we reached open farmland; and just a few hundred yards away was the silhouette of a farm house, large barn and other outbuildings. I paused, whispering to Richard, "We better steer clear. There could be soldiers or even dogs there." Then we hurried on.

We arrived at a fenced-in pasture, but kept to the outside of the fence, going slightly north and west around the farm. Here we came to another road, perhaps the main road leading to the farm, since it was a dirt road wide enough for only one vehicle. We climbed a small embankment and came face to face with a field planted with bushy plants. In the moonlight, Richard recognized it as a potato field. "Are you sure?" I demanded.

"Positive," said Richard.

My first impulse was to dig them out and eat them.

Richard said, "No. Let's wait until we get to the other side and pick a spot where we can dig without leaving too many marks."

So, we went clear around the field. Now Richard said, "Let's go in about a dozen rows from the end."

I was following Richard's lead, since he was the potato expert. He began digging about six inches down. And then, there they were: potatoes!

Richard felt the potatoes. "Hard, unripened, but good enough to eat."

We filled our pockets, replaced the dirt carefully around the plants, and took off, continuing in an easterly direction toward the hills in the distance.

We passed another farm, much larger than the first. No lights shone from the farm house. Either everyone was asleep or no one was home. "What do you think?" I asked Richard.

"I don't know," he mused aloud. "But it sure would be nice to find a place to eat the potatoes."

The faint barking of a dog reached our ears. We stopped dead in our tracks. A breeze blew in our direction from the farm; we felt sure no dog could've gotten our scent. But the dog kept barking and lights went on in the second floor of the farm house. That did it. We got going in a hurry, though we continued to glance over our shoulders. Soon the dog quit barking and the farm house lights were extinguished.

Another mile, and we came to a creek, not more than six feet wide. The water glistened in the moonlight, clean and clear. We dropped to our knees and plunged our heads in the stream, washing our faces and drinking at the same time. Refreshed, Richard suggested we wash the potatoes and enjoy them. We were on a nice grassy bank, so I wasn't too worried about leaving tracks. We washed the potatoes and each of us bit into a potato.

The potato was hard and not too tasty. But after chewing on it for a while, the potato was easy to swallow. "This is a hell of a way to eat a potato," I remarked, "with the skin on it. The damn things look green."

"All newly dug potatoes look green," said Richard. "The skin is the best part, believe me."

We stretched out on the bank. Each of us ate three potatoes. The hunger pangs ceased. There was hope.

The hills were still a couple of miles away. We had misjudged the distance. Now we faced open grazing land. We crouched low and took off across the field as fast as it was humanly possible. We came across another stream that seemed to lead into a larger body of water not far away. We followed the stream for a few hundred yards to a pond. There we turned to the right and continued in a westerly direction.

It was amazing how much water there was in the area. No wonder everything was so green. Meanwhile, it looked oddly peaceful and beautiful in the moonlight. I had difficulty imagining a war raged out there somewhere or that we were a couple of escaped prisoners on the run. Finally, we reached the foothills.

They hadn't looked big from far away. But they were a good 1200 to 1500 feet high, rocky and thick with brush and fallen trees. It was rough going. To make matters worse, we couldn't find a decent trail. In time we paused to rest.

While traveling, we hadn't heard a sound. Now the world was alive with hooting owls, crying animals, birds flapping their wings. But we took courage. Perhaps it was the potatoes or the prayers we had said on the island in the lake. But it was a superhuman effort, that mountain, and we made it to the top, zigzagging all the way through terrain that was truly impossible.

On top, about four o'clock in the morning, we found a well-traveled path along the ridge. We turned along the path in a southerly direction, and my leg began to throb. I wasn't about to squawk.

The moon had disappeared completely now, and the first faint rays of light became visible to the east. We were both physically and mentally exhausted to the point where we were ready to collapse. But our best bet was to keep going until full daylight, then find ourselves a good spot to hide. Perhaps we had lost the soldiers and the dogs.

The sun came up in all its glory. Even with the trees, the warmth was good. Inside my jacket I was soaking wet from perspiration. When we arrived at a spot with large boulders, I called a halt and told Richard, "I want to climb up and take a good look around." In the doing, I came up with a good idea. There was bound to be an overhang or a cave down the side, if only we could find it. I yelled to Richard, "Come on along." I wanted to stay on the rocks to keep from leaving a trail.

A little way down the mountain were a few pine trees and brush cover. Right below was a large growth of foliage. I followed the rocks down around the side of the trees and came back up on the other side; and I had found it!

A large flat outcropping of rocks about fifteen feet long and half as wide appeared to've broken from another section. It was a neat overhang, the perfect place, going several feet back into heavy brush on both sides!

In this natural hideaway, we broke branches from bushes and made ourselves a cushion for comfort. The nicest part about it was that it was open to the east with the sun shining down on us. Meanwhile, if a spotter plane flew over or someone looked down from the trail, either coming or going, we couldn't be seen. Further, we were protected by a boulder in front of us. I told Richard, "All we need now are two good looking gals, a blanket, and a picnic basket!"

We stripped off our wet clothes and settled in for a suntan on government time. "Just think," I said, "of those poor bastards flying combat!"

Richard nodded and fell asleep. I wasn't far behind.

A chilling breeze awakened us. The sun had slipped off to the other side of the mountain. It was perhaps late afternoon. I felt my clothes. They were dry. Before I dressed I walked over to the edge of the rock to take a leak.

Richard yawned and said, "What's going on?"

"I just woke up. How do you feel?"

He groaned and rolled over. "Hell, I could sleep forever. Since I can't, how about some potatoes?"

The potatoes tasted lousy. But what the hell? We needed energy. Then, we contemplated the future.

We decided to stay there the remainder of the day and take off that night. I said, "We should keep a sharp lookout. I don't hink we should look for water until after dark."

Richard was in agreement. We took it for granted that I knew what to do.

"I'll take the first watch," I said. "Get a couple of hours sleep. I'll wake you."

I sat on the edge of the boulder, the perfect vantage spot. The whole valley lay below me. By turning my head and looking over the brush, I could see the top of the mountain. Considering our situation, I felt secure. Even someone with binoculars would have a hard time spotting us.

For about an hour I sat there. Then, the temptation to sleep got the better of me. I stretched out on the rock and dozed off to be awakened by Richard saying, "Wake up, old chap, time to rise and shine. Wake up and piss. The whole bloody world's on fire." This was Richard's favorite expression. Nevertheless, I awakened with a start to a moon obscured by clouds. "It's what we call a bomber's moon," Richard said. "This is how our R.A.F. bombers like it, so the ack-ack guns can't pick us out of the sky."

I stretched and got to my feet. "Well, let's get going. Do you have to take a crap or anything?"

"Hell, no, Ed!"

Then we both laughed. Except for the cold frog legs and the potatoes, we'd had nothing to pass through our systems, and we were growing skinnier by the day. I dismissed the thought. We had work to do. We took the limbs we'd cut and stuffed them behind other foliage before climbing to the top of the ridge, once more heading south.

Our plan seemed logical: Travel as far as we could at night and hide during the daytime. But tonight we had lost valuable time. It must've been around midnight.

We journeyed along the ridge, stopping a few times to check my fly button compass. The mountain angled somewhat to the west and the moon was behind my left shoulder. Well, okay. We kept the pace for a good four hours, until the mountain flattened out, the trail heading downhill, the trees thinning out. Civilization was just around the corner. That's exactly what I dreaded, and I began to grow nervous.

As the trail turned slightly, a brief glint of moonlight caught my eye. I couldn't make it out at first. Then, there it was: a railroad line with a double set of tracks. A wonderful idea struck me!

Doing what we were doing now, we might evade capture for a while, but inevitably we would be caught, unless we acquired a swifter mode of transportation; and there was the railroad, a glimmer of hope.

The railroad lines appeared to run from a north or northeasterly direction to a south-southwesterly direction. The rails were well used, the beds firm rock gravel with well-kept wooden ties, heavily creosoted; the odor was unmistakable. Our steps quickened.

When we arrived at the tracks, like a couple of kids, we started jumping from railroad tie to tie. I remembered an old trick I had learned in Allentown when we hitched rides on freight trains of the Lehigh Valley Railroad. We could tell when a train was coming by putting an ear on the steel rail. I placed my ear on a rail; nothing was coming. We set off in a southerly direction, following the railroad.

Telegraph or telephone lines ran parallel to the tracks, up on poles about twenty feet from the ground. The poles were notched with wedges, making them easy to climb. A crazy thought ran through my head. Why not cut the lines and fuck up the German communication system? I promptly vetoed the idea. Why, on the other hand, call attention to ourselves?

We followed the tracks for a few more hours until we came to a small siding with a marker light and switchbox. Nearby was a large box next to the switches. Although it was padlocked we found an old tie bar and broke the padlock, looking for something that might be of use to us. Inside were sledgehammers, short shovels and crowbars. We took a crowbar and followed siding rails that ran right into a small shack. Only a piece of wood held the latch on the shack. We opened the doors cautiously, and here was something we hadn't expected to find, not in a 1000 years!

There sat a small handcar used by workers on the railroad line. I had seen them many times as a kid, and we had ridden them often, a hand-pumped job where two men worked by pushing the handle on top of the car up and down to propel it.

"Let's give it a try," I said eagerly.

We opened the doors wide, and we discovered it moved easily, much lighter than the ones I remembered from back home. We had no difficulty until we got it to the main rail line switchbox. But we were able to jump this by just pulling the handle and holding it, until we got the front of the car onto the main line. Then, we repeated the process with the rear wheels. That done, we found something else of interest in the shed: a lunch bucket. But it had nothing in it except a small cup. We took the lunch bucket and the crowbar, loaded our machine gun onto the car and began pumping. Immediately, we found ourselves heading in the wrong direction. We stopped to look for a lever. We found it: a simple forward and reverse gadget. Again we began to pump, slowly at first, then faster. It was great!

Joking and laughing, we became masters of the cart. If we pumped real hard for a bit we coasted along without effort for a ways, just as long as we kept our foot off the brake pedal. Of course, our worries weren't over. We might run into soldiers or a train might run into us. We kept our eyes and ears glued for any sound or flash of light.

We must've been moving along at a good 25 to 30 miles an hour. We covered a good distance over the next two hours. This was the break we needed, except that dawn was about to catch up with us. "It's a shame we didn't find this thing earlier in the evening," I told Richard.

"Beats walking," Richard laughed.

The sun had just got up when we spotted our first crossing. "We better coast and be on the alert. In fact, we better be ready with the machine gun."

Richard made sure the safety catch was off on the machine gun.

"Just as soon as we go a bit farther, we'll ditch this thing and get some sleep."

The crossing appeared all clear. Then, Richard yelled, "Oh my god, Ed!" and it was too late to do anything.

A small open truck was parked to the side of the crossing. Two guards stood by the truck and two others in the truck with dogs. I think we surprised them as much as they surprised us; and we both opened fire at the same time.

Richard caught the two in front of the truck with the first and only burst. Then, the gun went dead.

Christ! I thought. "Pump!" I yelled. "Pump! Let's get the hell out of here!"

We pumped that railroad car for all we were worth; we had a hell of a time getting it going again. Meanwhile, the other pair of soldiers had come off the truck and turned their dogs loose before firing. They each must've had a pair of dogs because four dogs were chasing us!

We kept pumping since quite obviously we couldn't lie down in an effort to avoid the bullets and still keep moving.

After they had released the dobermans they got into the truck. Evidently, it wouldn't start.

By now we were seventy to eighty yards down the line. We had been lucky. But the first pair of dogs was gaining on us. They were thirty feet away and closing in, baring their fangs and barking to high heaven. It was a terrifying sight, more terrifying than being shot at.

Richard had dropped the machine gun when it ran out of shells. Instinctively, I grabbed the heavy crowbar. "Keep pumping!" I yelled. "I'll try to fend them off!"

One of the dogs had caught up with us. He lunged, seeming to hang in midair. Wham! I caught him smack on the side of the head. He went down yelping. The second dog was about twenty feet behind. He kept coming, but he was intelligent enough to not come closer; he had seen what happened to the other dog.

The second pair of dogs was now fifty feet away, slowly closing the gap between them and the other dog from the first pair. Since none of them seemed to be gaining on us, I dropped the crowbar, and we pumped like crazy.

As our speed increased, the dogs increased their speed, staying behind, barking and yapping. Then, one of the dogs moved up. Richard yelled, "Watch out!"

I grabbed the crowbar again and swung at the same time. The dog was trying to board the car from the side, but I nailed him square in the chest; he hit the car and went down with a wild yelp. The remaining two dobermans dropped back. They turned away to join the second doberman I had knocked down. What a relief! But for how long?

– 13 –

The encounter with the guards and the dogs had sent adrenalin flying through our veins. It had been a superhuman effort, and nothing else accounted for our survival. Still, we weren't out of it. I knew damn well, since the other two soldiers hadn't been able to start their truck, they had some way of alerting their comrades in arms. Gasping for breath, I told Richard, "I think we oughta dump this car before long and take to the woods."

We began looking for a logical spot to implement our plan. At least thirty minutes had passed since our initial encounter with the Germans when we saw ourselves approaching a large bend in the railroad line. As we came out of the bend, off to the right were hills and a heavy woods which continued toward the hills. Here was the spot. But first . . .

"Let's go down a ways with the car," I told Richard, "ditch it, come back along the railroad and then head for the hills."

Right here we passed over a small trestle, going down a slight grade; beneath the trestle was a stream.

Simultaneously, we blurted out, "That's it!"

We pumped for another five minutes. If we ditched the car now, with its momentum it was bound to go another few miles or jump the track, and everyone would assume that we went with it. I grabbed the small lunch pail, ready to abandon the car.

"What about the crowbar?" Richard rasped, out of breath.

"To hell with it! Let's go!" I leaped from the car for the gravel bed to the side of the rails.

Within seconds, Richard jumped too.

Although the landing hurt like hell we pulled ourselves to our feet and climbed back on the track. "For God's sake, let's stay on the railroad ties. Don't step off of them!" I cautioned.

As fast as our legs would carry us we ran back toward the trestle. Fifteen minutes later we were there. We paused to see if the car was still in sight. It wasn't. Good! We dropped straight down into the water. Fortunately, the stream wasn't very rocky or deep.

The current seemed to be coming from the hill, a break for us. We stayed with the stream. When it came out into a meadow, we crouched low and kept at it. Once or twice we thought we heard vehicles and voices. But we didn't pause to listen. This was our best hope for escape and we scrambled onward, tripping and falling in the stream from time to time as we stumbled over rocks, but pressing ahead.

At least an hour passed before we reached the woods. It hadn't been easy going. Panting and soaking wet, we were delighted with the cool refuge of the trees.

As the stream grew more rocky, we noted many fish. They looked like food to me, but I had no idea how we would catch the fish, even if we could afford to rest. We couldn't. Then, the stream turned on us, making a sharp bend, heading back into the open field. This was where we had to get out. Our only chance lay with the hills.

We found ourselves a rocky spot and climbed atop the rocks. Suddenly I realized I was still carrying that lunch pail. I called a halt, rinsed it out and filled the pail with water. I closed the top and the water held. We began to run again.

My heart and temples were pounding from the exhaustion of running against the stream. I promised us a brief rest when we reached the hills.

A short way up the hill we found a big rock. Our muscles cried out for rest. But before I gave myself that luxury, I climbed up on the rock for a look around. I couldn't see the railroad line, but I could see the road, and three or four vehicles traveling in the direction we had taken the railroad car. Just what I wanted!

When I jumped down off the rock I found Richard stretched out, resting. As much as I hated to do it, I said, "We gotta rest standing up." Already I had left a puddle of water on the rock. "No telling how long it will take to dry off that rock."

"How right you are," he said and pushed himself upright.

We stood there for a brief interval, allowing our breathing to return to normal. Then, we made for the top of the hill.

The hill was heavily wooded. But we were blessed by not so much small foliage and brush. We were moving ahead well now, arriving at the top of the hill in about an hour, to find a small animal path which led us right to the ridge.

On the other side of the hill was one hell of a large canal, running north and south. Even from this distance the canal was huge. We couldn't believe the size of it. Never mind. We continued on, heading south, parallel to the canal, and every so often coming into open land where we caught sight of barges going in both directions.

Finally, we paused for a brief rest, watching two barges, one heading north and one heading south. An idea struck me!

"There," I said, in sudden revelation, "is our passport to freedom!"

"You've got to be crazy, my Yank buddy," Richard responded.

"You'll see," I said. "But first a drink of water." I opened the lunch pail and was disappointed. About half of the water had leaked out. Still, it was better than nothing. We each took a good swallow. I was so hungry, though, that I thought I was going to throw up. We held briefly. The feeling passed. But we were drained from hunger and physical exhaustion. We had to find a place to sack out. I looked around for a solution to our problem.

The ridge seemed to climb. We followed the ridge, glimpsing the canal off to our right now and then. The sun was directly over us. It must've been around noon. Finally, we stopped and discussed our situation, deciding to head down the mountain to the canal. Halfway down we found a spot, a small natural cave which had been used by animals.

Bushes had grown up around the cave's entrance. This was enough. We didn't bother to get leaves or limbs to cushion ourselves. We were done for. We dropped down, and we were out like a light. Believe me, no sleeping pills were required!

Sometime later I awakened. The sun had gone down. Richard was still sleeping. My clothes had dried pretty well. Only my shoes and socks were wet. I felt downright comfortable there. I rolled over and went back to sleep.

Richard awakened me, and I fairly jumped to my feet, figuring there was trouble. "Easy, Ed," he said. "I got up to take a leak. I could see the canal."

We moved from the cave and looked down. The canal shimmered below us in the light of a full moon. I wondered what time it was. But I had lost my watch and, hell, we'd even lost track of the days by now. When you're hunted, hungry and tired, time doesn't matter much. We made the decision to head toward the canal and scrounge around, hoping to find something to eat.

At the bottom of the hill was a wide, dirt road we had been unable to see from the top of the mountain. Richard spotted something by the side of the road. "Looks like wild rhubarb," he whispered. He pulled a couple of stalks, tasting it. "Genuine," he murmured, and stripped the leaves, cleaning the stems. Then he handed one to me. "Taste it, it's rhubarb. May be a little sour, but this is real."

I chewed on the stalk. It was a bit like celery, and it was a lot more than sour. Nevertheless, I forced myself to chew and swallow bite after bite. God, what I would have given for a big juicy hamburger!

Having dined on rhubarb we crossed the road. We were only a short distance from the canal, and it was even wider than we had thought. It was like a large river with tidy banks. Perhaps it had been a river once upon a time, until it had been dredged into a canal.

We crept closer, through bushes now, coming upon a foot path which carried, much to our surprise, hoof marks as well as footprints. Then, I remembered the mules which towed barges along the Lehigh Valley Canal back home. As a kid I'd hitched rides on the barges. But the barges we'd seen from the top of the hill had to be motorized.

A sharp bank dropped down about ten feet to the water. We decided to stay on the bank to see if any barges passed. Shortly, a barge appeared, coming from the south. We ducked back into the bushes. And, yes, the barge was motorized, though moving very, very slowly.

As the barge came abreast of us a lone man appeared on board. Otherwise, the barge seemed empty, riding high above the water line on its side. Still, we waited and watched. A couple of hours later a southbound barge came along, also motorized, with one man handling the barge. This barge, however, was different. The man on the barge controlled it from a forward position and the barge was loaded with cargo, and this barge was faster than the previous barge. Meanwhile, a long rope trailed off the backside near the rudder, giving me an idea. If we could find some way to latch onto one of those barges, we could hang on at night without anyone seeing us, especially since the pilot was up front. I was encouraged by the fact that the barges carried very little light; it was amazing how they could travel so well in the dark. Still, we waited, thinking . . .

Another barge came along. Low and behold, the pilot pulled over on the far side and threw out an anchor to hold the barge against the current. He walked back along the cargo to the rear and disappeared down a stairwell. He stayed below for about half an hour, only to appear again, go to the front of the boat, pull up anchor, adjust his engine and head south again.

We debated the matter of only one man aboard. Was it really so? Yes, it seemed to be so. But why? Then, it came to us: the manpower shortage from the war. How fortunate for us!

Now we considered the matter carefully. Evidently, sleeping quarters, perhaps even a kitchen, were below deck on these barges, since we could see light coming from small portholes. The place in which the barge had been anchored was forty to fifty feet downstream from us, much wider than the remainder of the canal. Here was a logical stopping point to rest, to eat. Meanwhile, there was also something which appeared to be a dock. I said, "We've got to get to the other side, since southbound boats seem to stay on the far side. Anyway, there might be something we could use to hitch a ride on a barge. We'll never know if we don't look."

"Christ, Ed, don't tell me we have to get in the bloody water again. I can't stand the thought."

I laughed. "Maybe we can find a log or a boat or something and

114

keep our clothes dry."

"That's for me," Richard said. "Let's look on this side first."

We walked along the foot path downstream, keeping a sharp eye out for both soldiers and boats. Then, we came upon a half-submerged barrel. We both slid down the bank, hoping to pull the barrel from the water.

The barrel was open on top, but in good shape. After emptying the water from it we pulled it onto the bank. The barrel carried the odor of brine and pickles. Hell, the thought of pickles nearly did me in. But we couldn't waste time over that. We were growing a bit desperate. Perhaps we had already lingered too long.

We undressed quickly, placing our clothes and the pail in the barrel, and set the barrel afloat. It didn't sink. We pushed off, the barrel ahead of us, swimming the canal.

"My balls," Richard yelled. "They're freezing!"

"Keep swimming!" I yelled back.

Though we reached the opposite bank without trouble we were downstream from the dock. We climbed up on the bank, pulling the barrel in behind us. At the top of the bank another foot path appeared, only this time there were more bushes and trees. We waited there for the air to dry our skin. Then, we plunged into our clothes, such as they were. We were getting pretty shabby. While Richard's R.A.F. uniform was in fairly good shape, we agreed he had to ditch it as soon as we could find civilian clothes for him. That uniform was like wearing a red flag.

We stashed the barrel in the brush and went off along the foot path to the dock. There we found a dock made from railroad ties, stacked atop each other, the deck about thirty feet long. Four pilings were along the side of the dock and two ropes were suspended from two pilings. The ropes, heavy duty boatline, about three-quarters of an inch thick, were coiled neatly and hung on the side. Meanwhile, several large old tires were hung along the dock to cushion boats which pulled into the dock. Now something else caught my eye . . .

At the far end of the dock, fifty feet away, was a homemade picnic table and benches. Beside this was a genuine water pump like those used on some American farms. The surprise was wonderful. We ran toward the picnic area, thinking we might find something to eat. But there was nothing, just an empty mesh garbage container and a small barbecue pit. While it was a hell of a nice spot for private boats, during war it wasn't getting much use. Then, I spied the swing. It was suspended from a tree near the water. Nostalgia caught up with me again. But I didn't linger long with it. We got busy priming the pump, and it worked. Fresh, clear water spurted out!

We took turns drinking, filling ourselves with good water. But again nausea swept over me. God, we had to find something to eat. The thought was promptly filed away by the appearance of another barge from the north.

Richard and I ducked into the bushes. The barge slowed to a walk, then, the pilot edged right up against the dock. That done, he slipped a tow line over one piling and ran back along the deck next to his cargo and slipped another line on the piling, handling it all easily.

We couldn't have been more than twenty feet from the barge, and I picked up the scent. My god, could it be coffee? Yes! My mouth watered. "Do you smell that?" I whispered.

Richard nodded his head vigorously. "Coffee!" he said.

Yes, yes, yes . . . There were living quarters in the barge. We could see too that there were controls in back as well as in front, and I understood how one man could handle the barge. "Richard," I muttered, "there's got to be food down there. Now how in hell do we get it?"

"We could kill the bloody Kraut bastard and take the barge . . ."

"That wouldn't be too smart. We don't know how to handle the barge, and they'd spot us immediately." Then, I looked up, and I'll be damned, the operator of the barge got off and walked toward the picnic area and the pump. He carried a big jug and smoked a pipe, passing within less than ten feet of us. He was a large man, slightly stooped for his age, wearing a sweater and a captain's hat.

He filled the jug with water, then took the metal cup which hung on the pump and drank two cups of water. Next he took a leak, puffing on his pipe and looking around as he did. Finally, he sat at the picnic table. That didn't last long. He headed back to the barge. On board, he moved to the rear, dropping down into a small hole behind the cargo. And, yes, yes, yes, there were living quarters there. And food! "Maybe," I whispered to Richard, "maybe we could take a chance and sneak down there when he goes back up to the front of the boat."

"Let's just wait and see," was Richard's hoarse response.

My heart was in my throat. I so wanted that coffee, I so wanted to rest, I so wanted to ride instead of walk. But we waited.

The barge was seventy to eighty feet long with a beam of about twenty feet, only the back half of the barge tied to the dock. "What do you think, Richard?"

"I don't know . . ."

"Look," I said. "One of us has to take a chance . . . sneak down into his cabin and steal some food. I'm going to try."

"What if he catches you?"

"I'll have to kill him!" I didn't have an option.

"He might be armed," Richard cautioned.

I still didn't have an option. "Look," I said, "keep an eye on the operator, and I'll take my chances."

The barge was two feet below the dock level. I stepped down onto the barge. Then, I dropped on all fours and crawled toward the back of the barge. I wanted to stop, turn back and see if the operator of

116

the barge saw me. But I resisted temptation and crawled onward. I made it beyond the cargo to a rear deck which led into his quarters. And there was the small hatch stairway. I dropped down into the compact room below, and facing me was a stove with a pot on it. The smell of food cooking in the pot was too much for me.

A large spoon lay next to the stove on a table. I picked it up and turned to the pot, a pot of stew, no less. I scooped out a large spoonful and shoved it all in my mouth. Ah, meat and potatoes and carrots, and, oh, it was good. Then, I remembered why I was here. I glanced around. Beside the stove was an old-fashioned box. There was a table with two chairs, a large bunk built into the wall, all made up and comfortable with a blanket, sheets, everything. I wanted to crawl into that bunk, but I resisted. I had my duty to do.

Next to the bunk was a closet and a built-in chest of drawers. I searched the drawers, looking for a gun, anything that might help. And I found it. An automatic pistol, made in Czechoslovakia and stamped: *Bohmiche Waffenbrik calibre–7.65*. Hell, there was even a swastika stamped on the pistol's side. I tried to remove the clip to see if it was loaded. Some kind of trick catch prevented me from removing it. I gave up and shoved the gun into my jacket pocket, going on with my search.

My next lucky find was a leather jacket for Richard. I grabbed it and pulled out the drawer under the table. Knives, forks and other utensils were there. I snatched a can opener and a small knife, dropping them into my pocket. Finally, I came to the shelf above the stove; assorted cans of food were stored there, some with English labels stamped, "Argentine Corned Beef" on one side, and in German on the other side. I grabbed two of the larger cans. Hanging right below the porthole was a canvas bag. I lifted it from its hook and stuffed the canned goods in it. I glanced around frantically one last time, wondering what I had missed. Then, I saw it, a bread box on the table. I opened it and removed a large loaf of dark bread. Remaining inside the bread box was something wrapped in heavy waxed paper. I took it too. Now I was beyond all hope, carried away. Hell, we might as well go first class. I reopened the drawer and took two spoons and another knife, dumping them into the canvas bag. Finally, one last look at the stew. God, it smelled good!

I dropped the bag and fed myself another large spoonful. I remembered smelling coffee. One more look, I told myself. There was the coffee pot, but it was empty. The damn fool had finished it off. Ah, but it didn't end here. A half-dozen white candles lay on a small shelf along with a box of matches. I grabbed these. Into the canvas bag they went. I had started out to steal just enough, so that I'd leave no notice. Now I couldn't get enough. I was like a kid turned loose in a candy store. Fortunately, right here, I stemmed the tide of further temptation with ramrod resolution. I turned away and began crawling back up the steps.

I made it out on deck okay. Suddenly, I was filled with nerves of steel. The stew had done it. I smiled to myself and crawled back along the narrow walkway toward the dock. When I reached the dock I lifted the canvas bag carefully, pushing it slowly onto the dock. Then, I crawled up. Here I thought I heard something. I lay flat on the dock, slowly turning my head . . . But, no, the captain of the barge was still where I had left him. I pulled myself infantry style across the dock, pushing the canvas bag ahead of me, slowly, surely.

I had just arrived at the bushes when a hand reached out and took the bag. It was Richard. Then, he pulled me into the bushes and, without a word, we sneaked off into the bushes, circling around, so that we could keep an eye on the barge captain, but not so close he could spot us.

Richard couldn't resist asking relentlessly, "What do you have? What did you get?"

"Plenty," I whispered back in excitement. "Plenty!" I threw the jacket at him.

"Hope it fits," he said softly, wistfully.

We settled in at our new location. I took out the loaf of bread, breaking it in half. Then, I unwrapped the object in the waxed paper. I thought it might be butter. It wasn't. It was Limburger cheese and it stank to high heaven, but it was a good stink. I handed one of the knives to Richard and with the other one, I cut the cheese in half.

Richard was like a wild man, chomping first on the bread and then the cheese. He wasn't alone. The stew hadn't filled me up, not by a long shot. I followed him right along, savoring every bite of wonderful, nourishing bread and cheese.

Richard paused in his pursuit of food, saying, "What else did you get?"

I just nodded and kept on eating. Food came first. Only a sound from the dock caused the festivities to come to a halt. The old man, the captain of the barge, had slipped off the tie ropes from the dock. He was leaving.

The engines on the barge started and the barge pulled straight out. As the barge went away I wondered how long before he'd go down into his living quarters. I hoped it would be a hell of a long time. Of course, I had left the stew. But the bread box was empty. To hell with that! I grabbed the two cans of corned beef, throwing one to Richard and keeping one for myself. The cans had keys on the bottom. We opened the cans and devoured the corned beef as the sun came up. My god, it was good!

We might have been wild animals on a feeding rampage. We couldn't stop for anything. Finally, we came to the end of the cheese, corned beef and bread. "We better not eat anything else," I ventured, common sense at last overcoming desire. "We'll get sick." It was daylight now. But I felt wonderful, safe and secure. "Let's get a drink from the pump."

At the pump we took a couple of long drinks, and the water was delicious. Then, we returned to the bushes, Richard demanding, "What else did you get?"

I reached into my left jacket pocket and took out the gun, displaying it with a smile.

Richard let out a low whistle. "Is it loaded?"

I shrugged and got busy finding the small catch. It worked. The clip slid out perfectly, and there were seven shells and one in the chamber.

"Beautiful," Richard breathed. "Just beautiful!"

Now I showed him the remainder of my treasure. I even told him about the stew, apologizing all the way for not having brought him any, while Richard demanded, "Why in the hell didn't you bring it with you?" until we broke down laughing. Of course, it was impossible. Of course.

Richard slipped off his R.A.F. jacket and pulled on the leather jacket. The sleeves were a little short, but it was okay. "I hate parting with my R.A.F. jacket . . ."

"You have to get rid of it. You'll be spotted."

He nodded, found a large rock, turned the jacket inside out, tied the sleeves around the rock tightly and dumped it in the canal. Slowly it sank from sight. Well, that was done.

It was broad, bright daylight now. We figured we better get the hell out of there and find a good hiding place. Just to cross anyone up who might look for us, we headed north, continuing on the west side of the canal for three or four miles until we saw hills off to the left. They weren't very high hills, but they were heavily wooded.

Within a short while we were in the foothills where we came into heavily wooded scrub brush. This would be our hiding place for the day.

We hadn't left any telltale signs behind us, even bringing the empty tin cans with us. But we were hungry again. I checked the canvas bag. We had two cans of saurkraut and three cans of soup. But only God knew when we would get an opportunity at more food. We decided to rest rather than eat.

Now I checked the gun, slipping on the safety. The gun was perfect in every detail with very small tolerances, a real dandy. It made our G.I. issue .45 automatic look like a piece of junk.

We stretched out on the ground, Richard insisting I use the canvas bag for a pillow. "You deserve it, Ed old boy. That was one hell of a good show. I just wish you'd brought back that bloody stew. God, it must've been terrific. Real hot stew. Tell me about it again . . ." He kept at it, asking for every detail of that goddamn stew. I felt like a dirty rat. But it was a hell of a lot nicer falling to sleep on a full stomach.

I woke several times during the day, tossing and turning. My stomach wasn't accustomed to food. Richard was moaning and groaning and thrashing in his sleep. We'd have to be careful about over-stuffing ourselves from here on in. But despite the discomfort, I didn't regret it. Oh, it felt good to be full.

I reflected on our last acquisition, prior to leaving the dock. We had taken one of the thick ropes. We didn't dare take both of them since we wanted it to appear that someone had taken one by accident in departing the dock. The rope was so thick it could be unraveled into three good pieces of rope. I had an idea that if we could latch onto a barge we might be able to use the rope to good advantage.

When we managed to bring ourselves awake and in good order, we spent the remainder of the day unraveling the heavy rope, and sure enough, we came up with three ropes which were quite strong. I used one to fashion the loop for two lines. After we had tied two lines to the individual line, we fashioned two harnesses plus another loop which could be slipped over the barge cleats easily. Next we made a short harness for the canvas bag, so that it could be looped over the shoulder. We wanted to take great care of the bag; it held all of our worldly possessions. Now, all we had to do was find ourselves a suitable barge.

At dark we journeyed down to the canal, traveling cautiously, circling the dock, going into the brush a ways and then, heading back down to the canal further along. Here we found a place in the brush on the bank in which to hide. We had just settled in, and here came a barge into view. We made our decision. This was it. We would slip into the canal, duck under water as the barge came closer, and catch ourselves a ride.

– 14 –

We entered the water up to our necks and waited. The barge was about 100 feet away. Yes, this was it. We started swimming. An eerie feeling caught up with me.

I could hold my breath under water for at least sixty seconds without trouble. But I had the canvas bag tied around my shoulder and over my neck; it seemed to drag me down, down, down.

I counted off a very slow sixty seconds, and I was genuinely pleased when I came up a scant three feet from the barge. The barge was moving faster in the water than anticipated. Quickly I glanced around for Richard. He popped up about ten feet away. Pressing, we swam to the side of the barge and latched on to its rub strip. Hand over hand, we made our way to the back of the barge, getting an assist from the water.

At the back, it was harder to hold on. I began to slip away toward the propeller. Richard grabbed my hand in the nick of time, pulling me back toward him. I found my rope, passed it to him, and he hooked this onto a cleat which protruded from the boat. And by god, it worked!

We were suspended in the water a few feet from the back. The barge operator could see us only if he walked back and peered over the edge. Still, the canvas bag gave me trouble. It was cutting into my neck. I slipped it off and hooked it to the tie-on. So far, so good. I whispered to Richard, "Everything's working fine. Let's hope it keeps on."

We relaxed in the water, the barge moving along at a fine clip, and we even dozed off from time to time. Eventually, the harness began to cut into our sides. We learned that we could ease the pain by reaching up and pulling on the rope, thus, removing the pressure. After a while, a bridge came into view. As we drew nearer the bridge soldiers were at both ends and two motorcycles with side cars were parked at one end. Swiftly, we pulled ourselves closer to the barge and ducked under water as we slipped beneath the bridge. We passed under two more bridges in like manner without detection.

God only knows how far we went that night. But we did some traveling. Finally, the faint rays of morning streaked the sky. It was time to get off. I pinched Richard. He nodded, and we pulled ourselves to the side of the barge, unhooked the loop from the tie-on along with the canvas bag and dropped away. We stayed in the water until the barge was downstream a considerable distance and swam to shore. In shallow water at last, we sprawled in exhaustion, getting our second wind. Then, we crawled up on the bank.

This was a heavily wooded area and beautiful at daybreak. But we had no time to enjoy the scenery. We hurried up the bank, crossed a foot path carefully and worked our way back into the dense brush. We were miserable from the soaking. Our hands and fingers felt as if they'd spent the night soaking in a swamp; they were shrivelled and chalk white. Even with the sun, we shivered. Throwing caution to the wind, we holed up in a thickly shrubbed gulley where we stretched out and tried to sleep in our wet clothing. It was damned uncomfortable, and we napped for only a short while. Yes, we were going to have to remove our clothes and spread them to dry. And, yes, we were hungry.

The clothing out to dry, we opened the canvas bag and removed the large can of sauerkraut, using the can opener. We had lost the spoons and one small knife. We took turns taking handsful of cold sauerkraut and eating it. Somewhere along the way we thought of heating up the sauerkraut in its can with a candle. But the matches were soaking wet.

Once we'd eaten, we packed up the candles and soaked matches in the empty tin can and buried them. Then, we sacked out in the nude; it wasn't half bad; the sun was out in full force. We joked lazily while we waited to drift off into sleep. "Sure glad this isn't winter," I murmured. "We'd freeze our balls off."

Richard's laughter was hearty and welcome. I had heard that Australians had a great sense of humor, and I was glad to have Richard as my companion, though we were both in a hell of a fix.

"If they caught us like this," I ventured, "they might think we were refugees from a nudist colony!"

Richard shook his head. "You Yanks are something else again!"

Yes, we got on famously, and that was nice — if you had to be on the run from the Nazis . . .

We slept until late afternoon. Although our clothes were slightly damp, we put them on, Richard suggesting that we eat another can of sauerkraut.

"I think we ought to stretch it out," I said.

"It'll be easier for you in the water without the sauerkraut," he argued. "It's the heaviest can . . ."

Hell, I was hungry too. "Let's open the second can of sauerkraut." I wasn't hard to convince.

I will say one thing for that sauerkraut; it tasted far better than American sauerkraut. Although it wasn't the greatest for breakfast, it was food, and it sure beat raw frog legs, raw potatoes or rhubarb.

The second can of sauerkraut eaten, we dug a hole and buried it too. It wasn't dark yet, so we had ourselves a light nap. It was bound to be a long night.

When we awakened, the sun had gone down and dusk had set in. If we could keep this up for a few nights minimum, hitching rides on the back of barges, hopefully we would find ourselves nearer the border and a sense of genuine safety.

As we set out for the canal, Richard was grumbling. He'd been away from home for over four years, and he felt it was going to be a hell of a lot longer before he saw home again.

"Don't worry. We're going to make it. I know we are."

He didn't respond; he just kept walking.

When we came to the spot where we'd climbed out of the canal that morning, I was appalled at our lack of thought. There were our marks where we had dug in coming up the bank. We were getting careless; like today, sleeping so close to the canal, not finding a better hiding place. I vowed not to let that happen again, and we settled in to wait. We waited well over an hour, admiring the bright moonlight night, me saying, "We've got to be careful not to be seen."

Finally, two empty northbounders came by. Then, a southbound barge came along, a double surprise since this was two barges hitched together. We scampered down the bank for a better look. The barges were piled high with coal that sparkled in the moonlight.

The double barge was moving slowly, its load heavy. We strained to see if there was more than one man aboard. As the barge came closer, yes, only one man stood at the front of the barge. "We might as well chance it," I whispered.

We swam out from the side, since the barge was only fifteen to twenty feet away. This seemed a hell of a lot better than going into the deep water. We hugged the bushes with our faces turned away from the moonlight, until we could stand it no longer. Then, we took a peek. The operator, eyes straight ahead, stood there puffing on a large pipe. Once the barge passed, we came out along beside the edge of the first barge and decided to duck in between the two barges, since there was a foot of space between them.

This was more comfortable and we didn't bother to hook up. But there was one problem. The barges were hooked together with double clamps on each side and over us; attached to the decks, a long gangplank about three feet wide crossed over from one barge to another. If the operator came our way, he was bound to see us. But never mind. We could pull ourselves up from the water slightly, especially where the rudder had been removed on the first barge.

Compared to the previous barge, this one was just snaking along. We eased under three or four small bridges and came to a point where the canal narrowed to only slightly wider than the barge. However, we didn't see anyone on the bridges or banks of the canal and this improved our spirits.

After several hours, we rigged our rope harnesses to the section where the rudder had been. Then, we braced our feet against the second barge. We had it made!

I noticed the road had gotten closer to the canal on the east side. Now and again, trucks went by. I wondered if we were getting close to a large city. Finally, I whispered to Richard, "While this is more comfortable, we can't see good enough from here."

Grudgingly, he responded, "Okay. You're the big Yank. I'm with you. What do you suggest?"

I suggested we move. We unhooked and pulled ourselves hand over hand on the rub strip to the back of the second barge. Here we found a good cleat to tie on about a foot from the end. So, now we resigned ourselves to hanging behind the barge. But at least we could see better, and suddenly, we seemed to be moving more swiftly . . . Then, unexpectedly, we came to a bend in the canal and the rudder was pulled very close to where we were. We must be heading in a deeper channel.

Although the canal had veered away from the road, it was still only a few hundred yards away, and the traffic had picked up. I spotted a weapon's carrier with a motorcycle escort. Richard whispered, "Maybe we're getting close to Munich." I didn't know. But wherever we were, I was growing worried.

Peeking around the side, I could see a large bridge looming ahead. Unlike the other bridges this bridge spanned the entire canal and was supported by a structure in the middle. Meanwhile, a railroad trestle crossed the canal, running east and west. As we approached, we heard a freight train coming.

We looked beyond the side of the barge. It was a hell of a long freight train. When we passed under the railroad trestle, we could see that it was a double trestle. We were in the big time!

We clung closer to the barge, trying to stay out of sight as much as possible, our heads just above the water. Even after we were downstream a hundred yards, we still heard that freight train passing over the trestle. I said to Richard, "We'll wait another five minutes then unhook ourselves."

He nodded in agreement.

Another five minutes from the trestle we unhooked, but stayed in the water until the barge disappeared from view. We didn't dare head for the bank too soon in the bright moonlight. The barge operator might spot us. Once he was gone, though, we swam to the bank.

Again, we were exhausted. But now, with thoughts of train travel in mind, I took both harnesses, wrapped them around a rock and threw them into the canal about ten feet from the shore. Now I had only the canvas bag, hanging over my shoulder, to drag up the bank with my body. This helped. But not much.

Finally, we plunged into the bushes, moving away from the canal, changing our course abruptly north, until we were in sight of the rail line, half an hour later. We approached the tracks with extreme caution, looking up and down the line for a minimum of ten minutes from the brush. Convinced it was safe, we stepped on the track, me reaching down to touch the rails; they were still warm, probably from the earlier freight train we'd seen. Then, I did my old trick of placing my ear on the rail. I heard and felt a distinct hum. "There's a train coming," I told Richard. Hurriedly, we crossed the tracks, scrambled up a slight incline and hid ourselves among the bushes, waiting . . .

A heavily laden train chugged toward us. We peeked from the bushes, watching for the large headlight. But when the train arrived, the light was blacked out, throwing a low sliver of silver light before the engine. Two men were in the engine cab, one firing up the boiler, the other apparently the engineer.

Behind the engine came the adjoining coal car, a closed car of some sort, then the freight cars. We didn't dare come from our hiding place until about twenty cars had gone by. The laboring of the engine told us the train was picking up speed. Then, Richard said, "All right, Ed. Now tell me. How do we get aboard this bloody train?"

I explained the procedure of running along and lunging for the ladder on the end of the car, yelling, "Let's look for an open car!"

Most of the freight cars were closed. Then, several open cars came toward us. "This is it!" I yelled, and I began running, making a lunge for the second open car, swinging myself up and barely grabbing the front ladder. Boy, was that train moving . . . But I hung on for dear life, glancing back to see how Richard fared.

He was having a hell of a time. He missed the first ladder. Finally, he lunged, grabbed the rung of the second ladder and pulled himself up, letting out a yell. I couldn't understand what he said, but he seemed okay.

I climbed to the top of the car. The cargo was covered with a heavy tarpaulin. Looking up, searching for Richard, I saw him crawling over the top of his car toward me. I held my breath as he crossed between the cars. He made it and I edged toward the rear. He reached out to me, pumping my hand wildly, saying, "We made it! We made it, Ed! We really made it!"

I swatted him on the back and we began to examine the tarpaulin. It was tied tightly at both ends and in the middle. However, we were able to pull the tarpaulin far enough away from the side to slip down under and crawl atop the numerous wooden crates.

There wasn't a hell of a lot of room, but we pushed a crate aside by bracing our backs against the side of the car and shoving with our feet, giving us enough room to sit down.

In all the excitement we'd forgotten how wet and uncomfortable we were. Once we calmed down, we began to shiver. Even if we wanted to take off our clothes, there wasn't enough room. We sat facing each other, our legs pulled up against our chins, shivering and praying the train was heading where we wanted to go: southwest.

Slowly, our little space beneath the tarpaulin grew warmer. We dozed off, sleeping fitfully, falling asleep and waking abruptly from the lurching of the cars. Once or twice we heard the roar of another freight train passing in the opposite direction. The Germans were making hay by the dark of night; during the day our fighter planes and light bombers were strafing the hell out of them.

At long last streaks of light filtered through the narrow opening between the tarpaulin and the car. It was daylight. I reached into my jacket and took out the fly button compass, placing it atop the small piece of wood I carried. Since there was so much metal around us the compass acted erratically. But the little notch kept swinging to the north, indicating we were heading west or possibly southwest. Thank God!

Eyeing the compass, I said, "Wouldn't it be terrific if this train was headed for France?"

Richard just nodded his head, mumbling, "We should be so lucky . . ."

He was hungry. I could tell. Well, so was I. We still had the cans of soup. I removed a can of soup from the canvas bag, gave it a good shake and opened it with my can opener. "Wonder if the guy on the barge has discovered we ripped him off."

Richard grinned, having brightened at the sight of the can. He accepted it eagerly, licking his lips in anticipation.

Right here the train slowed to a ponderous stop. Then, we heard someone walking on the gravel bed outside and the slamming of what sounded like a box. Suddenly, I realized what was happening. I signaled to Richard not to make a sound. A box slammed very near to us, then moved away, repeating itself every twenty or thirty seconds. Finally, the sound ceased. "They were checking the wheel boxes," I whispered to Richard.

"What in hell for?"

"To see if they're greased, not getting too hot."

"Ed, You're a bloody genius, a bloody Errol Flynn!"

After what was an interminable wait, the engine began to chug, chug, chug, straining to acquire the momentum to pull the heavy cars along behind it. With a sigh we relaxed, though the chugging had spilled half the can of soup. What the hell! We decided to go all the way and open a second can.

The soup wasn't half bad: noodles mixed with vegetables. We

relished the soup, though we wished for something hot, like that stew I'd sampled on board the barge. Dinner over, we didn't pitch the cans out. Instead we pushed them behind us, figuring to wait for night when dumping them couldn't be so easily seen.

Our clothes were dry now, our stomachs weren't growling, and we attended to our shoes. We removed them, placed them on top of a crate and hoped they would dry before we had to put them on again. Contemplating those shoes, I felt envy for Richard's R.A.F. high-top, grained leather footwear. They were a hell of a lot better than my heated flying shoes which had started to come apart.

We passed the remainder of the time dozing off. The clickety clack of the rails seemed to lull us into sleep now and then, and that was fine. The day wore away quickly, and dusk was near. Now for a look around.

I pulled myself up, forcing aside the tarpaulin just to the point I could see out. The sun had just gone down, but there was still plenty of light. The countryside was beautiful with rolling hills. Trees and foliage were in full bloom. Then, I spotted mountains in the distance; they were quite high. Where were we? I just plain didn't know.

Ducking my head down, I reached in and pulled out the fly button compass. It worked better holding it above the car, and it indicated we were heading west. I resumed my position in the cramped quarters, and Richard decided to stretch his legs and acquire a breath of fresh air by sticking his head out.

It was almost dark now. We could hardly see one another. But the darkness, as it became as black as pitch, made us feel safer. We had been on the freight train twelve to fifteen hours. Undoubtedly, we had covered real ground.

What had gone before seemed like a nightmare as I reflected on it. I wondered how we were holding up. Richard looked horrible; while he was fair, his beard was scraggily and unkempt. I imagined I appeared even worse with my dark beard. I ran a hand over my face and wished for some of the pleasures experienced at the Ournays. Would I ever go back there? I better not; they'd hook me sure as hell. But I enjoyed thinking about their daughter. I told Richard about her and he said, "You're a bloody cad, Ed!"

The train began to slow down. I took a quick peek. The train was climbing a steep grade. On top of the grade, it picked up speed again. If only we had a map or could see road signs.

Here Richard asked me, "Do you think we should stay on the train or take a chance and jump off when it slows next?"

"Hell, no!" was my response. "We stay on as long as it keeps going." Then I conceded, "I do need to take a leak."

We moved around, standing one at a time and aiming at the side of the car away from where we sat. Our little cubby-hole didn't exactly smell like a bed of roses now.

A short while later we stopped again. Once more I peeked. The engine was taking on water from a large water tower, and we were in the mountains. Steep hills lay on both sides of the tracks. Then, I heard footsteps on both sides of the train; they were checking the wheel boxes again.

After the train got moving we spent the better part of the night dozing until we stopped again. Light knifed through the opening between the tarp and the car. Then, I heard voices, and my heart jumped into my throat. I not only heard German, I heard French!

We had to be in France. "Do you hear that?" I whispered to Richard.

He nodded, his eyes wide in the dim light.

Finally, the train moved on. We traveled through the night and on into daylight, feeling better by the minute. We opened the other two cans of food, our last, and savored every drop, every noodle.

Early that morning the train slowed. Hell, daylight or not, take a look. We were entering a marshalling yard. I flushed with excitement. The sign ahead read: St. Etienne. We were in France!

I ducked down fast and shared the good news with Richard. His face went wide with a grin and his eyes sparkled with anticipation. "By god, Ed, you were right. This is a damn miracle. Maybe I'll get laid by one of those pretty French mademoiselles!"

We couldn't believe in our good fortune. St. Etienne was in Vichy France, deep in the southeastern part of France. We packed our empty cans into the canvas bag. I took out the *Bohmiche Waffenbrik* gun, and we climbed out into broad daylight. We had to get off that train before it stopped.

Ed Cury as an aviation cadet prior to takeoff. July, 1942.

Ed Cury and crew with new plane and equipment, prior to going overseas.

Lt. E. C. Cury, Allentown Fortress Bombardier, Distinguishes Himself When Six Bombs Stick in Bomb-bay

By JOHN DURSTON
(Copyright, 1944, New York Tribune, Inc.)

AT A FLYING FORTRESS BASE SOMEWHERE IN ENGLAND, Jan. 24.—For 15 minutes a Flying Fortress droned over the water today between the continent and England with six heavy incendiary bombs stuck fast in its bomb-bay and with the wind spinning the bomb vanes which, after a certain number of turns, automatically set off the bombs.

The bombs the plane was carrying were of a particularly devastating type invented by the British and

LIEUTENANT ENVER C. CURY

handled most gingerly by the American bomber crews, who are particularly not anxious to have to land planes loaded with them. When the plane approached the channel the bombardier, First Lieutenant Enver C. Cury, 23 years old, of Allentown, Pa., asked the pilot whether it would be all right to dump them in the water.

The pilot was a bit reluctant. He told Lieutenant Cury to go ahead and the bombardier pressed the toggle switch. He was greatly relieved and at peace with the world generally. Then he poked his head into the bomb-bay for a last look.

To his horror six of the incendiaries were stuck fast in a shackle on one side. The wind, rushing in the open bomb-bay doors, was spinning the vanes. Gently at first, then faster and faster.

Lieutenant Cury for one moment did not know what to do. He knew that the pin-like pieces of wire which held the vanes tight had been pulled out by the bomb-release mechanism. He kicked at the bombs and pushed at them. Nothing moved. Although he was wearing no parachute, and although 24,000 feet of empty space were between him and the water through the open doors, he placed one foot on the bomb shackle on one side of the bay, the other on the catwalk, grabbed the bomb-bay door with one hand and started fumbling with the other with the mechanism.

Lieutenant Cury was using a so-

called walk-around oxygen bottle. And as he bent over to work with the bombs, it swung back and forth on its hose like a pendulum. With every swing it nearly pulled him loose from his grip. In desperation he finally pulled off his oxygen mask, braving asphyxia. Meanwhile the ball turret gunner, Sergeant John E. Schaffer, 23, of Cullman, Ala., had come to his rescue and the pilot was standing by. The rest of the crew, parachutes on, were grouped around the windows ready to jump out.

"My God," said Lieutenant Cury, "I don't know how many turns of those things it took to set off the bomb. I was so busy crossing myself I hardly had time to work at the bombs. Then the lack of oxygen began to get me, and I felt myself fogging out."

When unconsciousness came it came with a rush. Lieutenant Cury suddenly slumped down on the catwalk like a rag doll, banging his head on the walk. The bang broke his goggles and raised a nasty bump on his forehead. He would have tumbled on through the open bomb-bay doors if the pilot had not grabbed him by the seat of the pants.

By the time the pilot and Sergeant Schaffer pulled him through, the plane had let down to 16,000 feet and Lieutenant Cury was able to work without his oxygen mask and gloves. Although his fingers were slightly frostbitten, he took up his place again, straddling the yawning bomb-bay and started plucking bombs out by main force. Between his efforts and those of the ball turret gunner, they pulled out six and tossed them through the doors.

They didn't know until then how narrowly the plane had escaped an especially unpleasant destruction. As they tossed out the bombs the incendiaries fell about 200 feet and then went off.

"By the grace of God," said Lieutenant Cury, shaking his head. "By the grace of God."

10 April 1944

GENERAL ORDERS)
:
NUMBER   263)

SECTION

I. Under the provisions of Army Regulations 600-45, 22 September 1943, pursuant to authority contained in Restricted TT Message #2139, Hq USSAFE, 11 January 1944, the SILVER STAR is awarded to the following-named Officers and listed Man:

II. Under the provisions of Army Regulations 600-45, 22 September 1943, and pursuant to authority contained in Restricted TT Message #2139, Hq USSAFE, 11 January 1944, the DISTINGUISHED FLYING CROSS is awarded to the following-named Officers and Enlisted Men:

ENVER CHARLES CURY, O-670027, Second Lieutenant, Army Air Forces, United States Army. For extraordinary achievement, while serving as Bombardier of a B-17 airplane on a mission over Germany, 24 January 1944. One of the bomb-bay doors failed to open over the target causing a large number of incendiaries to jam against the closed door. Realizing the danger of the armed bombs being detonated, Lieutenant Cury immediately set about releasing them. Working over the open bomb-bay without a parachute and with only an emergency supply of oxygen, Lieutenant Cury, assisted by two other members of the crew, stopped the arming vanes from spinning and threw the bombs out one by one. The courage, skill and disregard for his own safety displayed by Lieutenant Cury reflect highest credit upon himself and the Armed Forces of the United States. Entered military service from Pennsylvania.

ANDREW DROBYSH, O-677681, Second Lieutenant, Army Air Forces, United States Army. For extraordinary achievement, while serving as Pilot of a B-17 airplane on a bombing mission over Germany, 25 February 1944. Shortly after crossing the coast of Europe, a burst of flak knocked out one engine of his aircraft, severed the rudder control cable, seriously wounded the tail gunner and caused other damage to vital instruments in the plane. Unable to hold his position in the formation, Lieutenant Drobysh continued on into Germany and selected a target of importance, which he successfully bombed. With his plane thus lightened, he skilfully maneuvered it into another squadron and remained with the formation during the balance of the mission. As a direct result of this action by Lieutenant Drobysh, his crippled bomber received the added protection of the fire power of the other aircraft in the formation. His courage, determination and

- 4 -

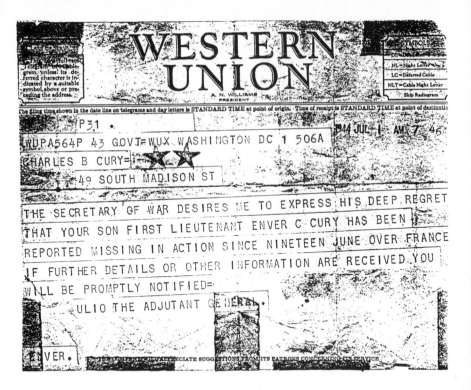

WESTERN UNION

A. N. WILLIAMS
PRESIDENT

The filing time shown in the date line on telegrams and day letters is STANDARD TIME at point of origin. Time of receipt is STANDARD TIME at point of destination

P31

1944 JUL 1 AM 7 46

WUPA564P 43 GOVT=WUX WASHINGTON DC 1 506A

CHARLES B CURY=

49 SOUTH MADISON ST

THE SECRETARY OF WAR DESIRES ME TO EXPRESS HIS DEEP REGRET
THAT YOUR SON FIRST LIEUTENANT ENVER C CURY HAS BEEN
REPORTED MISSING IN ACTION SINCE NINETEEN JUNE OVER FRANCE
IF FURTHER DETAILS OR OTHER INFORMATION ARE RECEIVED YOU
WILL BE PROMPTLY NOTIFIED=

ULIO THE ADJUTANT GENERAL.

VER.

LISTS OF PHRASES

FRENCH
DUTCH
GERMAN
SPANISH

FRENCH

ENGLISH	FRENCH	ENGLISH	FRENCH
One	Un	Twenty	Vingt
Two	Deux	Thirty	Trente
Three	Trois	Forty	Quarante
Four	Quatre	Fifty	Cinquante
Five	Cinq	Sixty	Soixante
Six	Six	Seventy	Soixante-dix
Seven	Sept	Eighty	Quatre-vingts
Eight	Huit	Ninety	Quatre-vingt-dix
Nine	Neuf	Hundred	Cent
Ten	Dix	Five Hundred	Cinq cents
Eleven	Onze	Thousand	Mille
Twelve	Douze		
Thirteen	Treize	Monday	Lundi
Fourteen	Quatorze	Tuesday	Mardi
Fifteen	Quinze	Wednesday	Mercredi
Sixteen	Seize	Thursday	Jeudi
Seventeen	Dix-Sept	Friday	Vendredi
Eighteen	Dix-huit	Saturday	Samedi
Nineteen	Dix-neuf	Sunday	Dimanche
Minutes	Minutes	Week	Semaine
Hours	Heures	Fortnight	Quinzaine
Day	Jour	Month	Mois
Night	Nuit	O'clock	heures

ENGLISH	FRENCH
I am (we are)	Je suis (nous sommes)
British (American)	Anglais; (Américain)
Where am I?	Où est-ce que je suis?
I am hungry; thirsty	J'ai faim. J'ai soif
Can you hide me?	Pouvez-vous me cacher?
I need civilian clothes	J'ai besoin de vêtements civils
How much do I owe you?	Combien vous dois-je?
Are the enemy nearby?	L'ennemi est-il près?
Where is the frontier?	Où est la frontière
BELGIAN	Belge
SWISS; SPANISH:	Suisse, Espagnole
Where are the nearest British (American) troops?	Où sont les forces anglaises (américaines) les plus proches?
Where can I cross this river?	Où est-ce-que je peux traverser cette rivière?
Is this a safe way?	Est-ce que ce chemin n'est pas dangéreux?
Will you please get me a third class ticket to . . .	Voulez-vous me prendre un billet de troisième classe pour . . . s'il vous plait.
Is this the train (bus) for . . ?	Est-ce-que c'est le train (autobus) (car) pour . . ?
Do I change (i.e. trains)?	Dois-je changer de train?
At what time does the train (bus) leave for . . . ?	A quelle heure est-ce-que le train (autobus) part pour . . . ?
Right; left; straight on	A droite; à gauche; tout droit
Turn back; stop	Revenez en arrière; arrêtez vous
Thank you; please	Merci; s'il vous plait
Yes; No	Oui; Non
Good morning; afternoon	Bonjour
Good evening; Night	Bonsoir
Consulate	Consulat
Out of bounds; Forbidden	Défense de pénétrer; défendu

133

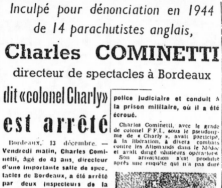

Inculpé pour dénonciation en 1944
de 14 parachutistes anglais,

Charles COMINETTI

directeur de spectacles à Bordeaux

dit «colonel Charly»
est arrêté

Bordeaux, 13 décembre. —
**Vendredi matin, Charles Comi-
netti, âgé de 43 ans, directeur
d'une importante salle de spec-
tacles de Bordeaux, a été arrêté
par deux inspecteurs de la**
police judiciaire et conduit à
la prison militaire, où il a été
écroué.

Charles Cominetti, avec le grade
de colonel F.F.I., sous le pseudony-
me de « Charly », avait participé,
à la libération, à divers combats
contre les Allemands dans le Médoc
et avait dirigé plusieurs opérations.
Son arrestation s'est produite
après une enquête qui n'a pas duré

Charles COMINETTI.

L'interrogatoire
de Charles COMINETTI
ne reprendra
que dans quelques jours

Bordeaux, 17 décembre — En attendant des confrontations pro-
chaines l'officier instructeur a sus-
pendu l'interrogatoire de Charles
Cominetti, qui reprendra cepen-
dant dans quelques jours.

LES PARACHUTISTES

Parmi les parachutistes alliés,
dénoncés et déportés, nous sommes
en mesure aujourd'hui de donner
les noms de onze d'entre eux qui
tentèrent à s'évader : lieutenant
Johnson et soldat Winston (Anglais), L. Parker, P. Conrad, William Armstrong, J. C. Schadler, E.
Tracy, J. C. Cory, S. W. Trimble,
J. Macquey, B. F. Lenke (améri-
cains).

C'est grâce à leur témoignage que
la justice militaire a pu éclaircir
la plus grande partie de cette affaire.

moins d'un an. En 1945, la justice
militaire était saisie par Paris, à
la suite de rapports transmis à la
France par des soldats anglais.
C'était en 1944; le débarquement
venait d'avoir lieu; des parachutistes, égarés dans le Sud-Ouest,
avaient pris contact à Bordeaux
avec la Résistance. Charles Cominetti connaissait leurs lieux de
traille. Brusquement, en juillet de
la même année les quatorze soldats
alliés, cachés à Bordeaux et en
banlieue, étaient arrêtés par la Gestapo et déportés en Allemagne.

(Voir la suite en quatrième page)

L'ARRESTATION
de Charles COMINETTI
dit « CHARLY »

(Suite de la première page.)

Pour prix de la dénonciation, il
avait été remis à un chauffeur,
50.000 francs, qui devaient être
transmis à l'homme qui avait télé-
phoné au commandant Dose, chef
régional de la Gestapo.

Les investigations ont permis de
retrouver, les uns après les autres,
les parachutistes qui ont tous té-
moigné sur cette affaire.

Il y a trois mois enfin, lorsque
Dose est arrivé à Bordeaux, et que
son interrogatoire a commencé, on
a appris de sa bouche que c'était
Charles Cominetti qui avait été
l'auteur de ces dénonciations.

Ce seul témoignage ne fut pas re-
pendant retenu pour la suite de
l'enquête et les officiers instruc-
teurs procédèrent à l'audition d'autres personnes, qui furent formel-
les quant à l'action de Cominetti.

C'est alors que, possédant des
preuves irréfutables, le capitaine

Lesueur signait, jeudi soir, un
mandat d'arrêt contre le colonel
« Charly », ce mandat a été aussi-
tôt exécuté.

Interrogé le matin et l'après-mi-
di, Charles Cominetti a nié avoir
force sa participation à une telle
forfaiture. L'enquête suit son cours
et l'inculpé a choisi comme défen-
seur, Me Lacquièze.

Bordeaux news article about "Colonel Charley's" arrest. He was later
tried, convicted and executed, May, 1945.

Scene of Incredible Human Massacre Remains
Exactly as It Was on the Day the Nazis Came

... So the World Will Always Remember

By NINO LO BELLO
Special to The Herald

ORADOUR-SUR-GLANE, France — Not a soul lives in Oradour-sur-Glane, and this is the stark drama that screams out at you.

You walk along the empty streets of this historic village, which the Nazis burned during the Second World War, and you are reminded, step by step as you roam among the charred ruins, of the incredible human tragedy that makes this place perhaps the most macabre tourist site in the world.

Six hundred and forty-two persons, of whom 247 were children, were shot or burned to death June 10, 1944, by the famous "Das Reich" S.S. division in revenge for the guerrilla murder of a German officer. So that the world will never forget, the French keep the burned-out town as a national monument.

A NEW, modern Oradour has sprung up a few hundred yards away from the wall-enclosed ruin that spreads over 300 acres. At the entrance of the wrecked village are

Every Building in the Village Was Set Afire by the Invaders
... more than 600 persons, many of them children, perished here

two signs that speak volumes: one reads, "SCENE OF EXECUTION," and the other says, "SILENCE." Behind these signs is a church with its

broken windows and its destroyed belfry, and beyond that lies the silent skeleton of a town. The stage is set for your visit — one of the grisliest sights in all Europe.

Booklets and folders giving historical details of the massacre, as well as color slides and other mementos, are available in a souvenir shop that has been set up in a shack near the entrance. If nothing else, a stop here before you proceed will help you understand better the stark message of Oradour — that war engenders inhuman and unhu-

man crime against human beings, crimes committed because war is the noblest of barbarians.

No historian is quite sure why Oradour-sur-Glane, 15 miles north of Limoges, was selected by the commanding officer of the S.S. unit, General Bernard Hentz. Lammerding, it is certain that Oradour did not house any of France's underground Maquis fighters, for it was off the beaten path and nearly all of the residents that never even saw a German soldier. Notwithstanding, Oradour was picked for the reprisal.

IT WAS Saturday afternoon, just after lunch-time, and the sun was shining when trucks full of Stormtroopers rumbled into Oradour. Everybody in town was quickly rounded up and paraded into the public square. The men were kept to one side, and the women and children were led away. The mayor was asked to single out 50 residents to be shot, and he refused, answering defiantly: "I name myself — and if that is not sufficient, then also my family."

This was not enough for the major in charge of the detail. He had all the men ushered into barns and sheds, where they were machinegunned. Though some of the victims were not killed outright, the Nazis spread straw over them and set fire to them so that those who were not dead were burned alive.

Meanwhile the women and children who had been packed into the village church met a similar fate. All of them were cut down by ma-

chinegun burst, and then the church was put to flame. To make sure there were no survivors, every building was set ablaze.

ONLY FIVE men and one woman survived the massacre — but of these only the woman actually witnessed any of the horror. Her name is Marguerite Rouffange, and she lives in virtual isolation just off the main square of New Oradour, refusing to this day to see anyone or allow any photographers to take any pictures of her.

Madame Rouffange, a farmer's wife, watched her small son, two daughters and a seven-month-old grandchild die under a hail of lead inside the church. She also lost her husband. Although she herself was hit by five bullets, she successfully played dead and while the church building was burning managed to get away and hide in the grass nearby until nightfall. Hers is the only authentic eyewitness account of what happened in Oradour, since the other survivors were not present in town on that fateful day.

Unlike the similar massacre of Lidice (Czechoslovakia) which also happened on a June 10th, but two years earlier, in which 192 people were killed, the events at Oradour were kept a secret and never publicized. To this day very few people outside France even know about it.

Where to Go?

Read These Pages

Oradour-sur-glane after the total destruction by the S.S. Waffen.

Some of the better memories of France — "Yvette".

Our escape airplane.

The author in Perigeuex.

The funeral parade for the Maquis in Perigeuex.

DÉCRET DU   (J. O. DU

DÉCISION N° 9/107....

Le Président du Gouvernement Provisoire de la République Française,

Chef des Armées,

CITE A L'ORDRE D E L A D I V I S I O N,

C U R Y   **e.**
- - - - -   Sous-Lieutenent

"Officier aviateur américain descendu au cours d'une mission
au dessus de BORDEAUX le 19.6.1944.
A servi avec bravoure les groupes F.F.I jusqu'au 1.9.44. S'est
particulièrement distingué dans le secteur de DORDOGNE et dans l'
ANGOUMOIS, au cours des combats de la LIBERATION."

Cette Citation comporte l'attribution de la Croix de Guerre 1939-1945

avec E T O I L E D ' A R G E N T.

Paris, le 9 Novembre 1946

LE MINISTRE DES ARMEES,

Four le Ministre et par son Ordre,
Le Général BONNEAU,
Délégué Général F.F.C.I :

signé : BONNEAU.

MINISTÈRE DES ARMÉES

DÉLÉGATION GENERALE F.F.C.I.

Référence à rappeler :

N° 514/ 9/107 D JC ST

/ED.

Paris, le 21 Novembre 1946.

Le Commandant COUDERT,
Chef du Bureau FFI "Air" :

POUR AMPLIATION

Award from the French Government of the "Croix de Guerre" with the
Etoile D'Argent.

Escape Map

HEADQUARTERS
EUROPEAN THEATER OF OPERATIONS
P/W and X Detachment
Military Intelligence Service

9 September 1944
(Date)

The following named officer/EM has been missing in action and proper
identification papers are being prepared. He is in London for official purposes
and is unable to conform with existing uniform regulations.

Cury, Enver C. 1st lt. 0-670027
401 Bomber Group; 615th Squadron

For the Commanding Officer:

JOHN F. WHITE, JR
Captain, AC
63 Brook Street
Regent 8484, Ext 2596

Special pass after return to England.

– 15 –

I climbed over the ladder at the rear of the car. Bracing myself, I jumped, tumbling to the gravel bed. I was so stunned I sat there for a few seconds, watching for Richard. Finally, I saw him jump. He was about a hundred feet away. He picked himself up and started coming toward me. I thought to get up. But my leg hurt like hell. Had the wound on my leg burst open? I hoped not.

Richard ran to help me to my feet. We snuck off into the bushes, and less than a few hundred feet away from the railroad line was a wide road with traffic on it. We dared not cross that highway. We traveled parallel to it until we reached a sign which read, "Rive-de-Geir 2 Km," and beneath it, "St. Etienne, 14 Km."

While we were all excited about being in France we weren't taking any chances. After all, this was still German occupied territory. The last we had heard the Allies were battling far to the north . . . And I was remembering the radio broadcasts at Ournay's: French news from London. We had listened to it right after our fine dinner. They kept the radio hidden, except for this brief interval each day. We heard the chimes of Big Ben, and the announcer in a deep resonant voice, saying, "This is London," in French; afterward, Armand had said, "General Patton has swung down as far as Nantes and is heading north again, possibly to encircle Paris." There I had asked how far Nantes was from where we were, north of Bordeaux.

Richard and I considered entering the village of Rive-de-Gier. But thought better of it. St. Etienne was much larger. We'd have a better chance there. So, we had a walk of fourteen kilometers ahead of us.

After being cramped in that freight car for so long it would be good to walk, in spite of my leg. But first we ditched the canvas bag and the cans. Since the cans had no labels on them, the labels having washed off in our journey along the canal, we just pitched them and

141

dumped the canvas bag under bushes. All that remained of my foray on the barge was a small knife and the gun.

"We've got to be extremely careful," I told Richard as we walked along. "Not all of the French are helpful." I described my first encounter with French people.

"You're kidding!" he said. "I thought they were all loyal."

"Some are. Some aren't. Anyway, we have a good shot now. We can get help to get us to the Pyrenees, Andorra and Spain. We do that and we got it made!"

Three hours of walking brought us to St. Etienne and the inevitable blockade and guard house on the highway. We cut away from the highway into deep woods, Richard mumbling his surprise at the four German guards.

"They're in every town. They blockade each road going into town and every main crossing and bridge. They don't take chances."

We arrived in St. Etienne and walked along the narrow streets. It was beautifully picturesque. But the people took one look at us and turned away. God! We must've been a sight. Of course, Richard still wore his R.A.F. trousers. We had to get some help or we'd be picked up.

I spotted a small butcher shop with poultry hanging in the windows. I said to Richard, "Wait here. I'll go inside and see what I can do."

I entered the shop as a little old lady carrying a small package came out. A short man in an apron stood behind a butcher block, trimming meat. He looked up at me, his glance curious.

I didn't give him a chance to say anything. *"Je suis Americain,"* I said.

He shook his head.

I repeated myself, adding *"J'ai faim; J'ai soif."* I wanted him to understand that I was not only an American, but also hungry and thirsty.

He stared at me, now muttering, *"Pas comprend,"* over and again, extending his hand in the doing. But his face was full of fear.

I reached in my jacket and pulled out the dog tags to show him, repeating, "I am American," in French.

Nothing.

"Comprendez vous anglaise?" I asked. Did he understand English?

He shook his head. *"Je ne comprend pas."* Then: *"Attendez."* "Wait," in French.

I waited, watching him go to the door. I motioned for Richard to come in, and the butcher opened the door for him. Once Richard had entered, the butcher locked the door and pulled the shades, both on the door and the window. He motioned for us to follow him.

We went with him to the rear of the shop and into an alley where he looked cautiously in each direction before moving on. We had a hard time keeping up with him. He zigzagged in one alley and out another, checking each crossing carefully. Finally, we crossed a very wide street. Down the street was a square, German soldiers and Vichy police. He saw them too, turned around, and we went the other way.

By this time I was so confused I didn't know where we were. Never mind. I tried to strike up a conversation. He quickly told me, "Don't talk to me now. Just walk," in French. We walked along beside him as if we didn't have a care in the world.

At a high stone and concrete wall with a door in the center our butcher opened the door and led us into a lovely garden. We passed through the garden and out a gate. Here we turned down an alley. Finally, he led us into a small garage, asking that we wait.

When he was gone I said to Richard, "I wonder what the hell is going on . . ." I was apprehensive; what if he had gone to get German soldiers? Then again, why had he taken the trouble to bring us here if he wasn't going to help us? Richard and I discussed this, deciding to wait.

Our French butcher returned. Three men accompanied him, and they didn't look the least bit friendly. I had my hand in my jacket pocket where I had taken the safety from the gun. Before I could remove the gun, one of the men had a Luger trained on us, telling us to get our hands up.

The three men searched us thoroughly. They came up with my knife and pistol. "Oh, hell," I complained.

In response, they muttered one word: "Boche."

I knew what that meant, the dirty name for a Kraut. I shook my head, saying, *"Je suis Americain."*

They shook their heads, muttering madly in French.

I got the drift of it; they were convinced we were Germans!

They set to work, tying our hands behind us, me complaining in English. "What in the hell is going on here? What's the matter with you damn frogs? I am an American, and he is English. We are escaped flyers . . ."

They gagged us with scarfs. Then they took out a large roll of adhesive tape and taped our mouths shut. God, I thought, they're crazy! Next, they bound our feet and we were thrown on the floor. The butcher gave me a swift kick in the side and spit on me, saying, *"Merde!"* with disgust. My spirits sank to an unprecedented low. Dear God, please make them understand . . .

The butcher's name was Pierre. Now he raged and raved like a madman, jumping up and down, and yelling, "I want to kill them. I want to kill them myself personally, to avenge my brother and his family. I insist!"

The tallest man, whose name was Albert, replied, "Pierre, my friend, I agree with you, and I would be the first to say kill them, if they are Boche. But we must consider. What if they are American or

American-English as they claim? What then? Would you have that on your conscience?"

"I swear by my mother's grave. They are Boche. I know they are!" And with that he ran to the opposite wall where he retrieved a short axe and a sharpening stone. He began to sharpen the edge of the axe. "This is why I brought them here. I want to kill them myself. By my own hand with the axe! I want to split their heads open from the front. I want to see their brains tumble out, like they did to my brother and his family at Oradour!" Though he was highly excited, his French was slow enough for me to understand.

The second man was Roger, and the third man, short like Pierre, was Jean. Now Jean and Roger were beginning to agree with Pierre. Oh, my God! But Albert was the voice of reason and seemingly the leader. He continued to shake his head, telling them he wouldn't have it on his conscience. Not unless the curate or the teacher sanctioned the execution, having proved we weren't Allies.

I rolled over, so that I could look directly into Albert's eyes. I kept nodding, as if to say, "Yes, get the priest or the teacher. Please help us," while trying to draw attention with muffled shouts from my throat. Then, I started to gag. I thought I was going to choke. My nose had become stuffed up during the train ride.

In response, Pierre kicked me again, turning me, so that I faced straight up. He threw the sharpener onto a small bench and raised the axe above me. His face was terrifying! Filled with hate.

Albert shoved him aside and yelled, "No, Pierre. I will not let you do this. We must have proof. I implore you. Think, Pierre, think!"

Jean paused in his cheering for Pierre and evidently began to think. He pitched in with Albert, and Roger followed. There was hope.

Now they let Jean out of the garage door. I rolled over again, trying to get Albert's attention. Finally, our eyes met.

"He's choking," said Albert.

"Let the dirty Boche choke!" Pierre screamed. "No, that way isn't painful enough. I want to split his head open!"

Albert said to Roger, "Come on, give me a hand."

Between them they sat us on the bench, Pierre objecting all the way. I straightened up against the wall, trying to control the gagging, and felt a hot searing burn across my face. Albert had snatched the adhesive away. Then, he pulled the scarf from my mouth. "What did I tell you?" Albert said to Pierre. "This man is choking to death . . ."

Pierre snorted. "Now he will scream to his filthy German friends and Vichy police. They are only a few blocks from here!"

Albert silenced him by pulling out his Luger again and removing the gag from Richard. As a persuader he now placed the gun in front of my mouth and said, "If you so much as let out a scream I guarantee you, I will put you out of your misery." Then he spoke in English: "The others think you are not American, as you say you are, nor your friend English. But I do." He enunciated his words carefully and slowly. "Tell me all you can to prove you are Allies, before Jean returns with the teacher."

"Who is the teacher?" I asked.

"She speaks English well. She studied in England. She knows much of the United States and England."

"Mon ami," I began, "I am an American." I was trying to bring credibility to my words and having a hard time maintaining my equilibrium before the Luger. "I was shot down . . ." I gave him the date and the target area. Then, I told him about being aided by the Maquis, mentioning a few names. I followed this by explaining about my capture. "Yes, I know there are Maquis of the F.F.I. operating in that area," he admitted. "But I do not know their names."

I let it all tumble out: being taken to Germany and escaping again with Richard, an Australian with the English R.A.F. I was on a roll, selling us. I could tell I was convincing him, but that little bastard Pierre kept yelling, "Lies! All lies! Filthy dirty Boche!" Finally, in despair, I turned to Pierre and pleaded, *"Mon ami,* if we were Germans, why would I come to you? Why would I have done the things I have done? How would I know of the Gironde and Bordeaux and other places in France? Would a German agent know of these things?"

He spat at me. "Filthy Boche know everything. That is why you are able to overrun our country, because of traitors and spies planted among us." He moved to kick me again.

Albert intervened, shoved him out of the way and yelled at him. Then, Albert said to me in English, "My friend, if you are American, and I hope you are: I am not bloodthirsty, but you must understand that Pierre lost some of his family at Oradour. The teacher will arrive soon . . ."

No more than half an hour passed before the teacher showed up, but it seemed like forever. The teacher was a slightly built woman with dark brown hair and matching eyes. She wore her hair pulled straight back with a bun at the nape of her neck. A pencil was sticking through the bun. She was a typical old maid school teacher in a long-sleeved and high-necked dress that fell well below her knee line. She wore heavy black shoes. "You are the American, are you not?" Her voice was precise, though very soft.

"Yes . . ." And I was off and running, trying to tell her everything.

"Wait." She held up a hand. "Let me ask you the questions, if you please. I will judge." She cleared her throat. "I am Mademoiselle Angeline, and I am the local teacher of the upper school. But now I am helping in the bakery shop of my brother." She was almost apologetic on that score. "The schools, of course, are closed at this time."

I said, "In America the schools are closed in summer."

"Oh, that is not the reason. We have school in summer. It is because the Germans push us for all the food we can produce and school children in the upper school are excused to help work in the fields." She smiled. "But if you are a German, you would know . . ."

I practically shouted, "No!" Then, I pleaded with her, explaining ourselves.

Albert interrupted, speaking to her in rapid French.

She turned to him, and they walked over to the other side of the garage to hold a private conversation. Finally, she returned to face me. "Albert has told me of his conversation with you. He is partly convinced you are what you say. But I have studied and know many things of your country. If you are American, let me ask . . . What is the capital of New York State?"

"Albany!" I responded quickly, imagining I was back in a school where the wrong answers brought worse than dire results.

She shook her head slowly. *"Non, mon ami.* It is New York City."

"No!" I cried. "New York City is the largest city of New York State and our country. Believe me, the capital is Albany!"

Once more she shook her head slowly. "What is the capital of Florida?"

"Tallahassee!" I said, spelling it out for her afterward.

"Non, mon ami, it is Miami."

My god, she must be crazy! "No, no. It is Tallahassee!"

"What is the capital of California?"

I hesitated. Should I tell her the truth or should I just go for the largest city? It was beginning to dawn on me that she wasn't as sharp as everyone gave her credit for being. No, this might be some kind of a trap. Only the truth would serve me. "Sacramento."

"Non, mon ami. It is Los Angeles."

Pierre, the little bastard, was busy sharpening the axe, spitting on the stone and rubbing it over the blade with an eager look in his eyes.

Quickly, I went over the territory we had just covered, spelling out each capital. I wanted no misunderstandings. It made no difference.

She plunged onward: "Now, tell me. What game does America play most?"

"Baseball!"

A smile bloomed on her face. "Correct. And what do Americans eat when they attend these games as spectators?"

"Hot dogs!"

"And how do they eat hot dogs?"

"With mustard and onions, though I prefer catsup instead of mustard."

She paused in her interrogation. "What is catsup? I am not familiar with this catsup. How do you spell it?"

I spelled the word quickly.

"Who makes this catsup? What company?"

"Heinz!" I yelled triumphantly.

"How do you spell it?"

I spelled it.

"*Mon ami*, I am starting to believe you. I know about catsup. But I wanted you to tell me. One more question. If you are truly an American, you will know the answer." She eyed me. "In fact, if you answer this correctly, I will be convinced."

I waited tensely.

"This question has three parts. First, what do Americans eat in summertime, or should I say, late in summer and early fall, that Europeans do not eat?"

I tried to think.

"For god's sake, old chap," Richard begged, "give her the answer!"

"But we eat many things then. There's watermelon . . ." I glanced at the teacher. I'd drawn a blank. "Ice cream . . ." No, that wasn't it. "And corn on the cob!"

She smiled and turned to the others. "Didn't I tell you?" Then, she returned to me and the quiz. "How do you eat corn on the cob?"

I described it with my hands still tied; I talked about the butter and salt on the corn; I licked my lips. I did my best.

"But," she pressed, "how do you prepare corn on the cob?"

Easy! I sighed. I told her just exactly how my mother prepared it.

She was all smiles. The others were smiling too, except for that little fucker, Pierre. She went to work explaining everything in French. Finally, even Pierre lowered his axe. But it wasn't over.

She whirled around and said, "I told you it was a three-part question. Why do we not eat corn in Europe as you Americans do?"

I was stumped. I assumed they ate corn. "I really don't know. I just took it for granted that you do eat corn, since your climate is much the same as ours. I can't understand it, if you don't eat it or have it . . ."

"Yes, yes, that is it, my good friend, my American friend. That is it!"

I was baffled. "I still don't know what you mean."

"We do not eat corn in Europe. Corn is raised only to feed cows and horses."

This was an emotional moment to say the least. Tears of relief came to my eyes. "Thank you," I murmured.

She placed a hand on either side of my face and kissed each cheek. "Yes, *mon ami*, I know how you feel. I can understand what you have been through, especially with our friend Pierre. Please try to understand his position. We have been tricked many times by the Gestapo agents posing as escaped flyers, then coming back to arrest the people and their families who helped. Executions. All this ends in executions, to impress on the people the penalty of aiding the Allies. Do you understand now, *mon ami?*"

I nodded my head and thought to add icing on the cake, saying to Pierre, "*Mon ami*, Pierre, I do understand. And I forgive you."

147

This was too much for Pierre. He began to cry. Over and over, he said, *"Mon ami, mon ami, pardonez moi, s'il vous plait."*

I felt like choking the little bastard. He had taken years off my life.

Then I was ready to forgive everybody, and we did. "But please take the binds off. They're cutting my hands and feet."

With relief, they laughed. Then, Albert cut me free while Pierre pulled out a large pig sticker knife and freed Richard's hands and feet deftly; he did know how to handle a switchblade, and I was grateful, very grateful we were on the right side of the proposition!

We all began patting each other on the shoulders, shaking hands now. We might have been at a convention. Of course, Mademoiselle Angeline was the real heroine. They thanked her, we thanked her; only her wit and intelligence had identified us. Frankly, I thought her questions a bit off the mark, but never mind. We were alive and well.

Albert said, "There is much to be done now." He spoke to Jean and Roger in French. They came over, shook our hands and told us goodbye. They departed, and Albert added, "They've gone to contact Marcel, the leader of the resistance forces of the F.T.P.F. and prepare a place for you to hide."

Pierre said something in French to Angeline and she said to us, "He says he should have known you were not Boche. The Boche would never go to such trouble as to pick up lice in their hair as you have!"

Lice? What next?

"Pierre says," said Angeline, "that he is going to make arrangements for the barber to get rid of the lice, cut your hair and give you a shave. Then, you will not look so much like wild animals."

A soft knock came at the door. It was a fellow named Michel. He didn't speak English but Albert said, "Eduarde, *mon ami,* you go first. It would be too obvious for both of you to go in the car with Michel at one time. Go quickly."

I hesitated. "What about my gun and the small knife?"

He laughed. "I have the gun. But the knife . . . one of the other men must have grabbed it. Here. Let me make you a gift of my knife. It is a special French *trente deux,* which means, '32.'" He handed me a small black folding knife. It seemed that every French man and boy carried a knife such as this.

I thanked him and Angeline embraced me, wishing me good luck and Godspeed. I turned to Michel, facing another future. What it might be, I couldn't guess.

– 16 –

A gray Citroen was parked in the alley near the garage. Michel reached under the front seat of the car and pulled out a small, folding-stock American machine gun. He handed it to me.

The car was big as a tank. I remembered seeing them in Bordeaux. Armand had told me about this make of car. It didn't have much power, burning off the fuel distilled by a charcoal burner. We climbed inside, and as soon as Michel got the thing running, he patted me on top of the head and motioned for me to stay down. I stayed down. After a bit, he motioned for me to sit up. We were leaving St. Etienne, heading south, since the sun was just off to my right. We passed a road sign: Monistrol 27 Km.

We traveled a few more kilometers and turned off onto a dirt road, continuing on this road for another ten minutes. Then, a sharp right into a very narrow dirt road with grass growing in the middle, to sail up over a small rise and down through a meadow. Then I saw it: a picturesque farm house almost hidden by trees with two large barns to the side. A fence which matched the house encompassed the pasture where several cows grazed in a field to our left. To the right was a large hen house with hundreds of white chickens squawking.

Michel drove the car across the lawn and stopped in front of the steps to the house. On the porch several people waited to greet us. *"Le premier Americain est arrive!"* they called out over and over again.

The only one who spoke English was a short, heavy set old man who wore a jaunty black beret pulled over his forehead. A large white handlebar moustache matched his hair, which stuck out from the sides of the beret. He was forceful, yet he had a kind face; and even for his age he was obviously strong as a bull.

"I am Messr. Jacques, *mon ami, le Americain*. We have eagerly awaited your arrival and our humble home is your home. Come." He took my arm, forcing me through the other people and introducing me as we passed. His wife looked as if she were poured from the same mold, minus the moustache, of course; she had a kindly round face, a typical grandmother. Crying, she embraced me, as if I might be her own. In fact, they all cried — emotional, very warm people.

Inside the house, my god! I could smell food. I turned my head in the direction of that heavenly aroma.

"Ah, *mon ami*," cried Messr. Jacques. "You smell the food. I know you are hungry. I have heard. Roger came here on his motorbike to get Michel. Michel is one of Colonel Marcel's trusted men; he had only arrived this evening."

Colonel Marcel's name carried respect and authority with it.

I looked around to see if Michel was following me.

The old man said, "Michel returns to St. Etienne."

Apparently Michel had gone to bring Richard here too.

The large parlor was impressive. Unlike the Ournays' home, here the furnishings were very plain, everything neat, quite homey, charming. Messr. Jacques fetched several bottles of wine and the inevitable bottle of cognac. The drinking and toasting began immediately. Dinner would be served as soon as my friend arrived. Meanwhile, Madame Jacques entered with a large plate; it was loaded with assorted cheeses, tomatoes, and homemade sausages with a large loaf of hot French bread. She placed the plate in front of me. I was to nibble on this until dinner. They didn't have to tell me twice.

I broke off an end piece of the bread, placed a slab of cheese on it and stuffed it into my mouth. With the wine, it was heaven. I relaxed. Nothing bothered me, except I kept itching. Perhaps Pierre was right. I had to scratch between my legs often, and I was embarrassed.

Messr. Jacques inquired about my friend. Between stuffing my face I gave him a brief rundown on Richard and our travels.

"Ah, *Anglaise*," said Messr. Jacques, and there was that coolness I had first noticed in the garage. When "American" was mentioned, their faces lit up like Christmas trees. In time, I was to learn that they respected the British and were appreciative of their help. But they were competitors in the world between wars. "Yes," he said, "they are good Allies, staunch and brave. But *Anglaise* are *Anglaise*." Then he told me the latest news.

Last night Free French Radio had said that General Patton was spearheading a drive, far ahead of the British under General Montgomery. Patton had swung south, breaking through the Falaise pocket and advancing 67 kilometers, stopping only a short way from the main north-south road to Nantes at the small town of Redon.

"General Patton," he said, "would have continued on to Nantes, if he had not run out of petrol, which is being supplied by the *Anglaise*." Otherwise, it seemed there was no stopping Patton. He would liberate France, swinging around and encircling Paris, freeing the city with General DeGaulle at his side. It was very exciting since the liberation of Paris appeared just around the corner.

Richard arrived along with Albert and the barber. We were invited into the kitchen. What a room!

It was at least 25 feet long and 25 feet wide. A large round table with eight chairs sat in an alcove. On the table rested a large plate of pork chops, a full plate of sliced ham, and a huge salad bowl filled with lettuce, tomatoes and raw onions. There was also hot bread, cooked onions, carrots, and even steamed celery. They had placed two large pitchers on the table, one of milk and the other filled with hot chocolate.

I asked if I might say a word of Grace. Permission was granted. Messr. Jacques would interpret.

I thanked God for bringing us through a seemingly endless nightmare safely. I thanked Him for bringing us to this home and for these beautiful people who were helping us. We had been through "The Valley of Death . . ."

When I said, "Amen," all hell broke loose. Tears flowed as they stood up to hug and kiss me. Finally, and at long last, we got beyond the hugging and kissing to the food.

I couldn't believe food would taste this good. Everything was perfect. The bread was even hot. Madame Jacques had baked it this morning, using her last ration of flour and yeast. But she said something had told her to do it, an inner feeling she couldn't explain.

I asked about rationing, surprised. I remembered the Ournays telling me that people on farms ate well, but people in the city were going through hell.

"Oh, yes. Everything. The Germans even check the production of the farms now," said Madame. Of late, most everything of use to the Germans back home was being confiscated and shipped to Germany.

"Things are not good for the Germans," Jacques told us. "They only started doing this several weeks ago."

Richard and I ate without end. In time, I noticed the others hardly touched the food. I began to ease off, though they insisted I eat more. If we ate any more, Richard and I were bound to get sick. I felt as if I were about to burst now, as I topped it all off with a final cup of hot chocolate.

Next came the white lightning: clear white cognac, homemade cognac. Messr. Jacques poured Richard and me each a glassful to settle our stomachs. I'd heard that one before. I sipped it slowly, but Richard gulped his right down and nearly choked to death.

The day was warm. The cognac made us warmer. I began to sweat. I apologized to our host and hostess. I knew we smelled terrible and hoped we didn't offend. "We lived like animals, getting out of Germany," I explained.

This set off another fit of crying among the women, while our hostess apologized for not having time to prepare dessert, but she brought forth a large bowl of grapes, apples and plums to make up for this oversight. God, what a wonder! "These grapes are the sweetest," I said as I tucked away the fruit. "I haven't had fruit like this in over two years."

It seemed they were eating grapes these days instead of making so much wine. I mentioned I had been shot down north of Bordeaux, in wine country, but this wine was better. I was the polite guest, bringing smiles to faces all around. They explained how the grapes in their area and west around Dijon were the greatest of all grapes grown worldwide. These grapes were made into fine champagne. A flurry of apologies appeared here for not having champagne on the table. But Albert said, "I have several bottles buried in my backyard. I promise to bring some champagne within a few days, and we will enjoy it together."

I was delighted at the prospect, but for now, I was busy scratching. Once more I apologized.

"First you must rest," Messr. Jacques said. "Then the barber will cut your hair, while we heat water for a bath."

Richard and I broke into big smiles.

"Ah, I knew this would please you," said Messr. Jacques.

"The barber," Albert pointed out, "is one of Colonel Marcel's men. He personally arranged for the barber to take care of you. We must prepare photos for your *identite* cards."

"I'd like to meet Colonel Marcel," I said.

"He has helped other English flyers, but never an American," Albert said. Then, shaking his head, he added, "There is a large price on Colonel Marcel's head. He is the leader of the F.T.P.F. and, in fact, of all resistance forces in this area, even as far east as Perigueux, as far south as Montpelier and as far north as Nevere."

Colonel Marcel could only travel at night, mostly by motorbike with his aides. The price on his head was $20,000 in gold. He must be quite a man, I thought, and inquired about his background.

Marcel had been born to nobility. He was a member of a leading French family, I was told.

"We keep in contact by phone," Albert said, explaining that limited phone service was still to be had. "We have our own codes and ways. Believe me, we are well organized. Many Vichy police and soldiers are on our side, with a little bribing of gold."

"Gold?"

"Yes, gold. That is the only thing acceptable for bribes. They have received many parachute drops with millions of francs printed in London, and the Germans do the same for their own use."

Meanwhile, the British Secret Service and our O.S.S. were making drops of guns, ammunition, plastique dynamite, bread and food rationing coupons. "They even drop us plum pudding and baloney!"

he added with a turned-up nose. "But the Maquis in the field need every bit of food they can get." He dipped his hand into his pocket and produced a few gold coins. "Look, this is the real money of France. They are Napoleons. All of our gold is in bank vaults in England, not only gold boullion, but gold Napoleons." He insisted I take the Napoleons as a reminder of this day. I couldn't refuse.

The barber was ready now. Someone else was bringing us proper clothing, and this person was to take back one of each of our shoes so that they could match our size. The photographer would arrive later in the evening. The barber said, "All the various groups of the Maquis, the F.T.P.F. and F.F.I. are preparing for something very big." He shrugged his shoulders and his eyes narrowed. "Something else is brewing too, something very big that only Marcel and a few top men know about. I suspect there will be another invasion . . ."

Here it dawned on me. No wonder the goddamn Krauts had given me such a rough time. Of course, it was true. There was another invasion on the way.

"What is wrong, Eduarde?" the barber asked.

I explained about the torture I'd experienced and the Germans' assumption that I was a special agent.

"Ah . . . I knew it. I could tell by all the activity, as you shall see."

The table was cleared and the food stored, the ladies placing the meat in crocks, pouring wine over it and covering the crocks with heavy wax paper. It was the only way to keep the meat since they had little refrigeration. When they were ready to eat again, they removed the meat and warmed it. Damn clever!

I followed the barber into a small room with a concrete floor. He had cleared away a space. A large kettle of hot water appeared. I sat on the indicated small bench in a large empty tub and an old towel was placed around me. The barber went to work, cursing every now and then as he scrounged around in my hair. It was lice, all right!

"Not to worry," said Albert, standing by. "The barber has a solution. When he is done cutting your hair and shaving you, he will also shave under your arms and around your genitals, and apply the solution there too. It will loosen up the lice and he will pick them off with tweezers."

The thought made me sick. But I had no choice, if I ever expected to stop itching. I became a good patient and the job was done, the barber muttering from time to time, "Ah ha! *Un otre!*" He had found another one.

He kept this up for about half an hour, pausing occasionally to show me what he had extracted. The critters were ugly as hell, but they were dead. The solution, which smelled like creosote, was doing its job.

Finally, the worst was over. Albert pitched my clothes in the yard, and another larger round tub of hot water was brought in. Then, they put the bench in the tub, had me sit on the bench to lather up with a big bar of brown homemade soap and a washrag of sisal. Madame Jacques brought in a couple more buckets of hot water. I was embarrassed. But beggars couldn't be choosers. Albert poured the hot water over me and had me lather up again, first my head, then, my body. Twice we followed this routine. Finally, Madame brought a large fluffy towel, and I dried myself, feeling good all over.

Here Albert suggested I go out on the back porch and allow the sun to dry my hair. We moved along, and the sun was heaven as I continued to dry myself and rub the feeling back into my body. I was alive and well, for the first time in a long, long while. "What time is it?" I asked, eyeing the sun.

"Don't you have a watch?"

I told him what had happened to my watch.

Albert removed his watch and insisted I take it. I refused. I felt bad enough already; he had given me the gold Napoleons. But he insisted. He had another watch at home. Albert was a gem.

A former electrician, he had been in the war in North Africa where he was captured and returned to France. He was fifty-eight years old, though his physique and appearance belonged to a man in his mid-thirties.

As I continued to rub myself with the towel, I began to feel my ribs. I looked down at myself. I was skinny. I couldn't've weighed more than 165.

Madame Jacques came out and handed me a pair of her husband's shorts. They were similar to American shorts, but instead of having elastic around the top, they had buttons and small adjustable buttons on the side. I slipped into them and they fit fine. Next she handed me a pair of light, knitted wool, gray socks. I had dropped into the lap of luxury. She gave me a big hug as I put them on.

While I was drying off, the barber was working on Richard. I walked around in my new shorts and socks until my hair dried, then they led me to a mirror in the kitchen above a small table holding a pitcher and a bowl. Messr. Jacques brought me a bottle of *eau de toilette*. I used it and smelled like a rose.

Meanwhile, Richard was yelling bloody murder. I went to see what was up. He had, so Albert testified, the worst case of lice they'd seen. They were cutting his hair very short; it was almost a crew cut. I watched as he went through the same trial and ritual I had survived. When it was done, and yes, Richard did survive the hair cut, we wanted to stretch out in the lawn chairs in the backyard. Albert vetoed the idea. That was where our clothes had been thrown, and he was afraid we might pick up lice again. He didn't have to tell us twice.

Richard spotted my new watch almost instantly.

"Where'd you get it?"

"Albert gave it to me."

"And I will bring you a watch too, Richard," said Albert, "from home. I have four or five of them." He gave us a sly wink. "To tell the truth, they are all German or Swiss watches taken from dead German soldiers killed by the Maquis."

Accepting the gift of the watch didn't seem so wrong to me now.

Roger arrived a half an hour later, carrying four fairly new suits, six shirts, assorted ties, and two pairs of shoes. "What's this?" I demanded.

"You need to be dressed for your photo, so we can make you false identity cards. All men and women over the ages of fifteen must carry such a card."

"How do you make them? The cards, I mean."

He smiled and winked; and that was all. Then, he motioned us into clothes.

It was no problem finding a shirt to fit each of us. In fact, the suits were okay too. The second one I tried on fit perfectly. Hell, even the sleeves were the right length. But the shoes were all bad luck; none of them fit me. Very few shoes exceeded size 10 in France. This had been going on from the days of Napoleon, when soldiers were conscripted by height, the tallest ones first. With all the wars, the tall fellows had been killed off and a man five feet six and over was considered tall these days. I was considered, *tres gros*, a freak, since I was five feet eleven.

Well, I was dressed fit to kill, but I was still barefooted. Roger said, "I will take the shoes back with me and bring you a pair of boots of a larger size. They are good boots. The previous owner no longer needs them." He winked at Albert.

"Yes," said Albert, "I took them from a German major, when we killed him. They are handcrafted, expensive boots. Though we don't usually remove shoes, Roger pulled them off. I was disappointed when they didn't fit me!"

They had dried out Richard's shoes and cleaned them; they looked positively new. The imprint on his shoes was "Church." Such English shoes made by Church were sold in France and carried an excellent reputation. If I ever got back to England, I promised myself a pair of Church shoes. Meanwhile, I felt like a real dude, walking around in my shirt, tie and suit, even in stockinged feet.

Madame Jacques said, "You look like a Parisian," the ultimate compliment in France; and I felt even better about myself.

Albert departed with Roger, and Messr. Jacques said, "You must be tired. You should have a rest."

Well, I was all dressed up with no place to go. I removed my tie and coat, stretching out on the rug in the parlor.

"You are welcome to use the bed in the bedroom," Messr. Jacques said.

"This is fine," I told him.

Richard joined me on the floor, asking, "Why didn't you take him up on the bed?"

"They've been so hospitable that, well, if there are still lice on us, I wouldn't want to leave them in their bed."

Madame brought us pillows and blankets then, and very soon we were sound asleep. I awakened to Messr. Jacques, shaking me gently.

Richard mumbled, "What time is it?"

I was so proud of my new watch I couldn't wait to tell him. "Well past eight o'clock!"

"Dinner is prepared," said Messr. Jacques. "But we will wait for Marcel." An hour later Marcel and Albert showed up with two other men.

Marcel was a very handsome chap; he resembled King George; in fact, I couldn't get over the similarity in their appearance. He spoke perfect English and could speak Spanish and German fluently too. The man reeked of such class, he stood out like a sore thumb, and I stood in awe of him.

Madame Jacques had warmed up what was left from lunch and baked a large casserole with meat, cheese, noodles and tomato sauce. Needless to say, the dinner was delicious, since along with all this we were served soup, salad, and hot rolls. To close out a perfect meal, Madame bustled in proudly, carrying a large cake fresh from the oven. I thought of their rationing; that cake, plus the two meals, must've blown their rations all to hell. I thanked them.

Colonel Marcel said, "We are happy to do this. You are part of the Resistance. Anyway, everything will be replenished. Do not worry. We take care of our own." Now he got down to brass tacks. "Since you don't speak French very well, your identity card will bear the sign: *Muet.*"

"What does that mean?"

"Mute. This is a frequent happening, if one is caught in a bombing raid." He turned to one of his aides and directed him to make notes on our height, weight, color of eyes and hair. That done, he turned back to me. My identity card would carry the profession of *cultivateur* and my name would be Jean LeGuern whose home was Brittany, far to the north. LeGuern, it seems, had been killed. Since Brittany was in the invasion area, with all the combat going on there, checking up on the name of LeGuern would be next to impossible.

After dinner we retired to the parlor. We sat around sipping brandy and drinking coffee, while Colonel Marcel made inquiries about everything that had happened to me since I'd bailed out from the plane. He showed the same interest in Richard. When the stories were done, he congratulated us, and turning to me, he said, "*Mon ami*, Eduarde, I wish I had officers with your resourcefulness, intelligence and courage." Then, he directed his remarks to Richard. "The courage of both of you."

Richard was generous to a flaw. "Without Ed, I'd probably be back there in the truck, dead or in prison. When I began to despair, it was

156

Ed's courage that kept me going. He was the leader. All the way."

Colonel Marcel responded by telling us how much he and his country were indebted to men like us, that our countries had sent brave men to aid the liberation of his nation. He was particularly emotional when he remembered how the Nazis were treating the French people. Then: "As soon as you receive your identity cards, you will be taken to my people, one town to another, until you arrive in Toulouse. Toulouse is quite some distance. But when you are there, a very close friend of mine, a man I served with for many years, is in charge of all the Resistance forces in the area. I will send word to him so that he may plan for Basque guides to take you across the Pyrenees. The trails will be difficult, but the Nazis can't follow, and you will be in Andorra, which is neutral. From there, the English Consul will get you throuugh Spain, into Portugal and back to England."

This was the Underground Railway, as he called it, set up to help Allied flyers escape. Many had escaped in just this fashion. Now the colonel leaned back in his chair and appeared to relax, until he began to talk again about the Nazis.

He spoke of a recent massacre of an entire village which had occurred only a few months earlier. And when he described what had happened, Richard and I were shocked. It was beyond belief, but it was quite obviously fact.

– 17 –

S.S. Waffen storm toopers under the command of a Major General Bernard Heinz Lammerding. Marcel said, had been incensed because of the revenge murder by the Resistance of Lammerding's nephew, an officer, Lammerding had ordered a major in his division to go into the town where the murdered officer, his nephew, had been found, and carry out complete reprisal if the town's people didn't surrender the killers of the young nephew, an S.S. oberleutnant.

A fifteen-year-old girl had been assaulted and raped by the oberleutnant. When she was found dying she told her parents the name of the Nazi officer. Two Maquis cousins heard about it. They trapped the Nazi officer not far from the village of Oradour-sur-glane, a village fifteen miles north of Limoges, a large city in southern France. They strung the Nazi officer up by his hands to a large tree limb, castrated him, stuffed his severed genitals into his mouth, sewed his lips shut and left him to bleed to death.

When General Lammerding heard of the killing of his nephew, he dispatched his favorite major with a special "Das Reich" unit into Oradour-sur-glane. Arriving on June 10, 1944, on a Saturday afternoon after lunch, came trucks full of storm troopers. Everyone in town was rounded up and paraded in the public square. There was an exact total of 642 people; 247 of them were children. This done, the Germans kept the men to one side, while the women and children were led to a nearby church and locked inside.

Now the mayor of Oradour was asked to produce the murderers of the oberleutnant. When he answered honestly, "I do not know," they told him to single out fifty residents to be shot. He refused, answering defiantly, "I name myself, and if that is not sufficient, then also my family."

"Not enough!" snapped the major.

The men were herded into a barn nearby and machine-gunned. When some men refused to die in the first blast of fire, the major ordered straw spread over them. Then, he set the straw on fire so that all those who were not dead would be burned alive.

That accomplished, the major ordered the heavy weapon carrier backed up to the front door of the church. Machine guns were aimed at the doors, the doors were swung open, and all of the women and children in the church were gunned down. Then, he had wagons loaded with straw backed up to the church. The straw was spread around the church, sprinkled with gasoline and set on fire. A few of the women and children who were only wounded tried to climb through the windows, but they were gunned down too.

One woman, Madame Marguerite Rouffange, crawled through a small back window. Five bullets struck her, toppling her body outside the church; she was left for dead. Inside that church she saw the horror of fire destroying her friends, neighbors and family. Her small son, two daughters and a seven-month-old grandchild perished inside the church, her husband having been killed earlier with the men.

Playing dead, Madame Rouffange watched as the fire drove the Nazis back. Then, she managed to crawl away and hide in the grass to watch the final destruction of Oradour-sur-glane. Every single building in the village was burned, leaving nothing but charred brick, stone walls and metal light poles. Only then did the storm troopers depart. (See photo and article in center section.)

Neighboring farmers, having seen the smoke from the fire, came to see what had happened and were shocked beyond words. The silence of the horrible holocaust was broken only by the cries of Madame Rouffange begging for help. She was rescued, given medical aid and hidden. Thus, Saturday came to an end for Oradour-sur-glane and its citizens. But Sunday lay in wait.

On Sunday morning the storm troopers returned with trucks and other equipment. Carefully, they went over the town, destroying and burning anything that had escaped the previous day's holocaust. To insure that no evidence remained, they bulldozed a large hole in the ground on the edge of town, burying bodies and bones which defied their destruction. Finally, units were sent into the country side to look for survivors or witnesses.

Actually, five men and one woman, visiting relatives in another village, were survivors. But they had not witnessed the massacre. Madame Rouffange was the only survivor of the horror. However, some people nearby had taken photographs before the storm troopers returned on Sunday. General Lammerding, evidently afraid of such acts, posted guards at Oradour. Signs were erected warning anyone who ventured into the devastation that the penalty was punishment by death. This went on for weeks until finally, only an occasional patrol came to the ruins.

Richard and I were stunned by the story.

Said Colonel Marcel, "We are accumulating all the evidence with the exact names of the storm trooper officers and their commanding general. The photos have all been authenticated with witnesses and certification, along with affidavits signed by Madame Rouffange. They will be punished at the end of the war." Here he paused to remove a leather folder from his pocket. From the folder he removed photographs, handing them to us. "See for yourself."

The photographs were explicit, showing every detail of the unholy massacre. It was sickening, sad and sickening. We sat in silence, shaking our heads.

"These are extra photos made from the negatives." Then, he dropped the blockbuster. "For a case against General Lammerding and his storm troopers, we need a witness from another country. Up to now, the only ones who have seen it are Frenchmen, although reconnaisance planes have flown over and taken photos . . ."

I held my breath. I sensed what was about to happen.

"If only you were not in such a hurry, *mon amis.* It would be a great help and a peace of mind to us to have someone like you witness this deed, especially you, Eduarde, since you are American. We want word of this massacre to reach America, which is so far away. Then, maybe next time, God forbid there is a next time, America will not wait to step on the yoke of tyranny until it gets started."

I don't know what the hell possessed me, but I didn't hesitate. "Colonel Marcel, after what you and the many French people have done for me and for Richard, I would consider it an honor to help in this small way."

Surprised, the colonel jumped to his feet, shook my hand, embraced me and kissed me on both cheeks.

I glanced at Richard. His face was expressionless and his jaw hung agape. Then, Albert, Messr. Jacques and the two Maquis who had arrived with Colonel Marcel, were shaking my hand, thanking me with the usual embraces and kisses. "When do we leave?" I managed to ask.

"Early tomorrow morning before dawn," said Colonel Marcel. "Now, I want you to rest. You will need your strength. I must warn you. The journey will not be easy. It is almost 200 kilometers."

I shook my head in dismay. I couldn't see myself walking that far. Not in my condition.

"Do not worry." He smiled. "We will travel on special motorbikes, you and I and one other man. His name is Paul. He's a trusted aide and a very brave man, while being a professional with motorcycles. I would feel safe if you rode with him."

The photographer arrived, did his duty and left. Then Marcel said, "I assure you that we will take every precaution. Meanwhile, we

160

will see that your friend Richard is taken care of. Others will bring him to a place where we will all meet after our return from Oradour. Now we must leave, *mon ami*. You must rest." Again, the handshaking and embracing began, only to be interrupted by a knock at the door.

It was Roger. He had returned by bicycle with my boots. Colonel Marcel and his group waited to see if the boots fit properly. They were a perfect fit, comfortable and well broken in. I smiled happily.

"Wear them in good health," said Colonel Marcel. He shook my hand and went through the door.

Albert was the last to leave the room. "I knew you were an American when I first laid eyes on you. I felt you had arrived among us for a purpose. Now I know, God has sent you to help us, not for us to help you. I add my humble thanks along with the others. Goodbye, *mon ami*. God bless and take care of you." Tears were in his eyes as he hurried to catch up with the others.

Messr. Jacques showed us to a bedroom. Richard and I didn't hesitate to undress and climb into bed. Jacques had brought along a bottle of brandy. Each of us took a few good slugs. Then Richard turned over and mumbled, "Good night, old buddy."

I tried to fall asleep. But I thought of all those people, those photographs. Such horror!

Yes, I must go. I really did want to go there. I had no second thoughts. If I could help bring justice to those murderers, I would be satisfied. I fell asleep.

Madame Jacques touched my shoulder gently. I opened my eyes and looked into her kind face. She held a small portable oil lamp. I nodded, knowing it was time to rise and shine.

Quickly I dressed and walked into the kitchen. Madame had prepared hot water for me to wash. Bless her heart, she must've stayed up all night. My breakfast was on the table: ham and eggs, hot bread and coffee. While I ate, Messr. Jacques sat with me, wishing me a pleasant good morning.

As I finished eating, he left the room to return with a jacket and beret. "You must wear these. You will look more like a Frenchman." He shrugged. "Too, it is cool in the morning. The ride before sunrise will be chilly."

I stood up, donned the jacket and beret, and stepped to the small table where I collected my gun, knife, and, of course, the wristwatch Albert had given me. Outside, we could hear the sound of a motorcycle approaching.

Madame threw her arms around me, sobbing. Messr. Jacques hurried to the door. Daniel, a Maquis, came in, asking for a bite of breakfast and a quick cup of coffee. Madame released me and set out food and coffee for Daniel. He ate swiftly, as if on the run. Then, Madame grabbed me again, sobbing, "My son, my son," and kissed me on the cheek.

Now it was Messr. Jacques' turn. He threw his arms around me, embraced me in a big hug, and kissed both my cheeks. These people had such warmth. I would never forget them.

Daniel handed me a small folding stock machine gun with an extra clip, compliments of Colonel Marcel. We went outside then, and Daniel showed me how I should hold onto the bike. He climbed aboard and started the engine, while everyone stood watching.

I remembered I hadn't said goodbye to Richard. Well, he was sound asleep. I had to trust that all would be well, and I would see him again soon. And so, Daniel and I were off, roaring down the dirt road from the farm where another fellow on a motorbike waited for us. Daniel gestured to him and he said to me, "He stayed there to keep a lookout for us."

He followed behind us as we turned into a field, picking up a footpath barely wide enough to walk on. The small seat I sat on wasn't too comfortable. We bounced often. But I hung on.

The day was misty and a slight fog hugged the ground. Never mind. I didn't have time for sightseeing. I was too busy keeping myself atop the cycle.

He wheeled up one hill and down another, over a field and through a woods. Hell, I had no idea where we were going or what direction. I didn't much care. I was in their hands and I had to trust them.

We must've passed St. Etienne far off to our right. We came out on a narrow road, following this for about ten minutes, then cut off into the fields again. By now, the fog had lifted and ahead was a small farm house set back in some trees; parked there was the Citroen car which had brought us to Jacques' farm house the day before, a motorcycle with a sidecar attached and two motorbikes with extra rear seats.

At the farm house I was escorted inside. Colonel Marcel was waiting, dressed in a black jacket and beret, much as he had been dressed the previous day. With him was Paul.

Of course, the colonel embraced me, saying, "Eduarde, I see you are ready to go. I now dub thee Colonel Eduarde of our Maquis!"

All three men stood at attention and gave me a snappy French salute.

At first I thought it was a joke. Not so. They were dead serious. I thanked them for the honor.

"Our thanks are to you," said the colonel. He brought out a map. It was like one of the rice cloth maps I had carried in my escape kit, the same in every detail, exactly like the one which had been taken from me when I'd been captured in Bordeaux. What I couldn't have done with that map in getting out of Germany. But, hell, I wasn't doing so badly now!

We were at a point called St. Marcellin. Holy smokes, Oradour looked like it was one-third of the way to Nantes, the point where I'd heard General Patton was heading.

"The route," said Colonel Marcel, "will be to Craponne, then, cross-country up to Clermont, then, cross-country down to Ussel, and then, just slightly north of Limoges, following east of the main highway from Limoges to Gueret." His finger traced the route. "See this dual highway running north and south? We will go east of this to the small town of Nieuf, then cross-country through the woods to Oradour-sur-glane. It is roughly 180 kilometers. We can arrive in Ussel in one day without trouble on motorbikes. Although we don't have many Maquis in the Clermont area, we have an excellent unit in Ussel. There are no German troops between Clermont and Tulle or around Ussel. We can spend the evening there in relative safety. They have been alerted."

"How did you alert them?" I asked.

"By telephone . . ."

"But aren't you afraid the Germans will listen in?"

He laughed. "Of course, they do. But we have everything coded. Another call will be made from St. Etienne to Clermont later today. And then, there will be a call from Clermont to Tulle. A courier will travel to Ussel since Ussel does not have phone service."

I studied the map and marveled at their ingenuity. Then, I traced the route of our escape for Colonel Marcel.

He nodded, saying, "It was not an easy journey."

I had to agree with that.

Now he asked, "Have you ever driven a motorbike?"

"Hell, no," I told him. "The only thing I've done, outside of riding a bike, is to get a ride with a friend of mine on a Harley-Davidson when I was about twelve years old."

"Come, then. Let us show you. I think it is best you learn how to operate one."

First, they demonstrated how to start the bike. Then they showed me where they had removed the key and fixed the switch on the other side of the handlebars so that all one had to do was flip the switch. No messing around, fumbling for a key. Next, turning the throttle which was on the handle, one depressed the starter wheel and it started simply. I was especially impressed by the sound of the engine. It purred like a kitten. I tried my hand at starting the bike a couple of times. I had no trouble. "Really quiet," I remarked.

He showed me the mufflers. "They are special so as to suppress sound. Without these mufflers, these bikes would be as noisy as motorcycles."

Now Paul gave me a lesson in riding. I should keep one foot down to balance myself, until I got moving. I tried my luck. I drove around the yard several times, each time coming back to apply the brakes in good order. Feeling cocky now, I decided to give the bike a real try. I sailed down behind the farm house, over a hill, following the path to a chicken coop, swooping around the coop and back. "Hell, there's nothing to it!" I said, braking to a halt.

All I had ever seen were American cycles and the ones the Germans used; they were heavy and cumbersome. This bike I could pick up; it was lightweight and manageable. Even the tires caught my eye. They were super grip tires, used by the Italians for hill climbing and field racing; they could carry a person over practically any terrain with their special treads.

I was to ride with Paul. He had performed in circuses all over the continent on this kind of bike, riding a sheer vertical wall, while live lions were released to roam the floor adjacent to the wall. He had even driven bikes through solid walls of fire. Paul had been with the colonel for three years, a valuable aide and a good friend.

"Now," said the colonel, "I will be ahead of you at all times. Should anything go wrong, this will give you enough time to escape. Remember, no matter what happens, you are the one who counts. If need be, Paul and I will not hesitate to sacrifice ourselves." Then, he handed me the map made of rice cloth, just in case.

I tucked it inside my boot, a map I treasure to this day; and we started off. I glanced at my watch. It was ten minutes after seven. It was a pleasant ride, without incident, to Craponne.

Leaving Craponne, we took a footpath, cutting across the hills. On the other side we stopped for an hour's rest, looking down on a dual, main railroad line running north and south from Tours, far to the north, and clear down to Arles on the Gulf de Lione in the Mediterranean. Then, we moved on, crossing the railroad and entering an open meadow with high grass. A few hours later we came back out on the main road for a few short miles, cutting off again at a sign which read: ISSOIT.

Shortly thereafter we turned into a narrow dirt road, stopping here to walk the bikes cautiously for the last few hundred yards. Marcel had gone ahead. Soon he was waving that it was all clear. We entered the farm of an elderly couple who were out to greet us.

The usual kissing and embracing followed. They couldn't speak English. But when Marcel and Paul told them about me, the embracing began. *"Vive, Americaine!"* they repeated over and over again. I was the first American they'd ever seen, and, of course, they broke out the wine. We rested, drinking the wine, then we said our goodbyes and traveled directly east on narrow pathways toward Ussel, since Colonel Marcel didn't want to take chances. I was with him all the way.

We stopped for another rest at two o'clock. I unslung the small sack I carried over my shoulder. In it was lunch, socks and handkerchiefs which Madame Jacques had packed. I shared the lunch with Paul and Marcel. Marcel added to the repast by producing two large bottles of red wine from a saddlebag slung across the back of his bike. He opened them with a bottle opener attached to a knife, wiping the tops off and handing the first bottle to me.

I took a healthy slug, and it tasted good. I was growing more and more like these Frenchmen. I had been drinking so much wine I hoped I wouldn't turn into a wino. But it went good with the delicious sandwiches prepared from left-overs by Madame.

The lunch vanquished, we traveled onward, and the going became rough. We journeyed down footpaths at a 45-degree angle, then up another hill, equally breathtaking. Paul was a super driver and I felt comfortable in his care. But going downhill brought anxious moments; and when he reached the top of a hill, he hesitated, only to apply power going downhill. The man was a whiz!

We approached the top of a long and arduous trail. Reaching the summit we looked down at Ussel, a picturesque village, seemingly untouched by modern civilization.

The closer we came to Ussel, the prettier it became. There were no billboards or signs. Its narrow streets were winding and hilly. It might have been a page from *National Geographic*. Ussel was that lovely.

The streets were brick, and there was not a car in sight, except for two small trucks. All other vehicles were horse-drawn carts. Someone might have turned back the clock fifty years. The town couldn't've had a population of more than few thousand.

We passed an inn, and a few blocks later, our inn presented itself at the top of a hill. People waved to us as they passed on bicycles. Young and old used bikes for transportation.

There were only two inns in the town. As we arrived at our inn an elderly couple rode by on a tandem bike. The old gent wore knickered pants with a matching cap. They were a sight to behold, and they didn't seem to have any trouble negotiating the hill as I watched them bicycle away. They had to be in their late seventies.

Two young boys, perhaps thirteen years old, came from the inn to embrace Marcel. He gave each of them a big hug. The boys took our bikes and walked them around the inn, and we went up the steps. The door opened and out came a short, portly, white-haired gentleman with a handlebar moustache on a round, ruddy, friendly face. He greeted the colonel and Paul warmly. Then, Marcel introduced me as Colonel Eduarde, the American.

The old fellow snapped to attention, giving me a quick side-handed French salute. At some point the old boy had served in the military; it was obvious. Then, he shook my hand firmly and kissed me on both cheeks.

The old man was dressed to the nines. He wore a striped shirt. The collar was white and stiff, and the long sleeves were buttoned, pulled up and held by two sleeve garters. Over this was a crazy white full-length apron. All of it was topped off by a jaunty bow tie. He looked like something from the Gay Nineties. His name was Rene Bonard; and, yes, he had formerly been Senior Sergeant Bonard of the French Army in Algiers.

His wife, Madame Bonard, appeared on the scene. They were perfectly mated. She was short and round with a kind face; her hair was as white as her husband's. She, too, wore an apron.

Next, a gentleman in a black robe, its collar turned up, approached us. The Bonards introduced him as Father Philippe, the local curate (Catholic priest); his vestments were similar to those worn by American priests, except for the old-fashioned, low, round hat.

Inside the inn we sat down at the same table as the curate. The conversation turned to French, everyone talking at once. I did, though, understand the conversation was about Oradour-sur-glane. Finally, the curate and the Bonards came around the table, each shaking my hand and kissing me on both cheeks. The priest, in beautiful English, said, "My dear American friend, it is a fine thing you do for our country, to be a witness to this dastardly deed. I know it will help to punish the criminals of this barbarous and inhuman act at war's end."

Then, Father Philippe spoke of Madame Rouffange. She was hidden in a convent far south of Limoges, healing physically, but spiritually and mentally she had a long way to go. Unfortunately, the Germans had heard of her escape; Gestapo agents were trying to locate her as we spoke.

I was amazed at the openness with which they talked. Several other people had come into the inn. After greetings all around, they sat at nearby tables. Everyone seemed to be on one side here, and I felt comfortable and safe.

The inn had six rooms upstairs and two real bathrooms with hot and cold running water. They were proud of this fact, and I was pleased to join in their pride. "Where is the *cabinet*?" I asked, needing to go to the bathroom.

Messr. Bonard pointed to a door under the stairs.

I hurried right along, the call of nature with me, and when I entered, I immediately wondered where the toilet was. I was faced by a contraption that looked like a trough with running water and two sets of metal feet pointing toward me. These metal feet were elevated about six inches above the water line. Directly above each set of feet were hangers (like those found on streetcars). Meanwhile, toilet tissue hung directly above the hangers. I finally gave up, baffled beyond words, and called to Paul for help.

He burst out laughing. In fact, he couldn't stop laughing. In fact, he called out to the others in French that I didn't know how to use the *trough de shoit cabinet*. Finally, the hilarity subsided, and Paul set to work showing me what to do.

One simply or not so simply straddled the trough with the running water in it, by placing first one foot on the elevated metal foot, then, the other. Now you were turned around, facing the door. Next, you unbuttoned your pants with one hand, squatted down, holding the strap in the other. That done, you let go of the strap. It was a feat for an acrobat. I couldn't believe it!

I practiced and finally got the hang of it, and just in time, while wondering how old people accomplished the feat. Although my legs hurt from squatting and trying to hold onto the strap, when I was finished I did manage to reach out, pull the toilet paper off, and finish the job.

My pants pulled up, I jumped off to contemplate the contraption. It was crazy. But the water had been running constantly. Now all I had to do was hit the plunger and the force of water increased, washing the rest away. At least there was a conventional small wash basin with a towel hanging beside it. I washed my hands and made my exit to laughter and congratulations. "This is crazy!" I said.

Madame Bonard said, "Why didn't you use the conventional bathroom upstairs?"

Paul laughed, saying, "I wanted to see if he could handle this one!"

Someone else said, "There are many *troughs de shoit* left in France."

"But what do the women use?" I asked stupidly.

"The same thing!" Paul said.

Madame Bonard appeared upset by this turn of events. "Come, Eduarde," she said briskly. Obviously, if she had realized this was foreign territory to me, she would not have allowed me to endure it, joke or no joke.

Marcel and Paul picked up our gear, and we followed her up an ornate stairway: several steps, a landing, and another six or seven steps, all open, so that one might look down into the dining room. It was a quaint old place, ceiling beams exposed, with a large stone fireplace.

At the first door on the second floor, Madame said to Colonel Marcel, "Colonel Eduarde will have the honor of the largest room since he is our American guest."

The room had a wash basin with hot and cold running water, and a big double metal bed. Everything was spick and span with beautiful, clean, white sheets turned down and waiting. A small chest and a chair completed the furnishings, and a large window with fluffy white tie-back curtains looked into the street.

I settled my gear: my guns, my cap and my jacket. Then I washed my hands again, combed my hair and came out into the hall. Marcel and Paul were in rooms at the far end of the hall. I went to look for them, but they had gone downstairs. Before I followed, I checked the bathroom directly across the hall from my room. It was exactly like home, except the bathroom was tiled in black and white marble.

At the top of the stairs now, I watched as Madame Bonard pushed three tables together to create one large table before the fireplace. A large white tablecloth was spread atop the table. Then, the customary wine and cognac came out, followed by a big bowl of hard-boiled eggs with beets, onions, and sausage cuts which looked

167

like ring bologna. The Bonards shuttled back and forth between the table and the kitchen. Still more food arrived: a large block of cheese on a board with a cheese knife. I couldn't contain myself any longer. I ran down the stairs to join the others.

We sat around talking, eating, sipping wine, waiting for other Maquis to join us. Every so often other people dropped in and paid their respects to Colonel Marcel. Always I was introduced. It appeared as if everyone in town had heard we were there.

After three glasses of wine, I excused myself, saying, "I'm afraid I'm tired." It had been a long day.

I dozed off on that lovely bed and began to dream about girls laughing. I had stretched out with my shirt and trousers on, but I had pulled off my boots. When I got up, I looked around for the boots. They were gone. Meanwhile I realized I had awakened with a blanket over me. I had not had a blanket over me when I went to bed. Someone had been in the room.

In my search for the boots I came upon a fine leather shaving kit with brush and soap on a shelf alongside the wash basin. There was also tooth paste, toothbrush, and a brush with a comb. I suspected I was being given a hint. I set to work immediately.

This was the first time I'd brushed my teeth since the morning I was shot down. While I was at it, I decided to shave. Talk about luxury, I was about to shave two days in a row!

Just inside the leather kit was a razor. When I withdrew it, I almost cried. It was an American Gillette razor; and a brand new package of Gillette Blue Blades accompanied it!

All washed, brushed and shaved, I decided to go downstairs and allow myself to be admired. I opened the door of my room, and there were the Nazi boots standing in front of the door, cleaned and polished. I slipped them on and hurried right along.

At the bottom of the stairs, Messr. Bonard exclaimed, "Ah, I am so happy you were able to sleep. You look so much better. All rested. *Voila!* It looks as if you took advantage of the toilet articles in your room."

"Yes, and thank you. I'll return them."

"No, my friend. They are for you. Some things were left in the inn from before the war. Only the toothbrush and tooth paste are French."

"The boots. Thank you for cleaning them."

"My young grandson took care of that. It is his pleasure. He is the one who approached you when you arrived. He put away the motorbikes. Come join us. Others have arrived who would like to meet you."

Those at the table all jumped to their feet as I approached. Then, Marcel came around to me and introduced me to the two ladies in the group. One of them was particularly stunning. She was probably in her early thirties. The other was slightly older. They were both attractive, though, and what struck me was that they had the same color eyes and hair. In fact, their complexions and smiles were identical. But the younger one was absolutely striking!

Her beautiful auburn hair fell in soft waves around her face, and her eyes were a deep green that looked right through you. She was well endowed in every other way too.

I tried not to be too obvious, since Father Philippe stood next to them. But I couldn't help noticing her well-shaped legs, full hips, and the bosom which jutted out in the tight dress she wore.

Marcel said, "Eduarde, this charming female is Yvette. And this is her sister, Denise."

They chattered away madly in French. I could hardly understand a word they spoke. Father Philippe acted as interpreter.

"They are pleased and thrilled to meet you as you are the first American they have ever met. They think you are quite handsome." While he had translated, Yvette had reached over and felt my arms and chest, as if examining a horse.

Now she said, *"Ooh la la, tres solide."* Then, she slipped her arm around me and said, "Come sit with me," in French.

I had no trouble translating for myself at this point.

Several bottles of wine were on the table. Everyone seemed to be enjoying themselves. A few of the men to whom I was introduced were from Oradour-sur-glane. They were, so Father Philippe said, honored to meet me and praised my willingness to travel to the scene of the massacre. But this subsided quickly in the face of Yvette asking questions.

Where are you from in the United States? Are you married? What did you do before the war? As swiftly as Father translated, I replied. Then, came the real shocker: Have you had the pleasure of a French woman sleeping with you? I couldn't believe Father Philippe would translate such a question. But he had. Still, to be on the safe side, I pretended not to understand, forcing him to repeat it. He did!

Then he said, "My dear Eduarde, sex is a thing taken for granted among our people. But I must admit Yvette is quite formidable and brazen. I am only interpreting what she is saying, but, then again, my young friend, think kindly of us for we have gone through a horrible time these last years. The Nazis have been cruel. We do not know from day to day whether there will be a tomorrow on this earth. As a result, attitudes have changed considerably."

Hell, I thought, he didn't need to apologize! I liked this gal, though she was slightly older. At twenty-three, I considered anyone over thirty older.

The usual toasts were made to me now and things began to settle down. Soon dinner would be ready, and I was looking forward to that rack of lamb the old gent had mentioned.

Paul and Colonel Marcel excused themselves. They wanted to freshen up before dinner. The two Maquis from Oradour-sur-glane engaged me in conversation. They seemed annoyed with Yvette. It was only after Father Philippe had said something to her that she quieted down verbally. As I spoke with the Maquis, she looped her leg over my right leg and began to swing her leg, tantalizing me. I felt the warmth of manhood rise up in my loins.

Flushed, I said to the two Maquis, "Speak more slowly."

They talked about the massacre, breaking down in several places and crying.

They were from the village of Conofolens, northeast of Oradour-sur-glane. One of them, named Jean, told me his sister's entire family perished in the massacre: the sister, husband and four children. The other chap, Robert, had been born and raised in Oradour. He had left the village at the age of sixteen to work in Limoges at a factory which manufactured Limoges china; he had lost his mother, father and small brother in the massacre.

Dinner was served, and it was unbelievable: wines, magnificent onion soup, salad, a rack of lamb cooked with vegetables, coffee. It was all marvelous, an epicurean delight.

Messr. Bonard reminisced, "Before the war, every day was a different specialty!" as if to apologize for what was being served.

I stuffed myself, leaving not a nook and cranny of my being empty. In time, though, I found my nose irritated from all the smoke. Since I didn't smoke, this was understandable. They all smoked like stacks.

Anyway, Yvette took my arm and volunteered to show me around town. "Come," she said, "you can take Denise's bike, and we will ride all around."

I hesitated, looking to Marcel for his approval.

He nodded his head and smiled. "Go, my friend. It is perfectly safe. There isn't a Boche within thirty kilometers in any direction."

It was dark outside. But a few oil lamps imposed themselves on the Nazi blackout, and it was light enough for me to see that Yvette had pulled up her skirt and tucked it in her panties to ride the bike!

We rode all over the village, up and down narrow, winding streets. The village was like a picture book. Magnificent! But I felt embarrassed that Yvette could pedal up the hills without trouble, while I had to get off and walk. I gathered that Yvette had bicycled from her home thirty kilometers away, and practically all of it was uphill. Meanwhile, it had only taken two hours for the trip. Enough said.

People sat on their front steps, taking the cool evening air. Many of them called out cheerful greetings to Yvette. But I was anxious to get back to the inn. Yvette had told me, *"Je desire coucher avec vous."* I wish to sleep with you; and she had made it quite clear that I should make an excuse to retire to my room early. She would, of course, follow, since she and her sister had planned to remain at the inn; they were related to the Bonards.

170

We returned to the inn to sit at the table again. I couldn't keep my mind on the conversation. I had something else on my mind and so did that little vixen Yvette. She sat beside me, her hand running up and down the inside of my thigh, driving me out of my mind. Finally, I admitted my fatigue to Marcel.

"Relax and enjoy yourself," he said.

I could read meaning into his words.

"Yes, enjoy. We will not leave for Oradour until tomorrow afternoon. You have time for all the rest you may need."

I glanced at my watch. It was ten o'clock. I excused myself, bidding everyone, *"Bon nuit, "*but I wasn't kidding anyone. Sly grins and winks were the response from almost everyone at the table.

Upstairs I washed up again, even brushing my teeth twice. Then, I hurried to my room, undressed, pulled back the covers and climbed into that snowy white bed. The electricity had been cut off earlier, so I reached out and turned down the wick on the oil lamp until it was barely discernable. Then, I lay back, breathing in the fresh air that flowed over the sill from the half-open window, enjoying the moonlight which filled the room now. Meanwhile, I couldn't believe my good fortune.

All those weeks of living a nightmare, and here I was well fed, clean and comfortable, awaiting that saucy, redheaded vixen. Footsteps sounded down the hall. They entered the bathroom. Was it Yvette? Water ran. The usual bathroom sounds. Then, my door opened, and yes, it was Yvette.

"Eduarde," she whispered. *"Vous etes couche?"*

"Oui," I answered.

"Bon, Attendez, mon cheri." Good, wait for me.

Then, I'll be damned if she didn't walk over to the window to undress, the moonlight revealing her every curve as she removed her clothing, until nude. Slowly, she ran her hands up her body, cupping her breasts. "Do you like what you see?"

Did I like what I saw? Only a blind man couldn't've liked it.

She came to the bed and drew back the covers, her mouth quickly on mine. She kissed me like a woman on fire, her mouth wide open, her tongue exploring. Unexpectedly, though, she ceased to kiss me, and brushed her full, firm breasts all over me. The delicate touch and the exotic scent of her perfumed body was driving me absolutely crazy. I grabbed a tit in my mouth, and this turned her into a wild animal.

She reached down with her free hand to caress my manhood. I tried to stop her; she was playing with fire. But there was no controlling her. Her lips found mine again, searching, exploring, enticing. Oh my god. Then, another unexpected event. She turned around, placing her mound against my face. "Eduarde," she pleaded, *"mangez me, s'il vous plait.* Let us enjoy *soixante neuf."* Sixty-nine! "I have washed, especially for you."

I didn't care what she had washed. I'd never done anything like that before and I wasn't about to start. How little I knew . . .

Here she muttered something about Americans, and I couldn't very well blame her since she was quite obviously hotter than the proverbial pistol. Now I felt her sensuous lips engulfing me, sucking violently. She was unbelievable, and I thought I might explode forthwith, but Yvette sensed everything. Quickly, she turned and mounted me . . .

I felt her beautiful wetness; it was like a hot furnace, and she began moving, grinding, as if there might be no end to it, moaning, *"Maintenant, maintenant . . ."* Now, now!

She didn't have to say it more than twice. I exploded!

She yelled, screamed, moaned. Her violent motions almost shook the bed from the floor.

I kept coming. Then, it was over, and I couldn't believe we both came so hard.

She fell on top of me, moaning gently now, kissing and whispering, *"Merci beaucoup,"* again and again.

I should have been thanking her. Well, I did. But she kept me within her, twitching and kissing me all over.

It had been so long since my last encounter, I was embarrassed that I'd been unable to hold back longer. I told her so.

Said Yvette, "Do not worry. It will be even better next time!"

She rolled over and cuddled up against me, throwing her leg over me. My god, she was a lot of woman!

For a short while, we lay there, Yvette murmuring words of love in French. But, hell, anyone can understand the language of love. Finally, she got up, went to the wash basin, took a small towel and let hot water run over it, squeezed out the towel and came to place the hot towel over my still throbbing member!

I'd never had or seen anything like this before, and I was intrigued as she wrapped the towel tightly, squeezing it every now and then over a period of perhaps three or four minutes. Finally, she removed the towel, wiped me gently all over and threw the towel aside to lower her mouth to mine.

What she did with her tongue next was unreal. She went all over me, up, down, clear down to the insides of my thighs, then, back up. Suddenly, I was hard rock again. She was a tigress! Such aggressiveness!

She lowered herself upon me; she was soaking wet. Then, she started it all again, and within a few minutes, she was climaxing, moaning, groaning, shaking the hell out of me and the bed. She stopped only to reach for the towel and wipe herself off, saying, "Now, *mon cheri*, you mount me quick, quick. I can hardly wait."

I got on top, penetrating the still hot furnace. She drew her legs high, placing her hands on my buttocks, and pulling me into her. Again, the same thing, only this time the event was even more violent.

She came twice more before I felt I could come again. Then, each time I felt like coming, she stopped me, moving very slowly, telling me, *"Attendez!"* Wait!

We went on like this for about a half-hour. Finally, I couldn't have stopped if I wanted and all hell broke loose. She bucked and threw me around like a toy. A crazy wild woman, I thought to myself. I hope they can't hear us downstairs!

Finally, I collapsed on top of her. We were both soaking wet from perspiration and passion. But what a beautiful way to perspire.

Much to my surprise we only stayed in this embrace for about thirty minutes. Once more she rose to go back to the wash basin and soak the towel in hot water. This time she bathed and wiped my face, my body, my genitals first before repeating the hot water trick with the towel. That towel was really hot, almost burning. But she seemed to know what she was doing. I felt like a king, lying there, her taking care of me. And there I was, getting erect again.

When she removed the towel, I was about half hard. Immediately, she took me into her mouth, not only sucking, but biting every so often. It hurt, but it was a pleasant hurt and made me harder. I couldn't believe myself. Sure, I had done it three or four times a night before, but never in so short a time and never with such intensity. When I became hard as a rock, I wondered what was next.

Now, she got up, went to the wash basin, mounting it as if she might be going to ride it, and turned on the water. She was washing herself. Then, she wiped herself and returned to bed, saying, "Eduarde, please play *soixante neuf* with me."

I tried to explain to her that I had never done this before.

"You mean, they do not do this in America?"

"Yes, I've heard of it, but I've never done it."

"You will like it. Please try it."

I couldn't.

"Well, then, at least kiss and suck inside my thighs and play with me."

Hell, I could at least do that, and we started up all over again.

Every inch of her was velvet smooth and firm. Her soft silken hair was so close to me . . . I loved it . . . I bit and kissed inside her thighs; her scent was not offensive. She was a truly exotic woman, turning me on relentlessly as she sucked me in return.

Finally, she whispered, "I cannot stand it longer. Put your fingers inside."

I placed my fingers there, rubbing her clitoris. She gyrated madly, moaning and groaning, coming again, and I was right there with her, coming myself. What a feeling . . . I had never imagined the intensity could be so great!

Beaten to a pulp, I tried to roll her off me. But she kept on sucking. I realized that she was swallowing every drop of me. It was beginning to hurt. So, I tried to stop her. She slowed down a little, but never mind. I was a toy in her hands.

Soon I was hard again. She was the aggressor, on top again. Hell, I was being raped, and it wasn't funny. I hurt, but I stayed hard, and that's all she wanted. She climaxed like a wild woman again. Oh, my god!

Now she used her vagina muscles on me, contracting herself, twitching, then releasing me. Again and again, her timing perfect. My cock didn't dare go soft. The gal was a nymphomaniac, sitting straight up now, her hands on the back of her hips. Her breasts jutted straight out; she glistened with perspiration in the moonlight. I reached up, placing my hands on her breasts, kneading those magnificent tits. They were the firmest I had ever held.

The tantalizing motion continued. Then, after a while, she lifted first one leg, then the other, so that she was turned around, her back to me. She placed her hands firmly on my ankles and rotated up and down. Here was a new feeling. I was turned on again.

She came twice more, the supreme nympho, and I loved it. I was starting to swell, and now it was my turn. The woman was a magician.

Faster and faster she moved; I shot up into her with such force that she responded, moaning and shaking her head. She kept on doing it, and I watched as our love juices ran out of her and down on me. Finally and at long last, she collapsed on top of me, purring sounds of satisfaction.

She stayed on top, still throbbing, until I went soft, slipping out of her. She started to kiss me, saying, "*Magnifique*," but all I wanted to do was roll over and go to sleep. I turned around, embracing her, and we fell asleep in each other's arms.

When I awakened, the soft rays of morning light were peeking through the window. I don't know what Yvette had done, but I was erect again. She had shoved her rear end up against me and was putting me inside her from the back. It felt good as I slipped into her. Finally, we did the whole thing over, coming together like this, then falling asleep.

The second time we awakened bright sun came through the window. I checked my watch. It was nine o'clock. I marveled at myself. I had come five times since about eleven o'clock last evening.

I could hear voices and activity downstairs. I thought we better rise and dress. I got up, put on my undershorts, grabbed a large bath towel, heading for the bathroom. I had seen that large tub, and I was looking forward to it. I paused at the door, looking back at that beautifully serene face. She was curled up in a ball, that firm round derriere turned toward me. The sight of her silken haired mound, peeking out between her thighs, gave me a feeling of arousal. I had enjoyed the encounter with Yvette, but one thing bothered me: She had been the aggressor; I had been seduced!

There was no one in the large bathroom. I went through my morning rituals. I felt guilty, using all that hot water. I had just stepped into the tub, when a knock came at the door.

"Open, please open!" It was Yvette. She came in the door, wearing only her bra and panties.

I wrapped a towel around me, thinking she wanted to use the toilet. I prepared to step from the tub and leave her to her privacy. But she turned around and locked the door. I dropped the towel and sat in the tub, while she sat on the toilet, did what she had to do and douched right in front of me. Then, she gave me a pixie smile and climbed into the tub with me.

I had never taken a bath with a girl, let alone a girl like Yvette. She took the washcloth, lathered it with soap, and handed it to me, indicating she wanted her back washed. I scrubbed her back all over; then, she did the same for me, lingering here and there to play with me. It was crazy, but all the hot water and rubbing had its effects. She pushed me back and took me into her mouth and started sucking. This brought on the results she wanted.

Satisfied, she reached up, wrapped a towel around her hair and straddled me, taking me into her. It was awkward, but it was wonderful. Still, I kept popping out. She reached for another towel, placed it in the tub, put her knees on it, and said, "Mount me from the back."

It worked.

My knees hurt like hell, but I didn't want her to think Americans were quitters.

We splashed water all over the place, but I gave it to her a sixth time, and she came with me, yelling, "Encore! Encore! Encore!"

Damn it to hell, I fell back in the tub and she sat down in front of me.

We soaked for about fifteen minutes more. Most of the water from the tub was on the floor and walls. So, I ran more hot water, luxuriating a while longer. I tried to get up, but she begged me not to move.

"Look," I said, "I gotta get up and get dressed."

Evidently, she got the gist of it. She followed me from the tub and we dried one another off. I was grateful Madame Bonard was so generous with towels. Then, we wiped up the mess we had made and returned to my bedroom.

To my surprise, I felt energetic as all hell. When I finished dressing, I turned around to see if Yvette was ready. She sat on the bed and asked me to come to her. I did. She kissed me long and well, hugging me and saying, "Thank you very, very much. You are my first American, and I loved every minute of it. You made me climax many times and satisfied me. I wish you could stay." She told me this was the first time she'd made love to a man in over two months, and I had been *tres formidable* to satisfy her so well.

Convinced I was king — well, all the French women made me feel kingly — I combed my hair and went downstairs. There stood Messr. and Madame Bonard, Father Philippe, Marcel, Paul, two other Maquis and Denise. At the sight of me they broke out in applause, shouting, *"Magnifique,* six times, *magnifique!"*

I was so embarrassed I began backing up the stairs, but *"Viva la France!"*

– 18 –

Breakfast was on the table. Seeing I was embarrassed, they all sat down and dug in. I joined them in a wonderful breakfast of sausage, ham, and scrambled eggs fried with onions and peas. Even a fresh pitcher of milk sat on the table, American-style coffee, and the inevitable bottle of cognac. They were having a drink before breakfast, perhaps in celebration of those six times, and I joined them.

They continued to kid me. Madame Bonard and Denise kept saying, "Eat, eat, you need it to replace the strength taken from you last evening." Then, they all had another big laugh.

Shortly, Yvette came down. They gave her the same treatment, whistling, clapping, telling her she had met her match. Little did they know that I was the lamb and she the tigress.

Said Yvette, "Eduarde is a masterful man." She paused to give me a big hug and kiss. "No man has ever made me feel so wonderful." She went on to say that she could not wait for the arrival of other Americans. All French women should be so happy.

I smiled. Boy, what a public relations officer she'd make! Meanwhile, my ego assumed monumental proportions as Yvette continued to extol my virtues in bed. Their attitude toward sex was phenomenal, and frankly, I liked it.

As we finished breakfast, the Bonards and the two girls cleared the table, leaving the men alone. Marcel got down to business. "I have," he said, "received word this morning that no German troops are in the village. In fact, they're sending Nazi patrols into and round the village only once or twice a day. I would prefer that you see Oradour in daylight."

"You should have awakened me earlier," I said.

"Ah, *votre jour d'amour*. I did not want to interrupt you. There is time enough. We will leave within the hour."

Back in my room, I packed the toilet articles in the black leather kit the Bonards had given me and slipped it into my jacket pocket along with the extra ammo clip for my machine gun. When we all came down to the dining room again, we were loaded and armed to the teeth. I wondered, What will this day bring? One thing for sure: I had made up my mind that I wasn't going to be taken prisoner again. I would fight until killed rather than go to prison.

The women came in to bid us goodbye. Yvette embraced me, saying, "Please try to come to our house on your return. Marcel knows the way."

I smiled and waved goodbye. I doubted I could handle another session with her!

The motorbikes had been gassed up. Our two new Maquis had a motorcycle and sidecar. "Did you get it from the Boche?" I asked.

"No, this is the genuine French article."

Marcel handed me a small brown folder the size of a wallet. I opened it, and there was my identification card with all necessary information, my photo in the upper left corner. In the bottom righthand corner was the official signature and seal of the *Commisare de Police*. "How did you get it so soon?" I asked.

"By messenger, early this morning from St. Etienne along with the word that they are taking Richard to Brive where he will meet us. It will take a few days to get there. They must travel over mountains to avoid German troops. But when they arrive, they will wait for us at least two days. If we are delayed, they will go to Perigeuex."

I felt concern for Richard; it must've showed.

"Do not worry. We will meet him. I can assure you." And with that, we began our journey.

The two Maquis who had joined us went ahead a half-mile or so, then, stopped and waited on us. They weren't taking chances.

We left Ussel, heading due north along a fairly good road for an hour. Then, much to my dismay, we followed a rugged footpath across the fields and up into the hills. We traveled this path until we came to a wide dual-lane highway. A sign indicated we were nine kilometers from Bourganeuf to the north of us.

We crossed the highway, staying in the hills until we reached Amburac, there keeping to the woods and footpaths, until we arrived at a very high point. Looking down from there, we could see Limoges four or five miles away. It was a big city. Paul estimated its population at well over 200,000.

"I wish I could take you there," said Paul. "It is a beautiful city. I have many friends, among them Robert DeHavilland of the DeHavilland china family. But Limoges is occupied by the Germans, unfortunately by the S.S. Division of that bastard General Lammerding, the ones responsible for the massacre of Oradour."

We had been moving along at a good clip for about three hours. We decided to have the lunch the Bonards had sent along. We dined on delicious roast lamb sandwiches (from the lamb cooked the night before), fruit and half a dozen bottles of wine. We even had napkins. Then, we moved on.

Now we went down the hill, following a steep footpath to cross a large north-south highway between Limoges and Chateauroux. A while later we crossed another large highway, leading to Poitiers. Within another half-hour, we were close to Oradour-sur-glane.

The two Maquis went ahead to make sure it was safe. We were but minutes away, and my heart pounded with excitement, since I didn't know what to expect. The Maquis scouts returned in ten minutes. All was clear. Not a soul was in sight as we approached along the only road leading to the village from the south, up a slight curving grade. Then, there it was, enveloped in an eerie silence.

Every single building had been burned and gutted. Only brick or stone, or the metal light poles survived. The stench of fire and flesh still hung in the air, smacking of death, yes, death, permeating everything. I thought I might throw up.

We rode through the village, street by street. Above the soft purr of the motorbike I could hear Paul sobbing quietly. Nobody spoke a word.

Every single home, building, human being, animal had died. It was heartbreaking.

We passed the small square. We passed the site where the church had been. Only the charred walls remained. It was unreal. No human could have done this. But the Nazis didn't belong to the human race. They were insane animals.

Finally we parked the motorbikes and entered the debris. Jean said, "Despite the rains of the past weeks, the stench of death is with us."

Yes, it was unmistakable.

My foot kicked up a metal object. Paul picked it up. It was a small toy car made of metal. I looked around; there wasn't a dry eye among us, including mine.

It was one thing for soldiers to kill each other and even to kill the Maquis who fought the Germans. But do not doubt that the Nazis murdered many thousands of Jewish men, women and children, methodically shooting, burning and gassing them. Many, these days, like to imagine that none of it happened. Not so. I saw evidence of this insane mentality myself. Here it was, right before my eyes.

Paul said, "There is another town, Rouinac, in which S.S. troopers chased Maquis soldiers. When they were unable to catch them, they executed everyone in town, but they did it nicely. They hung all the men and only machine-gunned the women and children."

Having seen Oradour, I, for one, will never put down the torch, and I cannot understand why this most horrible of massacres has never been publicized more. It was not until thirty-one years later that a major newspaper told the story. On Sunday, March 30, 1975,

The Miami Herald ran a feature story titled, "So the World Will Always Remember," by Nino Lobello, the truth at last, the story highlighted by a photograph of the destroyed village. In the interim, a wall has been erected around the ruins of the village and a new Oradour built a few hundred yards from the wall. A large plaque graces the entrance to the 300-acre monument; it reads: "Silence-Scene of the Execution." Inside is a small museum with photographs and relics, all pertaining to this mass murder. (See photos in center section.)

With Marcel and his men I visited the crude gravesite of the victims. Later I signed affidavits that I had seen the remains of the village along with photographs, attesting to the fact that I was the first American witness to the tragic site.

In leaving, we picked up another road to the south. This road ran parallel to a well-traveled railroad line which led to St. Yrieix. Marcel said, "We will leave this road and travel along the railroad after we pass St. Yrieix. If possible, we will spend the night at a farm house near Lubersac. So far, so good. We have gotten through all the blockades." And we stopped to rest. "We have something to attend to," added Marcel.

That something was a tunnel which the major railroad line ran through. One of his Maquis units had attempted to blow it up, but they had not succeeded since there were more S.S. troops than normal guarding the tunnel. He had learned from Maquis friends in Oradour that only two were at each end of the tunnel now. He and Paul would take care of the matter. I was to wait at a distance. They had brought plastique and fuses along, just in case, in the saddlebags on his motorbike.

I considered and yelled back at him, "Like hell, I'll wait. I'm going with you."

"This is not your concern, *mon ami*. Anyway, Paul and I are experts with plastique explosives."

After what I'd seen this day, there was no way they were leaving me behind. I said as much.

Marcel rattled something to Paul in French. Then, he turned to me, saying, "Eduarde, we have gone through all this so you could witness Oradour. We cannot take any chances with you."

"I'm going!" I said stubbornly.

Marcel threw up his hands, smiled and said, *"Mon ami, Eduarde, c'est tres dificil."*

I looked him straight in the eye. "I'm going," I said.

Obviously, there was no arguing with me. He nodded his head.

We continued off the road until we came to a place where we could hide the motorbikes. Our other two Maquis friends had left us at St. Yrieix, so there were just the three of us.

Marcel took out the plastique explosives, the first I had seen. They were packaged in a box similar to a student's pencil set. When opened, it looked like blocks of carmel candy with wax paper wrap. Marcel claimed it was very easy to handle, not really dangerous without fuses. The fuses had been packed in a separate box, and when they were inserted into the plastique explosive with a timer device, they ignited the explosive. "It is," said Marcel, "much more powerful than dynamite."

Marcel would handle the explosives; Paul and I would attend to the guards at each end. One guard usually stayed in a small guardhouse, the other guard outside. The main thing, I gathered, was to get them before they could set off the alarm signal which alerted the nearest units of Storm Troopers.

Marcel and I would go to one end of the tunnel, and Paul to the other. We synchronized our watches and set up a time. Then, exactly to the second, we would throw a rock on the track. As the guards investigated, we would cut them down. Here, Marcel would enter the tunnel to find a crack in the wall or a place where we could set the plastique explosive, setting the fuses for four minutes, giving us time enough to get away. By now we were atop a steep rise, looking down on the tunnel.

We finally arrived on the bank at the north entrance of the tunnel, directly opposite the small guardhouse at the side of the tracks. We noticed the glow of three cigarettes outside the guardhouse. Marcel whispered to me, "Increased protection. I hope Paul will notice if there are more at his end. Now do be careful to watch for trip wires. They run along both sides of the rails and set off mines or alarms. Follow my signals to the letter."

Since the guards were outside we wouldn't have to throw a rock on the rails to arouse their curiosity. We could see them clearly; they were only about fifty feet away. We moved cautiously down the steep bank, and I released the safety catch on my machine gun. Marcel didn't have to give a signal. We heard the loud chatter of automatic weapons at the other end.

I was about half way down the bank and starting to slide when the Germans spun around and opened fire on us. I stopped my slide at a large rock and returned their fire. I had the advantage. They were concentrating on Marcel; he was almost to the tracks.

My first bullet caught the German nearest the guardhouse. Then, I leveled at the other two Germans. I was screaming and yelling like a wild man as they went down, having lost control of myself. I kept my finger on the trigger and the gun became hot to my hands. But I kept firing.

Marcel had reached the tunnel and was waiting for me, gingerly holding the fuses and plastiques. I followed him across the tracks to where the guards went down. Marcel picked up a flashlight which had fallen from one of the guards.

I thought I saw one of the bastards move. I opened fire, letting the rest of the clip go into him. I was that furious. I wanted to tear the bastards apart.

We could still hear firing at the other end of the tunnel. Marcel yelled angrily, "Paul must be having difficulty!" We both plunged into the tunnel which was lighted up toward the center.

We stayed close to the walls until Marcel came upon a place to set off his plastique. I left him behind then, continuing to the other end of the tunnel, trying to stay out of the light by hugging the walls. As I approached Paul's end of the tunnel I could see he was pinned down by two Germans crouched behind a large toolbox while another German stood in the tunnel, ready to throw a grenade. I smiled. I was less than twenty feet away and they hadn't heard me.

I opened fire with the full clip I'd inserted, yelling, "Turn around, you fucking murderers!"

Paul opened up and we cut them to ribbons!

Only after we both stopped firing did I realize there had been four guards. Paul had gotten the first one near the guardhouse, and the other three had taken cover behind the box and in the tunnel.

"Do you think they set off the alarm?" I asked Paul.

"I don't know. Come along."

We hurried back to Marcel; he was finishing with the explosives. Quickly, he set the fuses, and we ran from the tunnel. We had less than four minutes to get away. I began counting the seconds off.

Climbing up the bank was tough going. We scrambled like mad, nobody speaking, and we'd just reached the top when the explosives went off. It was terrifying. Even the ground shook around us. We turned, looking down. Smoke and dust came out of the tunnel.

Marcel yelled, "It sounded like a good hit. I put enough plastique in there to keep the tunnel closed for some time."

We headed back toward our motorbikes. We still hadn't heard any other troops. The motorbikes retrieved, we walked them toward the wider path we had followed in, only starting the bikes when we reached level ground. But Marcel's motorbike flooded out. It took us a few worried minutes to get it started.

The path led down to the narrow hard road. We had just started turning south on the road when we heard the rumble of trucks. Immediately, we retreated, heading back to the footpath. We just made it under cover when two trucks loaded with troops roared by. Yes, the guard at Paul's end of the tunnel had sounded the alarm.

We had no choice now but to continue on down the road in the dark, keeping our eyes and ears strained, so that we could get out of the way of any oncoming trucks or motorcycles. We stayed on the road for another ten minutes. Then, we heard the sound of approaching traffic. We repeated our previous action. We had warning enough; the moonlight had shown us the vehicles in the distance, even to the point of revealing S.S. Waffen Storm Troopers, probably belonging to the same division that destroyed Oradour-sur-glane.

Once they passed, we were about ready to leave, when an armored car and two motorcycles with sidecars came along. We knew there was too much activity now for us to stay on the road. We had no choice. We took to the woods again, finding a small dirt road overgrown with weeds. We followed this path, walking the bikes. We didn't dare start them up.

It was slow going, getting away from there. But Paul said, "We'll soon come to another main road. When we cross it, there is a dirt road that we can follow. It may be safe enough there to start the motorbikes again."

Half an hour later, we reached the road. I, for one, was happy to be riding again. It was amazing how fast we traveled in the dark with only the moonlight to guide us. But believe me, we had reason to move on out. We were scared that the Nazis would be all over the place very quickly, covering all bridges and roads leading away from the tunnel. To encourage me, I think, Paul said, "This road isn't even on the map."

An hour later, after traveling about thirty kilometers, we arrived outside what should have been the town of Excideiul. Friends in the Resistance lived there. They would hide the motorbikes and hide us for a while. We had to lay low during the next few days, like it or not. The area would be hot, crawling with Germans.

Here Marcel decided that we should wait in the woods, while Paul contacted his friends on foot. We had to be especially careful. There was a curfew throughout France. Anyone seen this late at night would be shot. Meanwhile, we had no way of knowing whether there were any German troops in the village.

Paul didn't return for a good hour. But when he came he had two friends in his company. The men took the motorbikes and walked them back to the village where they planned to hide them. We were to go on around the town to a hideout of other members of the F.T.P.F.

The men had spoken with Marcel in French extensively. Now he told me, "They are not happy with us. They wished we had not blown up the tunnel. They have word that the Germans were planning to move out of Perigeuex, leaving only a small token force. The blowing up of the tunnel will alert troops in the area, especially since they heard over the Londres Free French radio earlier in the evening that General Patton has turned north from Nantes and is heading for Paris from the south. Further, the Americans and British have broken through the Falaise Pocket and are approaching Paris from three points. The German troops would have been heading north to help repel the invasion."

I remarked, "Blowing up the tunnel could prevent many troops from going north."

Marcel agreed. At least several days would be required to clear the tunnel.

As we walked, daylight was catching up with us from behind. I felt a hell of a lot better physically and mentally than the last time I'd watched daylight come up while escaping. I had good friends, was well clothed, and more important, I was dry and wore a comfortable pair of good German boots.

Marcel joked with Paul, "Eduarde must be *tres fatigue* after his *affair de Ussel.*"

I wasn't. But I did admit she had been formidable.

We reached the hiding place at about nine o'clock that morning and were picked up by lookouts immediately. We entered the camp, the ruins of an old chateau, and were greeted with the usual hugs and kisses.

Marcel was treated with much respect. Paul whispered to me, "These men are all part of his command. They are under the local command of a Captain Jacques." We soon were introduced to Captain Jacques. He insisted we come to breakfast with him.

Breakfast was cognac, wine, cheese, onions and bread. Afterwards, Marcel went off for a meeting with Jacques and two of his lieutenants. When Marcel returned a short time later he had much news of the last forty-eight hours. The breakthrough by General Patton at Nantes was true; so was the breakout from the German hold up at the Falaise Pocket by the American and British troops; all were heading toward Paris.

Meanwhile, they had been informed by code over Londres radio that the Germans were starting to panic. Within the last few days many officers had packed up their wives, mistresses, or families with what loot they could grab and were starting to leave Vichy France.

Jacques had told Colonel Marcel that the previous day the Maquis had intercepted a German colonel in a Mercedes sedan. The car was loaded with his mistress and an aide. Two trucks filled with stolen loot and an escort of a dozen or so S.S. troops followed. They had ripped the Nazis apart, killing all of them. One truck carried fine French antiques, priceless oil paintings and works of art, crated and packed. The Maquis had salvaged almost everything for later return to their rightful places.

I was surprised about the looting. But I was informed that the Germans had been doing this since their occupation of France. They had stripped almost every museum and gallery. Marcel said, "High-ranking German officers, especially those of the S.S. Waffen and the Gestapo, can do as they please. I know of one field colonel who flew to Switzerland regularly, taking vast amounts of money, gold and jewelry to deposit in his personal vault. They are all doing it, from Generals Goehring and Goebbels on down. None can accuse the other."

Then, we fell to discussing Patton. The breakthrough was the news the Maquis had been waiting to hear. Evidently General Patton, in his daring, hell-bent manner, had been advancing from twenty to thirty kilometers daily, often leaving the British and other

American forces behind. In his mad dash to Nantes, it was said that he had gone ahead forty-seven kilometers beyond the British and American lines. The only thing that had stopped him was lack of petrol.

I remembered an incident about Patton and I shared it with Marcel and the others. I had been in London at Selfridge's, the main officers' PX for uniforms, shoes, etc., with Fred Swantz a few months before I was shot down. I was trying on a battle jacket and Freddy was trying out some new shoes. In rushed two M.P.s in white helmets, leggings and gun belts. They ran to each end of the large room; then, one of them screamed, "Attention!" In sauntered this tall general with his aide. He was ramrod straight, wearing a combat helmet with three stars, a beribboned battle jacket, pink officer's jodhpurs and high-topped riding boots. The thing, though, that caught our eye was the gun belt with two pearl-handled Army .45s slung at each side. It was General Patton.

The general sauntered through the PX, and he caught sight of Freddy. Freddy was in his stocking feet, wandering around with his collar loosened and his blouse unbuttoned, trying to put the make on the English salesgirl.

Patton roared, "Lieutenant, what in the hell army are you in?" His teeth were tobacco-stained and ugly, and, damned if he wasn't chewing tobacco.

I stood rigid, hoping he wouldn't notice me.

Freddy said, "Army Air Corps."

General Patton exploded, "You're in the goddamn United States Army, and you're supposed to dress like an army officer. What do you mean walking around like a nudist without shoes, your collar open, and that hat! Who in hell gave you authority to wear a sloppy hat like that, all wrinkled up and without a grommet ring in it? Don't you know that's not regulation?" He might have been a mad dog. He bared his teeth.

Freddy mumbled the reply, "Buying shoes."

"Dammit man, you're in the United States Army! Just remember that. Do you understand?"

Freddy nodded.

Then, Patton yelled, "And you stand at attention when you are talking to a superior officer. Do you understand?"

Freddy froze.

Now Patton saw me, ten feet away, without a blouse. Oh, my god, I thought.

So, the general had a go at me, tearing me apart, then, turning to his aide, a lieutenant colonel, and snapping, "Get their names, rank, serial number and unit. See that they are reported to their proper commanders."

The lieutenant colonel snapped, "Yes, sir!"

Patton turned around and walked to the rear of the store,

yelling, "Carry on," and slapping his swagger stick against the side of his boots.

The lieutenant colonel came over and did his duty, collecting the necessary information. But he winked and whispered to us, "Don't worry. The old man blows off, then forgets. He is, though, the greatest general in the whole world, and don't forget it!"

Freddy and I got properly dressed in a hurry and got out of there, as did many other junior officers.

Colonel Marcel enjoyed the story, laughing and saying to Jacques, "No wonder he has terrorized the German High Command. It is no military secret that he could have torn the German army apart and gone all the way to Russia if they'd turned him loose. But he has constantly been held back by lack of gas, supplies, and more than anything else, protocol, for the Allies and especially General Montgomery. Montgomery, who fought so brilliantly in North Africa, is envious of General Patton."

We made the decision to rest a few hours while the other Maquis kept watch. But before we slept, all of the Maquis came to shake my hand and thank me as the first American to witness Oradour-sur-glane. They addressed me as Colonel Eduarde, and I realized how much weight Colonel Marcel carried.

On the shady side of the wall we made our beds on straw, the sun shining full force. We were not awakened until afternoon.

– 19 –

I glanced at my watch. It was 2:30. Paul and I went over to an old well, pulled up a bucket of water and washed in it. I even took out my treasured toothbrush and with the tooth paste brushed my teeth. I would have shaved, if I'd had a mirror.

I was hungry again, and more so, when I saw the men had set up a large board on top of rocks; they were slicing bread and ham. The ham was French jambone, a moist French ham that's salted and hung to dry. It's delicious. Meanwhile, of all the damn things, they had several large jars of hot peppers, and, of course, many gallons of red wine. I made some sandwiches for Paul and me. Paul grabbed a bottle of wine, and we went over to a large tree to enjoy our lunch. We weren't leaving until nightfall. We were waiting for a messenger from the Maquis unit command in Perigeuex. At that point we'd move out in small groups.

The courier arrived at dusk with good news. There was to be a large air drop that night at a predetermined location, and one of the leaders we would meet was Richarde Rene Baccard; Baccard was the liaison man who worked with Free French Radio and British Intelligence in London. We were to meet him at an old chateau high above the Dordogne River where he lived and operated secret radio equipment. Baccard was a large cattle dealer and food broker before the war, dealing with Germany, and he continued supplying the Germans after the occupation. The Germans thought he collaborated with them and they trusted him completely. In fact, Baccard was a main agent of the Resistance.

At dark we left camp in small groups within ten minutes of each other. Marcel, Paul, Jacques and I, along with several of Jacques' men, were the third group to go. We were to head south of town where there was a German truck used to haul supplies for the Germans by Messr. Baccard's company. We would travel in the truck, hidden under the supplies. We reached the truck within an hour.

I was shocked to see two men by the truck in German uniforms. I was even more shocked to learn that they were genuine. They had been bribed with gold to work with Baccard and had the proper papers to get through the many blockades. I felt uneasy being near the bastards, but they both spoke French fluently and got on with Jacques and the other Maquis.

There was a message for Marcel from Baccard. The envelope was handed over to Marcel by one of the Germans. Marcel borrowed a flashlight to read it. Then, he told us our plans were changed.

We were to meet Baccard near the location where the plane would drop much needed supplies. Meanwhile, the Maquis had been ordered to move in and liberate Perigeuex. Here was the beginning of *la liberacion*; everyone was excited and elated.

We took off in the Nazi truck, hidden under supplies with canvas thrown over us. The truck stopped three times, and each time I tensed up until we moved on. Yet, it did occur to me that the Germans must have the right answers and papers, or someone would have searched the truck. At length, I felt secure enough to doze off, catching up on much needed sleep. But when I awoke, I began to worry about Richard. I asked Marcel, "Any word of him?"

"No. But you will meet him in Perigeuex."

The truck came to a stop. The tarpaulin was pulled off. We climbed out. Standing to the side of a clearing were two heavily armed men, and I was introduced to Baccard.

He was a slender, fair-haired man; he didn't look French. He reminded me of a German or Englishman. More uneasiness. And when he spoke, he said in French that he could not speak English very well, excused himself, and took Marcel aside. When Marcel returned he said, "We're going directly to the drop spot, not too far away."

We all climbed on the truck again, not bothering to hide or pull the tarp over us. Baccard had given each of the German drivers a small bag before we departed. I learned later they were given about fifty French gold pieces, worth about $54.00 each.

We reached the drop location in half an hour, a large open meadow at the bottom of a very steep hill. We had traveled over a mountain, then, cautiously followed a winding road down into the valley. A swift river made its way through the valley connecting itself to the larger Dordogne River.

Baccard had brought along a dozen or so smudge pots. After we found the estimated location of the air drop, the smudge pots were placed, ready to be lighted at the appropriate time. While we waited, Baccard fingered a light signal gun. Finally, we heard the sound of planes, the pots were lit and the light gun signal given. Within seconds, two planes came into view, made a pass over the area and swung back, flying parallel to the smudge pots.

The planes flew at approximately 1000 to 1500 feet in altitude, no doubt fearful of hitting the mountain if they flew lower. Their silhouettes looked like Lockheed Hudsons. Then, several parachutes, dyed brown, blossomed and floated down.

Here was the beginning of many drops of much needed equipment: automatic weapons, plastique explosives, guns, grenades, ammo, rationing coupons, millions of francs and probably gold Napoleons for additional items needed, plus gold for bribes. The loaded parachutes fell quickly. As they touched the ground we ran out to dismantle the harnesses, pull the padded cartons away and hide the parachutes and harnesses under the bushes. We retrieved all the chutes except one which had dropped straight down and fallen near the river. Then, a Maquis let out a yell and pointed to the top of the hill. Vehicles, lights burning, were coming down the mountainside. It could only mean one thing: Nazis!

The drivers were told to take off; they had plenty of time to get away on the road in the other direction. Paul and I were at the far end of the field. Marcel yelled to Paul, "Take Eduarde and Robert. Robert will guide you to the Chateau of Baccard. I'll join you there when the supplies are safe."

Paul, Robert, who was the Maquis guide, and I took off across the field. By now, the lights of the vehicles were halfway down the mountain on the winding road we had followed. Then, I stumbled over something. It was the parachute dropped near the river. I unhooked it, yelling at Paul, "Give me a hand." The container was small but very heavy.

Robert had gone ahead, saying he'd meet us at the river. He wanted to be sure it was clear. We were to meet him at a large tree about half a mile downstream.

We picked up the container with difficulty. Since it was so heavy, we decided to carry it to the edge of the river and hide it along the bank. That container was damned heavy, but after a struggle we found the perfect spot. There were two exceptionally large rocks, among others, about five feet from the bank in fairly deep water. We figured the heavy package was probably much-needed ammo, though we were surprised at its small size. Paul and I lifted its straps and swung it out, dropping it in the water, so that it landed between the two large rocks, the perfect shot.

The container hit with a heavy splash and disappeared. We aimed the flashlight on the spot. The water was deep enough, hiding the container fully. We took off, running downstream to find Robert.

Robert led us to a quite rocky crossing of the river. Someone had built a dam across the large rocks, so one could jump from rock to rock to cross. Meanwhile, the river was narrower here, which helped.

We traveled for a few hours, not stopping even for a short rest, at all times staying near the river. Then, we came to a spot where we looked down upon a narrow bridge across the river. Robert had gone ahead. Sure it was clear, he signaled us to follow.

I said to Paul, "Why are we going back to the other side?"

"Marcel gave Robert instructions. Since the Germans will probably be chasing the main body, we are to take the safest route to Baccard's chateau." It seemed Marcel was taking the Maquis and delaying the Boche, so that the truck could get the supplies to their hideout. Since they were going in the opposite direction from us, we didn't think we'd have any trouble.

Robert went to the edge of the bridge. About fifty yards ahead of us, he waved for us to come on. It was steep going in the dark. Unfortunately, though, we felt safe, throwing caution to the wind, going downhill very fast and noisily. When we reached the bridge, all hell broke loose.

A large searchlight hit us. Much too late we saw a car parked at the other end of the bridge. Then, came the German command to halt. It was the S.S. Waffen!

We spun around and dashed back across the bridge as they opened fire. I yelled for Paul to zigzag. I didn't have to. Both Robert and Paul were experienced.

We reached the end of the bridge and ducked behind rocks there. Bullets were flying, soldiers were running across the wooden floor of the bridge, and we opened fire on them.

We cut down the first few Germans, then, noticed that the car had driven to the center of the road, aiming its large spotlight directly at us from a hundred yards away. We had no idea how many soldiers there were. But it was like a miniature war. Of all the goddamn times, none of us had a grenade, only our light machine guns and pistols. We kept firing, but it didn't seem to do much good. We couldn't even reach the spotlight.

I was on the left side of Robert, and Paul was slightly ahead of us on the right side of the road at the edge of the bridge. The soldiers were drawing closer and the firing was more intense. Paul yelled, "I'm going to try to get grenades and rifles from the fallen Krauts."

I yelled back, "Don't do it! Let's run for the woods!" But I was too late.

Paul was running, crouching low, toward the dead soldiers. He was almost there . . . Then, he had to leave the cover at the side of the bridge and run to the middle of the bridge where the German soldiers had fallen. Paul reached the fallen soldiers and was starting to pick something up, when they dropped their light away from us and aimed directly at Paul. Paul tried to dive away. The heavy rifle fire cut him down . . . But not before he had grabbed a grenade, pulled the pin and thrown it in their direction.

We were still firing at the spotlight without luck when the grenade went off, creating one hell of a flash-fire. It blew out timbers in the bridge, the floor of the bridge splitting open and the dry timbers catching fire. While that was a plus, we could see that Paul was down, apparently dead. What a brave man he had been!

My thoughts were short lived. The Germans had moved the car to the middle of the bridge and continued to fire. Robert yelled to me, "Let's get out of here!" and I followed.

The Germans couldn't tell from the fire and noise if we were still there. We crawled to the bushes a few feet away, then into the trees, not going up the steep hill but down along the river. Next, we cut across the road into the hills, where we looked back. The bridge was on fire and the Krauts couldn't cross to chase us!

Continuing over the hill to the other side, we ran at full speed. I couldn't help thinking of Paul. I had grown very fond of him and knew how much he meant to Marcel. I kept thinking: It could have been me! And I wondered how long we would be alive . . .

We reached another fairly high point. The bridge was still burning and the spotlight was aimed at the end of the bridge. No doubt about it. Paul had saved us.

Robert couldn't speak good English. But I could understand most of what he said in French. I made out that we would follow the river for about fifteen kilometers, then cross at another point he knew. When I had first seen Robert I guessed he was probably in his mid-forties. I was half his age but had a hard time keeping up with him.

We reached the point we were aiming for in about three hours. It was similar to the place we had crossed originally, large rocks and smaller rocks in between. We stepped from rock to rock.

We had no trouble crossing until we came to the very end. Here was an open space of about fifteen to twenty feet. Robert stepped into the shallow water, not quite up to his knees, and I followed. On the other side, we picked up a footpath and began running at a steady pace.

We continued like this for hours, until daylight, coming out on a fairly wide road. Robert pointed to the left, saying, "Perigeueux, *vingt sept.*" Twenty-seven kilometers. In the other direction was Libourne, seventy kilometers. I remembered Marcel telling me 15,000 German troops were stationed at Libourne, and I remembered Libourne was about 100 kilometers east of Bordeaux. What a hell of a note! I thought; all the way to Germany and back, and I was practically in the same place. I also knew that Toulouse couldn't be too far to the south. Perhaps I should just take my chances and head for Toulouse. I had been told there was a French underground network to contact the Basque guides who helped escaped flyers across the Pyrenees. Then, I thought of Richard. Since we had come this far together . . .

We crossed the road and followed another footpath. After a

while we came across one of the most beautiful rivers I've ever seen. It was the Dordogne, looking like it belonged in the Rockies or the Alps. It wasn't an especially wide river and probably wasn't deep, but the river ran fast and furious, hitting rock after rock which jutted from the water, throwing up white spray. Simply beautiful!

On the other side of the river were steep mountains. I asked Robert in French, "Are we going up the mountains?"

He smiled, pointing up the sheer side, saying, *"Madame Arlienne et Baccard."*

We came to a very narrow wooden bridge which crossed the river to follow a gravel road; and the road began to climb, straight up, winding from side to side. Wow!

Up the mountain I couldn't see anything until at last we turned a bend near the top. Here was a place out of a medieval French painting, a chateau built into the mountainside.

We left the gravel road, going along a narrow dirt road to continue up the mountainside. Finally we came out on the inner side of the stone chateau. The side we had seen from below appeared straight up and down, but this side had a large level area with gardens, fountains, a small barn and garage. It was magnificent.

A Citroen sedan sat in the parking area which was large enough to accommodate a dozen cars. The terraced lawn with mountain shrubbery accented the stone walkway which led to the entrance of the house. The oak door was heavily carved with large thick hand-hammered hinges. The whole place was unmistakably old, and it was beautiful!

The door opened before we reached it. We were welcomed by a charming lady in her early forties. She was a tall, strikingly beautiful woman with long silver blonde hair which, in the sunlight, looked silver-blue; her hair matched the large deeply-set blue eyes. She smiled a welcome, and in the doing, she reeked of class.

Robert removed his beret and I followed suit. Her greeting was warm, yet aloof. In French, Robert explained what had happened, indicating I was the American. She extended her hand, saying in English, "I am Danielle Arlienne and I speak English quite well. Messr. Baccard did not tell me to expect our first American. I feel terribly embarrassed that we are not prepared for your coming."

She invited us into the chateau.

I couldn't keep from admiring the beautiful appointments, including Madame Arlienne. The entrance foyer was impressive; all of the woodwork and high-beamed ceilings along with the large curving stairway were in solid oak and elegantly carved. The furniture was carved Gothic oak. Magnificent paintings and tapestries were everywhere. Without doubt, many were original furnishings.

Madame Arlienne noticed my admiring glances and said, "Come, my American friend, I know you and Robert could not have had breakfast. I will show you through the chateau later." An elderly servant woman had come into the hall, and Madame Arlienne gave instructions to her in French; the servant smiled and disappeared.

We were led into a large dining room. It was breathtaking, having the same motif with a tremendously large, bronze chandelier. A large tapestry carried a coat of arms woven into it; one could tell it was quite old.

We sat down, and she asked what had happened. Robert told her about Paul, Messr. Baccard, Colonel Marcel, etc. She then asked me questions in English. Most people who spoke English in France had a British accent. She didn't. I said, "Have you ever been in America?"

"Yes," she replied, "but not since years before the war when my family spent some time in Palm Beach, Florida. But I was educated in Switzerland at the University of Berne and I studied English and German."

I marveled at her natural beauty. She was obviously quite intelligent.

The old servant woman brought ham and eggs French style, small, fresh, homemade loaves of French bread, butter and coffee, along with the usual bottle of white cognac and a large bottle of Courvoissier brandy. While we ate, Madame carried on a conversation in French with Robert. I could understand her asking him about the drop. Had we gotten everything? Robert told her we had gotten all but one parachute, but he was certain the Germans had found it by now.

I started to say something . . . then, I stopped. For some reason I held back on saying, "Oh, no, it's hidden in the water."

After the good food, she took us on a tour of the chateau. We went upstairs, moving from one bedroom to another; there were six in all. Amazingly, almost every room had a window that looked over the mountain and down on the river. These were great views, but I wouldn't've recommended them to anyone afraid of heights.

We climbed to the top of the tower and into a small room which had a small winding stairway that led to the very top. The room held sophisticated radio equipment. Madame saw me looking at it and said, "It is Messr. Baccard's equipment. I'm sure, since you are with Colonel Marcel, you are aware of Messr. Baccard's activities."

Heading down the narrow winding stairs, she explained that this was her family's chateau. "Rene" Baccard rented a part of it before the war and had stayed on during the occupation.

I said, "Isn't his name Richard?"

"Oh, yes," she said. "But his friends came him Rene, and he prefers it to Richard."

We walked past the bedrooms, and she opened the door to the bedroom at the very end, saying, "This will be your room while you are my guest. It will be an honor to host our first American."

It was a magnificent room with a large stone fireplace. The floor was planked oak with Oriental rugs. The furniture was massive with a large dresser and two large commode tables with marble tops. There were two carved oak armchairs with a matching round table by the window next to the fireplace. But what really caught my eye was the bed: a beautiful Tudor four-poster which soared almost to the ceiling with a ceiling-framed canopy that covered the bed with red velvet swags all around, then, dropping in panels over the headboard. The draperies were made of the same red velvet. I couldn't believe I'd be sleeping in this elegant room!

She said, "I chose this room for you since it is so very masculine, and it is across from the only full bathroom in the chateau." There were two toilets on the first floor and it seemed strange to me that this was the only bathroom upstairs. Needless to say, it was extraordinary, as large as some bedrooms, everything was in Florentine marble, the large tub, both washstands, commode and bidet. I turned the spigot and felt the hot water coming out.

"There is plenty," she said, smiling. "We heat our water with liquid gas since we cannot depend on the electricity."

We went downstairs through the great parlor and into the lower level of the chateau. Here was a large wine cellar with all kinds of wine bottles. This collection had been made by Madame's father; he was a connoisseur of fine wines. She removed three bottles of champagne from the rack. "These are 'Tattinger Rose Reme,' my father's favorite, and mine too." She handed them to me to carry upstairs.

Next, she reached up to a rack and pulled a section of it down. To my surprise, the entire section swung open, revealing a passageway behind the rack which led to a steep stairway. "This, Eduarde, is our secret escapeway that leads down to the side of the mountain to a pathway that leads to the Dordogne. We use it only in a real emergency. The Germans trust us completely." Then, showing me how to close it, she led us out to a large storage room and upstairs.

Robert slumped down on the sofa and was soon catching a catnap. I couldn't stop myself from yawning.

"Why don't you rest also, Eduarde? I will show you the grounds later. It will give me a chance to see about lunch."

I stretched out on the other sofa, exhausted, and fell into a sound sleep, only to awaken a short while later, feeling uneasy. Robert was still asleep and Madame Arlienne had returned.

"Oh, I hope I didn't awaken you."

"I slept for a while."

"Good." She took my arm, adding, "Come along, then."

She took me out into the gardens, up around the terraced-drop waterfall, then back to the stables, which had been partly converted into a garage. They had kept horses until two years earlier; the last two horses had been stolen for food. When I looked up with a question in my eyes, she said, "Yes, horse meat has become quite popular since the occupation. Many people cannot get fresh meat at all." I remembered the black market juicy steaks I had eaten in

London, which had tasted suspiciously like something other than beef.

Two motorbikes sat in the garage, similar to those we had used. Apparently Baccard rated highly with the Germans to be able to keep all of this.

We returned to the chateau. Robert was sitting up on his sofa with a bottle of brandy next to him, sipping a large glass. "Come join me," he called out.

I obliged him, figuring we deserved a drink after what we'd been through, not to mention the loss of our friend Paul.

Robert was feeling no pain. He must've been doing more drinking than resting. I sat down and poured myself a glass of Courvoissier brandy, and Robert tried to carry on a conversation, but he was slurring and his French just wouldn't slow down. He was talking of Paul and how needless his death had been. Tears came to his eyes. I was able to understand. Of the many, many men of the Resistance who had died fighting the Boche to liberate France, Paul was the best. He had been a member of the Resistance for three years, since his escape from a slave labor factory in Germany.

Madame Arlienne returned to the room. She sat beside Robert, placing a consoling arm around his shoulders. She also had known Paul well. Robert rattled on and she interpreted.

Robert had served in the regular French army for twenty years and had last been stationed at the Maginot Line. This was the so-called impregnable line of fortifications that the French had built to keep out the Germans after World War I. The Germans overran the Maginot Line in less than three days at the outbreak of the war. So much for invincibility. Robert had been captured, then released after two years in prison to be assigned to work in a munitions factory for the Germans. He had worked in this factory for over a year, fifteen to eighteen hours a day, while being paid very little and fed less. He had slept in barracks that were like a prison. After the first three months, he received honor passes so that he could go into town and spend his meager earnings. He had worked with Czechs, Poles, White Russians, yes, White Russians, who hated Russia and were all for Germany winning the war, as well as Moroccans and Algerians.

The White Russians, Algerians and Moroccans were given much freedom. After their capture the Germans had indoctrinated them, telling them they had been subjugated by the French for hundreds of years, the French treating them as inferiors. Unfortunately, this was true; but after Germany won the war, they would be free.

Robert had also served in North Africa and could speak the Berber language. When he was able to go into town he passed himself off as one of them. The Algerians gave him one of their identity cards, passes, food and extra money so he could escape. It was very simple. All he had to do was get on a train, say he was going to visit Vichy France, and he reached Marseilles without any trouble to join the French Resistance Forces of the F.T.P.F.

Now Madame Arlienne explained how difficult it had been for the people of France. Immediately after the German occupation, both in northern France and Vichy France, the Germans imprisoned all the soldiers of fighting capabilities. They forced technicians and professional men to stay at their posts and work for the Germans. Every male between sixteen and fifty-five had to have special work papers, stating their work was essential to the occupation of France. All others were shipped to Germany as slave laborers. The farmers were given special permits; if they didn't produce more than their quota of produce, crops or cattle, they were sent to Germany too.

One could see what a sacrifice it was to be a member of the Resistance. One had to be alert at all times, and even with proper identity cards, the Germans were suspicious. The Germans had a simple penalty for any member of the Resistance captured; it was simply death!

Robert's fifteen-year-old nephew had been cut down for a minor violation by two S.S. officers. The nephew had gone to a cinema still open during the first year of occupation. Only movies approved by the German High Command and Propaganda Minister Goebels were shown. A documentary of the French workers in Germany was being run, showing how nicely the French were treated, they enjoyed the food, pay and privileges as other Germans, and how they were able to come and go as they pleased. The boy made a casual remark to his girlfriend: "That is not true. My uncle was treated horribly, until he escaped." Two S.S. officers in the theatre with their mistresses heard the remark. When the young couple was leaving, one of the officers grabbed the boy by his throat and slapped him across the face several times, calling the boy a liar. The boy was so angered, he spit on the officer. With that the German pulled his pistol and shot the boy to death in front of his girlfriend, then casually replaced his holster, took his mistress by the arm and walked away, leaving the body lying in front of the theatre. The German officers in occupied territory had to account to no one for their actions . . .

Robert had become so emotional and drunk that we stretched him out on the sofa to sleep it off.

I had told Madame Arlienne very little of how I had gotten here or what I had done before. But Robert had told her what I had done and what Colonel Marcel had said. Some of her haughty aloofness had disappeared. She commented, "Eduarde, you must be very formidable." And she came over to me. "You must be quite a man for one of such youth." She embraced me, then surprised me by placing her mouth on mine and giving me a long kiss, while pressing her body to mine.

This was not the usual French hug and congratulations, and I found myself aroused. Here I was with a woman almost twice my age and . . . She sensed my hardness and responded by pressing closer to me and reaching down to feel me!

I tried to push her hand away. I had no idea what her situation was, and I wasn't about to get involved. Quickly, I sat down again.

She must've sensed my embarrassment. "Let us have another glass of brandy. I know you have been through much, and it will make you feel better."

My face was warm; the brandy was having its effect. I apologized.

"Please, Eduarde, stop calling me Madame Arlienne. Please call me Danielle. That is my name. I prefer to be called that by those whom I like."

I pretended to grow drowsy, and it was only half a lie. I *was* sleepy.

She came to me, saying, "Eduarde, you did not nap long. Why don't you take an afternoon siesta? You will feel much more refreshed for dinner this evening." She was a strikingly beautiful woman, well endowed and very well groomed. Here in this chateau in the wilderness, her skin and make-up were flawless and her hair was well styled. Needless to say, her tailored clothing set every bit of her off to good advantage. "Eduarde," she added, "I will turn down the bed for you, make sure there are clean sheets and pillows."

"I'll just stretch out on the sofa," I told her. "I don't want to take a chance of being caught off guard by the Germans."

"Do not fear," she said. "I sent one of our servants to the bottom of the hill, and we have our secret alarm that will give you time to hide in the secret passageway. The Germans think Rene is a collaborator, and they like him. They seldom ever bother us, except to stop by for an occasional visit." She turned and walked away.

I couldn't help reviewing her tall voluptuous figure, and since I had always been a fanny man, I watched her well proportioned derriere swing from side to side as she moved away. I would have sworn that walk was deliberate. While Robert and I had been having our drinkathon, she had changed into a fitted beige moire robe that went clear to her ankles; the robe was belted tightly and I couldn't help wondering what her legs were like.

I placed my feet on the table, closed my eyes and began to doze off. Then, a delicate hand began stroking my face, and Danielle was saying, "Please do not fall asleep here. I have turned back the bed for you." She led me upstairs and into the bedroom, telling me to undress and get into bed.

While I removed my shoes and socks, she went off to return with a large pitcher and bowl which she placed on the marble-topped dresser. Then, she made a second trip from the room to come back with a bowl of fruit which she placed on the round table by the window. "Sleep well, *mon cheri*," she said and walked from the room, closing the door behind her.

I had planned to remove only my shoes and socks, but now that she was gone I felt better and decided to undress and wash up. I removed the toilet articles from my jacket and went to the dresser, pouring hot water from the pitcher into the bowl. I lathered up with a small washcloth she'd placed there. But then I thought, "This is crazy when there's a bathroom across the hall. I slipped on my trousers, picked up my toilet articles and opened the door cautiously, looking into the hall. It was empty. I tiptoed to the bathroom.

There I brushed my teeth and shaved. Danielle's explanation about my safety encouraged me to enjoy that beautiful marble bathtub. I ran water slowly; I didn't want to make much noise. Then, I climbed in and relished the luxury of hot water again, almost falling asleep in the tub, until I caught myself as my head slid downward and hit the fixture. Enough! I stepped from the tub, toweled myself, slipped into my trousers, gathered up my toilet articles and then, actually stopped to wipe the tub out with the towel, so that she wouldn't know I'd taken a bath. How ridiculous!

Back in my room, I undressed, pulled the heavy, velvet draperies closed and climbed between those beautiful white sheets. I felt clean and tingled all over, a pleasant change from the last few nights. Then, I realized the sheets were silk satin!

I looked up at that canopy and smiled to myself. I would've loved to have a picture of me sleeping in that bed to send back to my buddies in England, especially the wild Dempsey crew of Dolan, Mitchel and Dempsey. They'd die of jealousy.

I went out like a light and I thought I was dreaming when I heard the door open and someone walk in. I rolled over on my right side and dreamed of feeling someone warm beside me, firm breasts against my back, an arm slipping around me, fingers caressing my chest, my stomach and down between my legs, then, gently playing with me. What a dream . . . Only it wasn't a dream. It was Danielle, Madame Arlienne. I would've known her perfume anywhere!

I was too embarrassed to turn around. Naively, I thought, maybe I'll let her think I'm fast asleep, see what happens, although I had an erection so hard it hurt. I was overcome with a passionate craving for this woman.

She continued caressing me a while longer, stopping only to roll me over on my back and draw the satin sheet aside. I kept my eyes closed, pretending sleep, though I was leaking sperm as her supple fingers removed it from its head rubbed it down my shaft. God, it felt good. But I feigned sleep until a beautiful warm feeling enveloped me, and I started to throb. This was crazy, being jerked off by a lady, but . . . What the hell! Come I did, trying to lie very still in the process, and failing.

I imagined she would stop now. But she kept on. Then, her breasts were touching me. I took a peek. She had knelt over me and was rubbing herself all over my still throbbing member, moaning softly to herself. The game was over. I opened my eyes and lifted myself on my elbows; she had bent over me as I came, allowing my sperm to shoot all over her breasts. Now she was rubbing her breasts all over me. It was a delightful new sensation.Her eyes rose to meet mine and she smiled quietly. "I'm sorry," I said, fumbling for words apologetically. "I thought I was dreaming."

She smiled knowingly, put a finger over her mouth and bent over me, placing her mouth on mine with deep passionate ardor, her tongue probing mine, running deep into my mouth in a slow sucking motion. Finally, she came up for air, saying, "You aroused me so much I actually had a magnificent orgasm when you came. Oh, how delightful to feel the strength of your ejaculation. It hit me with such force! I had long forgotten the strength of a young man. Thank you so much." Before I could try the apology bit again, her mouth was on mine, her tongue flicking my lips, then my chin, my neck, my ears, and yes, my armpits. Of all the damn things!

Now she worked her way downward to my loins, my legs, my toes . . . I thought I had done everything, but this was unreal. What next? She asked me to roll over on my stomach. I obliged her, intrigued.

She kissed my legs, my buttocks, between my cheeks, a new sensation there! That does it! I thought. I won't let her kiss me again. But so much for resolution. I didn't stop her.

She came back between my legs, my testicles next, then up my back and all over me, her tongue the touch of a million pleasurable needles. Then gently, she asked me to roll over again, continuing the exploration of my body with her tongue down my stomach, all over my belly button, until she took me into her mouth. Everything she did was slow and gentle. She spread my legs apart, fingers probing around my backside. I wondered what she was doing. Then, I felt it. She had inserted her finger into my anus. I tensed, but she moved gently, whispering, "Please, *cheri*, please relax." I tried to pull away from her. "No, please, let me . . ."

Her soft massaging finally relaxed me completely. Then, she was on me again, enveloping me completely in her warm mouth which, along with her finger, was unreal. The sensation was mind blowing. She moaned, I groaned, about to come, but she stopped, pulled her finger away, sat up on her legs and placed her hands on her hips. "No, you don't, my young American. Not this time. This one you are saving for me." With that, she snapped her finger against my penis.

I was throbbing, but that did it . . . Cold turkey.

She smiled and reached over to the night table. A small bowl of water sat there, a towel soaking in it. She squeezed water from the towel and wrapped the towel around my penis. I expected it to be hot. But it was ice cold . . . I pulled back.

"Ah, *cheri*, did you like that? It is very cold water from my spring house!" She removed the towel and massaged my face and entire body, then put the towel aside to plump up a pillow. She placed it beside my head and stretched out along side me.

"Why did you stop?" I ventured.

"Do not be impatient. This is the way a real French woman makes love. We draw it out and enjoy it." She felt of me. I was harder than ever. "Oooh, la, la, but let us talk for a while to calm him down."

I propped myself on an elbow, turning toward her. Somewhere I had gotten the idea that a woman in her forties lost her figure. I was wrong. Her breasts were so large and firm they jutted out like watermelons; her nipples were unusually large, almost brown, with a dark circle around them. I couldn't take my eyes away.

"Do you like them, *cheri*?" she said, leaning over to place a breast in my mouth.

I just did the natural thing.

After several minutes of this delightful sucking, she said, "Eduarde, please, my other one is jealous," and she pulled away, placing the other breast in my mouth. Then, she asked, "Do you like my body?"

"Danielle," I said, "you're absolutely beautiful."

She stretched against the pillow with her arms extended. "Then, make love to me all over, the way I made love to you," and she was gentle, not wild and domineering like Yvette had been.

I wanted to make love to her, to please her. I kissed her the way she had kissed me, exploring, touching, fondling every part of her body. The tantalizing scent of her excited me. She spread her legs apart and gently pushed my head down. But the 1944 American in me hesitated.

She pushed my head down again gently, firmly. Since I just couldn't do what she wanted, I kissed inside her thigh down to her knees and back up again. She pulled her legs up and spread them apart. "Eduarde, do you not wish to eat me?"

I mumbled, embarrassed. "I've never done it. I don't know if I can . . ."

"Do they not do this in America?"

"No, hardly anyone does that . . ."

"But there is nothing wrong. A woman who takes care of herself is beautiful and clean. A woman's vagina is like an instrument. It responds when one knows how to handle it. Have you ever looked at a woman closely?"

I didn't reply, though I'm sure the truth was evident on my face. I hadn't. Like most Americans, I made love in the dark.

She rose from the bed, went to the window and pulled the draperies open to allow light into the room. As she returned to the bed, she reached back and let her long hair fall free over her shoulders and to the middle of her back. Gently she pushed me down between her legs, pulled up her knees and spread her legs apart. "Look, please, look. I want to show you it is no mystery. It was the way God has made a woman, and it is something to be loved and enjoyed." Then, she took both hands, holding her vagina lips apart, explaining to me, showing me her vagina, the vulva, the opening and the small apperture at the top of the opening. She took my hand and made it touch the apperture, showing me how hard it was. "This is my clitoris, and this is what excites a woman. Many men do not know that. They are innocent blunderers." She rubbed my finger over it. "See. It is hard. I am aroused and my blood has rushed there, causing it to become erect just as the man does." She spread her vagina lips further apart and had me look into the depths of the opening. "Does it not look good?"

By now I was so aroused, I couldn't stand it. Bluntly I said, "I want to fuck you!" I couldn't stand to be tantalized any longer.

"I know, and I want to do the same to you. But you are too aroused. You would come in a hurry." She reached over to the bowl and removed the towel, repeating the cold water treatment. When she completed her work, I was still erect, but the throbbing had stopped. Now she knelt beside me and fondled her breasts, showing me how a woman likes to be touched, massaging the hard nipples with her fingertips. Then, she bent over, showing me how she looked from the back. Even the small puckered opening of her anus was beautiful. She was right. There was nothing dirty or vulgar about making love like this.

She lay down again and asked me to play with her, massage her clitoris, before I penetrated her. I kissed her, and with my free hand I did her bidding. She guided my fingers, moving them the way she liked. She was the master, and I was the student. And I was ready to graduate.

Danielle moaned and sighed. I started to mount her. She said, "Keep doing that, make me come first." She lifted off, grinding hard against my hand. I started to pull away. "No, no, continue."

My hand and fingers were growing wetter and wetter. She opened and closed her legs on my hand; then, she broke away from my mouth and yelled, "I am coming!"

I could feel her contractions on my fingers; it was a beautiful sensation, knowing exactly what was happening. I felt her passion run out and down her cheeks, as she moaned and screamed, throwing her head wildly from side to side.

I had thought Yvette was wild and orgasmic, but she couldn't compare to this beautiful woman. Her slow, gentle ways became a volcano, and the contrast was exciting. She placed her hand on top of mine and kept my fingers inside her. I felt her twitch, contract and pulsate slower and slower . . .

Next she pulled my head down against her breast and held me there like a baby at its mother's breast. I felt cheated. I wanted her badly. I began to move, but she said, "No, wait just a few moments." She pulled me down beside her.

Now I understood how she had felt when I had come. I was wet from my own secretion but still hard. She felt of me, reaching for the cold towel again and repeating the process of cooling me down. That done, she smiled at me, and without saying a word, straddled me, lowering herself down hard, almost slamming me.

The unexpected heat of her vagina enveloped me. I rose up to meet her, thrusting as hard as I could. "Lie still," she murmured, leaning over and pushing her enormous breasts against me; then, placing her mouth on mine, she began contracting, holding for several seconds, letting go, contracting, letting go. The woman was unbelievable; and I was going crazy.

Finally she sat up, asking, "How does that feel, *mon cheri*? Do you like me?"

What could I say?

Then, she explained exactly where I was inside of her, where my penis head was, and taking my hand pushed it against her small stomach, until I could almost feel myself . . . She started moving, rubbing her clitoris hard against me. For the first time, I realized what sex was all about; and it was tremendously exciting.

She started moving up and down, turned around and bent over, so that her breasts were against my shins. She urged me to prop my head up with a pillow; she wanted me to watch myself penetrating her. I did as instructed. Each time she drew away, she contracted, then, came down hard on me . . . Suddenly I wanted to be the master; I wanted to be in command. But each time I tried to squirm from under her, she stopped moving and began to talk. To keep me from coming, she talked about the weather, the river, the mountains, any damn thing.

How I kept up like this for so damn long without exploding, I'll never know. Finally, I said to hell with it. I toppled her over, forcing her down, and I'll be damned if she didn't pull her legs together, all the while laughing, tantalizing me, keeping me from spreading her legs apart to enter her.

We played around like this for a few minutes. I was absolutely crazy. Then, unexpectedly she opened wide and drew her legs back, her knees against my chest. I didn't need a guide as I penetrated her. It was magnificent!

She wrapped her strong legs around my back and started rotating. I penetrated her hard and fast, and she responded. She knew just how to move, pushing up against me. As I pulled back, she pulled away, all the time holding me tightly with those strong legs, still rotating gently. I couldn't keep this up forever, though. I said, "I have to come . . ."

"Wait, wait. Just a few more seconds."

I waited.

She yelled, "Now!" and the strength with which she grabbed me was unbelievable. She reached up and pulled my mouth down to hers, yelling, "Now, now, I am coming!"

I exploded as if there was no end to it.

Her hands clawed my back, digging in.

The pain was beautiful, and I collapsed on top of her, still throbbing.

We were both soaking wet. Perspiration rolled down my face and across my lips. She held me tighter than ever, never letting go, her legs wrapped firmly around me. I felt her pulsating and throbbing. She was the best I had ever had.

We stayed locked in each other's arms, until I went soft. She kept kissing me. Her hair tumbled over my face, covering me completely. Finally, I rolled over; we lay that way with her head against my chest . . . and I fell asleep, drained of everything!

– 20 –

I was awakened by a cool breeze blowing through the window and the last glow of the sun setting. Danielle lay beside me in sleep. A smile of contentment graced her beautiful face, and this was satisfying to me. Someone might have spilled a bucket of water in the bed, but never mind. Impulsively I reached over and touched her beautiful womanhood. No longer was it a mystery.

Gently I spread her legs, feeling how wet she was. Heat emanated from between her legs, and she awakened. "What are you doing, *mon cheri*?" she said with a smile.

"I can't believe how wet you are . . ."

"I have never been aroused like this before," she murmured. "You brought to me sensations I have never had before."

I knew she was lying through her teeth. But I appreciated her generosity.

I understood now why French women had the reputation they did. They knew the secret of making a man feel superior and performing beyond his capacity; and it certainly boosted the ego . . . I glanced at my wristwatch on the night table. I was stunned. It was a quarter of six; I mentioned the time to her.

She sat up quickly. "I had planned a magnificent dinner tonight. I wanted to cook it myself. Now look what you have done. You are a naughty boy, making me forget time."

All her flattery had its effect on me. I had grown erect again, though I knew I was just a boy in this marvelous woman's hands.

Smiling, she reached over and grabbed me. "What is this? Did I not satisfy you?" She leaned over, kissed me and whispered, "Do not worry, *mon amour*. I will not let that go to waste." She brought her head right down on me and started sucking. She pushed my skin down hard and sucked with such intensity, just drawing up on me, harder each time, steadily. I propped myself up to watch. I loved watching now. Each time she drew up her cheeks hollowed out from the force of suction. Soon I started coming. This time there was no tantalizing, no holding back, just that beautiful motion of hers, as she drew up on me. I thought I would go out of my mind as I exploded inside her mouth. But she kept on, not stopping, although she had drained me dry.

Somehow she had kept me firm. Then, before I knew what happened, she had stopped and mounted me quickly. She had been playing with herself while sucking me, and she came within minutes. The intensity of her orgasm hurt me, as she bounced up and down on me, screaming and moaning French phrases I didn't understand. Finally, she collapsed on top of me, her warm juices running down my leg and she moaned weirdly. I was afraid she was going to have a heart attack, but, no, she threw her arms around me, kissed me, her fingers digging into my shoulders. She was shaking . . .

At long last we both sat up and stared at one another. The contented look on her face was gratifying. I was proud. The student had pleased the teacher.

We had difficulty standing up. But we made it. Then, she embraced me. I was exhausted. But I knew damn well this magnificent woman had taught me a lesson, one that I'd never forget, not only teaching me the art and magnificence of a beautiful relationship, but the openness and frankness possible between man and woman. A woman, like a fine wine, is enhanced by age; a woman isn't in full bloom until she reaches her thirties. All others paled in comparison to Danielle.

Danielle wrapped a large towel around herself. She twisted her hair back and wrapped a small towel around her head. She looked divine and inviting as she stood there. Then, a quick parting kiss, *"Merci beaucoup,"* and she was gone.

I collapsed on the bed. Then, I realized what damage we had done. Those fine sheets were absolutely soaking wet and we had pulled runs in them. They were a mess. But I smiled to myself, thinking: I know damn well she won't mind!

Outside it had grown dark. I lit the small oil lamp on the night table. After a while, I acquired the strength to get up, put on my shorts and stumble across the hall to the bathroom. I'll be damned. I could tell the lady had taken a bath and used the bidet. But she had refilled the tub with hot water, laid out fresh towels, a washcloth and soap. Talk about knowing how to treat a man!

After a luxurious bath, I walked into the living room to find Robert still asleep and snoring. I moved on into the kitchen. And there she was, back to the original Madame Arlienne.

Her hair was pulled back and tied in a braided bun at the nape of her neck. She wore high heels and a beautiful low cut dress with a ruffled skirt that hung slightly above her knees. She didn't have to take a back seat to anyone with those legs, and I told her so.

She kissed my cheek and said, "Ooh la, la, Eduarde, *merci beaucoup*. I think you are becoming a Frenchman with your flattery." She was preparing dinner by herself, a fancy apron tied around her waist.

I felt at home here, pleasantly so. I stepped over to the stove and lifted the lid on a pan. "What smells so good?"

"That is our appetizer, *mon cheri*. I am fixing frog legs, sauteed in onions and wine.

With "frog legs" I lost my appetite, remembering those horrible raw frog legs Richard and I had eaten at the lake. Quickly I replaced the lid on the pan.

"Our main dish will be veal and ham cooked on top of one another and smothered in a special sauce. I haven't cooked in over a year, no desire and no energy. But our delightful *amour de matinee* has rejuvenated me. I feel like a carefree, young bride!"

"Why have you been so despondent?" I inquired delicately, feeling I must bring consolation to the conversation.

"Since I returned to the chateau, yes, I have been despondent," she admitted. "The chateau has been in my family for over 200 years. But my main home is outside Paris, near Versailles. Just a typical French Normandy home of twelve rooms. The chateau has nineteen rooms. My husband died a few months before the surrender of France. When the Germans came, I had to close the house. I couldn't get help. Even food was a problem. That was why I decided to return to the chateau." Then, very casually, she added, "It is here that I met Richard Baccard. As a matter of convenience he moved in with me. I know of his activities with the Resistance . . ." She stopped, as if she had already gone too far.

"Where is your help now?" I asked, for want of something better to say; after all, I had seen the old lady at breakfast along with several other servants.

"Only two of the men and the old lady stay at the chateau. The old lady is seventy-eight. She's worked for my family for sixty-one years. She raised me as a little girl. How time goes! I left to go away to school at seventeen. This is really the old lady's home more than it is mine. She's a member of the family. She can do as she pleases. I told Grandmere Anne to go to bed early. She wanted to cook dinner. In France even the old ladies enjoy romance. She told me that she had heard the sounds of love. She was happy to see me blossom like a beautiful flower in the spring after a cold winter."

I smiled at her fondly, enjoying this kitchen talk.

She went on, "Rene rented the chateau before the war. If I hadn't returned from Paris, he was going to get a woman to live with him. He doesn't want to arouse the suspicions of the Nazis."

"How does the old lady feel about the occupation?" I wanted to be certain of everyone's loyalty.

"Oh, she is so loyal they could cut out her tongue. She hates the Boche . . ." Here she shrugged. "It was inevitable that Rene and I should become intimate. But it is strictly a business relationship that I don't enjoy. There is more to Rene than I know, I suspect. What do you know of him?"

"I met him at the Maquis camp. I was amazed at his ability to have the German army truck with two German soldiers as drivers . . ."

She laughed. "Yes, he is most amazing in every respect. He has done more for the Resistance than practically any man in the south of France. I just hope he can get away with it until the war ends. Only a few weeks before you arrived, Rene went to the tower and extended antennas outside the small windows. He sent wireless radio messages — to where, I have no idea. I have seen him do this often. He is driving the Germans crazy. For over a year now they hear and intercept the coded signals, then try to shoot a fix on the location. But the high elevation of the chateau makes it difficult for them. The Gestapo, you know, use automobiles with rotating antennas. They actually threw a fix, whatever that is, around the chateau."

I explained a fix to her.

"Oh, I see. Rene says that it takes them ten to fifteen minutes to locate a signal. He transmits for about ten minutes, then he gets off the air."

On the occasion of the fix around the chateau, it seemed that a Colonel Heinrich of the Gestapo had driven up the mountain to the chateau. She and Rene were sitting on the porch by the time he arrived. They politely invited the colonel to have an afternoon aperitif with them. After settling down with his drink, the colonel had asked Baccard to help them; the Germans were sure the radio transmission signals were coming from somewhere on the mountain; the horrible Maquis had a portable transmitter, and they were sending from one location and moving to another.

The colonel had gone on to ask Rene if he would object to a truck with a rotating compass beacon and two men staying at the chateau for several days in an effort to pick up the signals.

Rene had agreed, arranged for the soldiers' quarters, and departed the next day, leaving Danielle alone with the soldiers. She was terrified they might find the radio in the tower. But after two days the transmissions began from another location some distance away. The two storm trooper technicians got a fix on the new signal: ten to fifteen kilometers away on another mountain range. They packed up and left to track the signal, convinced that the signal wasn't coming from anywhere near the chateau, deciding what had been happening was a "bounce effect" of the signals!

When Rene returned, he was very casual about the whole affair. "He has only ice water in his veins," Danielle said with a laugh.

"I hope ice water doesn't affect his sex life," I joked.

She shrugged. "Everything he does is mechanical. He can't keep his mind on making love, even for a few moments. He is also like you. He will not *mange le boire*."

I smiled, answering, "Give me time. I'm sure I'll learn . . ."

She snapped back quickly, "How about tonight?"

Dinner was prepared. I hurried to arouse Robert. He didn't want to be bothered. So, Danielle and I enjoyed the delicious dinner by candlelight and I pleased her by eating some of the frog legs.

We had finished our after-dinner brandy and had cleared away the dining room table. Danielle said, "Would you like to come to my bedroom and enjoy a drink of Napoleon cherry brandy on my private balcony? The balcony extends out over the valley. My father had it added to the master bedroom when I was a little girl. It is the most peaceful place on earth, my private world. I have never shared it with anyone, not even Rene."

As we prepared to go upstairs, I said, "Should we lock the doors?"

"Those doors have never been locked, unless Rene locked them when I wasn't here. Only the two wine cellars, the tower and the garage are locked."

Robert was half awake now. But all he wanted was another bottle of cognac. Danielle retrieved a bottle from the kitchen. A small oil lamp burned in the parlor. Leaving Robert, we went upstairs to the far end of the chateau in a small wing which jutted out on an angle to conform with the contours of the mountain. She had not shown this area to me in our earlier tour of the house.

We lit two oil lamps, turning the wicks up brightly. Though there were several paintings on the walls, mainly the walls were adorned with photos of her family and her childhood. I examined the photos. Some were of her great grandparents, all done up in early tintypes.

The fireplace was immense, floor to ceiling, dominating the master suite, and faced in Florentine marble. The hearth, mantle and fireplace, as well as the entire wall behind it, were stone. "It is," she said, "sexy and cozy here, especially when a fire is lit."

Inwardly I groaned. I was worn out.

We walked onto the little balcony, and, yes, the view was breathtaking . . . A bit of moonlight filtered through scattered clouds and the Dordogne River sparkled in the valley. Below the balcony was a sheer drop of perhaps 600 feet. I felt uneasy sitting out there since the balcony had been built away from the wall, though angle supports secured it to the stone walls, and there it had stood for many years.

I glanced down, and I wished she hadn't told me. The floor of the balcony had pulled away from the stone wall about an inch. "Let's go inside," I said. It was almost eleven o'clock, and the night had turned cool. "Is the wood in the fireplace ready to go?"

"Yes, all it needs is a match." She handed me a small pot with the lighter dipped in a liquid. I put a match to it and touched its flame to the bottom of the dry firewood. It burst into flame instantly. At first the heat was almost unbearable. But after the first intense heat, the fire became a thing of beauty. The draft and height of the chimney didn't allow a bit of smoke into the room.

As I stood enjoying the fire, she went off to return with a large bowl and pitcher, towels and other things. I wondered what she had in mind. The temperature was perfect, though the French doors were open.

She turned out the oil lamps. The fireplace was just enough light. The two large logs stacked on the kindling had settled down and burned slowly; they looked as if they might burn for hours.

Danielle came over, slipped her arms around me and kissed me softly. "Eduarde, will we go to bed?"

I was easy to persuade.

For a long while, on that beautiful bed, we lay on our stomachs, pillows propped at the foot, watching the fire. Quite naturally, we resorted to our delightful games of early afternoon. We pleased one another for a few hours, until we fell asleep entwined in one another's arms, sleeping lovingly, cozily together, until Grandmere tiptoed in the next morning to place a large tray on a round table which she moved to the bed. My keen nose picked up the aroma of hot coffee, rolls and pastry, French toast, honey and warm goat's milk. She had even placed a rose vase which matched the room on the table. It was filled with fresh flowers . . . And she left the room as quietly as she had come.

After the door closed, Danielle, a contented smile on her face, gave me a warm, lasting embrace. Then, we sat on the edge of the bed, enjoying our breakfast, nude. She thanked me for giving in to her needs and told me I was *tres expertise*.

Danielle instructed me as we ate; the goat's milk would restore my spent passion. Meanwhile, the honey came from the hives in the garden; these were the boxes I had seen behind the fountains. I said, "This place could become self-sustaining. You could even produce your own electricity without depending on the Germans." I had seen the spring which came down alongside the chateau; part of it was diverted into the spring house. "The drop of the water and the swiftness of the current could turn a small generator," I added.

Danielle laughed softly. "You have a mind like my father. He often mentioned such an idea and planned to do it himself. But there was always something else to do."

My watch told me it was almost ten o'clock. "It's late," I said.

"It doesn't matter." She yawned and sighed happily. "All I want to do is go back to bed, stay in bed and rest all day."

I wondered about that goat's milk as I dropped back against the bed.

Again, it was the towel treatment, only hot water this time. She played with me, biting and teasing me, and within minutes I was hard. She turned on her side, her back to me, and said, "Eduarde, enter me from the back, so I can feel you holding me. I love it so much that way."

I did, slipping my arm under her to cup her breast, my other hands fingering her from the front. She was a tight, wet furnace, and it was sensational. Soon we came together in a wild thrashing climax.

As we relaxed she murmured, "This is a beautiful way to awaken." She kept me within her with her contractions. But we fell asleep for a short while to awaken . . . And I found myself still inside of her, her warm round derriere pushed up tightly against me.

Said Danielle, "Let's bathe together."

How could I resist?

The one thing, I decided as we entered the bathroom together, to which I'd never become accustomed, was the ease with which she went to the bathroom in front of me, then used the bidet without embarrassment. She asked me if I'd seen a bidet before. I couldn't help telling her about our initial encounter with a bidet.

We were on our first visit to the Dorchester Hotel in London. The two rooms assigned to us had a large step-up bathroom between them with a bidet next to the washstand. Our navigator, Bob Lemuewell, had never seen one though he was a college graduate with a master's degree. So, Bill and I decided we'd pull a good one on him since he was like a little old lady, even doing his own washing, ironing and sewing.

I started off by telling Bob that the English were ahead of us in bathroom facilities. The way to use it was to turn on the spray so it shot up about two feet. Then you could wash your face without using the same water again. We also told him it was the proper way in which to brush his teeth. I'll be damned if our "little old lady" navigator, a confirmed bachelor, didn't go for it, thinking it was delightful.

Bill and I rolled on the floor, laughing our heads off. We had to tell him, though. While Bob wasn't thrilled by the joke, he took it well.

Danielle laughed at the story, her sense of humor was delicious. God, I thought, if this gal was my age I'd pack her up and take her home. Then, we had a wonderful bath together, another unforgettable moment with Danielle.

We dressed and went downstairs. Robert was sitting at the kitchen table, having breakfast and looking hung over, his hair tussled, his face unshaved, his eyes bloodshot. Danielle and I sat at the table, and Grandmere Anne placed a large oval plate before each of us. On my plate were three pieces of bun with all kinds of sauce and a piece of ham on each. On top of the ham were three eggs with more sauce atop the eggs. Danielle was served the same, except she had two eggs. I had never tasted anything like this back in the states, and I became an Eggs Benedict fan right then and there.

We were eating, enjoying ourselves just fine, Danielle and I bantering back and forth about goat's milk and its wonders, when the buzzer alarm sounded from the guard at the bottom of the hill . . . One long buzz and two short. I sat alert, all ears.

Danielle said, "Relax. That is the signal that everything is fine and a friend is coming up. It must be Rene, Marcel and the others."

Some minutes later, they pulled into the courtyard behind the chateau. They were driving Baccard's gray Citroen. Danielle and I greeted them, acting disappointed that they'd not arrived the day before.

We all congregated at the table, and they were served breakfast. Then, the story came tumbling out. The truck had gotten away with the supplies dropped by the British planes. Baccard had left with two Maquis, while Marcel and about a dozen other men set up a blockade for the Germans at the bottom of the hill. I remembered that several of the men had dropped off the truck when we had reached the bottom of the hill and they had built a roadblock across the narrow road quickly, mining large boulders with plastique explosives above on the side of the hill. So, when the Germans reached the blockade, everything was set.

The German armored car had plowed right into the blockade, the second car hitting the first. The two motorcycle riders beside the first car went over the steep bank. Then, the Maquis opened up with automatic weapons from the hills above, cutting the Germans to ribbons. When the second German unit heard the firing, they came rushing right along. They stopped and their troops went ahead on foot, attacking. Here the explosives were set off, sending the large boulders down on the first unit. Marcel was embarrassed. "It is the first tactical error I have made in a long time. My professor of military tactics at St. Cyr would have failed me." Marcel was a graduate of the French military academy, similar to our West Point.

Baccard joked, "Everyone is entitled to a mistake or two." Then, he casually mentioned they had killed about thirty of the German Storm Troopers and destroyed most of the German vehicles. "We had the advantage of being up on the hill."

"We lobbed mortars on them. Only five Maquis were killed and a few injured," Marcel put in. "We needed those supplies. The men did their job well."

"Yes," said Baccard. "But we didn't get the gold. I cannot understand it. We had been promised gold Napoleons to buy food and supplies for the Maquis in the Dordogne sector. Plus, we need that gold to bribe the Germans. They like to salt the gold away for after the war. Millions of dollars in gold have been paid via these drops."

I sat listening; then, it hit me why that container had been so heavy which Paul and I had hidden in the river. It was gold! "How much gold do they usually send?" I asked.

"Around 180,000 pounds!"

I felt the blood rush to my head. That was about $720,000! Only Paul and I knew the whereabouts of that gold, and Paul was dead. Robert had gone ahead to meet us down at the large oak tree along the river. I hesitated.

I had come from a family of ordinary means. The thought of that gold was beyond my comprehension, but I couldn't help recollecting all I had heard of secret agents, French, British and German, buying up property, jewelry, gems and objects of art under false names to profit after the war. Why, Marcel himself had told me in Ussel in Father Philippe's presence about an intelligence agent in the Dijon sector secretly buying a large champagne-producing company with gold. No one knew for sure the man was an agent, but he kept coming up with gold. Case closed. Real money was scarce and most banks were closed. Evidently it was a vicious circle. The Germans bribed many of the French with gold, setting up their own agents, and these agents in turn used the gold to buy up valuable properties. And the same held true with some Allied agents.

I wondered: Since the Germans were starting to transfer and flee north, how long would the war last? Would the Maquis really need the gold?

Subconsciously my hand slipped into my jacket pocket where I fingered the two Napoleons I had. Solid gold, soft, beautiful gold. I removed a Napoleon from my pocket and asked innocently, "Are they like this?" I showed them the gold pieces given to me.

Baccard answered, "Yes. When Germany overran France almost all of the gold stored by the French government was in Napoleons. These were by far the most popular of gold pieces, and all of them, along with the bullion, were transferred and stored in banks in England. Actually, it is France's own money being used. There were billions of dollars in gold bullion . . ."

"What about the paper money I see everywhere?"

He laughed. "There are several suitcases of it in the garage . . ." Then, he sobered, as if the matter of the missing gold weighed heavily on his mind, and puffed at an empty pipe. The calm he usually carried with him was gone.

Perhaps something else is worrying him, I thought . . . Then, I realized if I told them about the gold now, I'd look like a traitor to their eyes. What to do? Finally I decided to wait a day or two and say that I remembered Paul had seen a parachute floating toward the river.

Marcel said bleakly, "The Germans have probably found it. They were still fighting savagely until almost daylight, when more reinforcements came up. Even a German spotter plane started to cover the top of the mountain where we were. We were lucky as hell to get out of there . . . those of us who did. After we got away, we crossed the river and went up into the hills. With Jacques' binoculars I looked down and I could see dozens of German soldiers combing the fields, covering every spot. They knew a drop had occurred and didn't think we'd gotten away. They wouldn't dream their own truck participated, let alone their own men."

One part of me told me to keep quiet about the gold; the other part, listening to Marcel, told me differently. Then, I considered a year or two after the war. If I volunteered to stay in the service and help in the army of occupation, it would be easy for me to come back here again. I would have an excuse: a luscious French woman named Danielle. Now I considered what she had told me about Baccard. I thought I could use her, since she was bound to be rid of him, once the war ended.

My mind was fantasizing, I suppose. All I had to do was keep my mouth shut. I would come back, spend a few months with Danielle, get the proper equipment and salvage the gold. Then, I began to wonder how I could get the gold back to the states. Nothing to it! I could dispose of it through black markets for American currency. Marcel had told me that Marseilles was almost an open port; all kinds of smuggling, black market, exchange of currency, and even hard drugs were processed and sold there. Hell, I could leave the gold there for four or five years, if necessary. I had earned it. I was entitled to it. Without me,the gold might not have been saved from the Germans.

Finally Baccard said, "We'll wait for things to cool down. Then, we'll all go look for it in daylight.I've already alerted a couple of my German agents at headquarters. I'll get word from them on what has been found."

That was it. I made up my mind. Sure . . . I had done my share. I had flown twenty-nine of the deadliest combat missions, been wounded, shot down on my thirtieth and last mission, spent all these months fighting the Germans, and fighting for the French. Better that I have the gold than those bastard Germans!

Only one thing bothered me now. We would be leaving tonight. Brive, which wasn't far away, was to be the scene of another air drop. Baccard was to contact Free French Radio and set it up.

Danielle and Grandmere Anne prepared a beautiful dinner for us. The large dining room was filled with wonderful food, compliments, drinking and toasting. Danielle sat next to me, and I was uncomfortable under her constant attention. Colonel Marcel's sharp eyes didn't fail to notice, and his smile for me was one of amused understanding.

After our final after-dinner drink, a fine rare aged brandy, Marcel said to me casually, "Her beauty is like this brandy; it improves in taste, quality and body each day it grows older." Then, his eyes leveled with mine. "I do so hope you enjoyed the fine bouquet and taste of this brandy."

I felt my face flush; and I sensed Baccard looking at me curiously.

So, now it was time to go, say our farewells. After much ado, exchanging knowing glances with Danielle, hugs and embraces, I stepped into Baccard's car with Marcel, Robert, and a new arrival, Charles. The plan was simple. Baccard knew the checkpoints. He would let us out before each stop. We would take to the woods and go around the checkpoints to meet him down the road.

Marcel apologized to me for the delay in getting to Perigeuex. But that would definitely be our next destination after Brive. Soon we were at the first checkpoint, a main intersection of two highways, blockaded with gates and a guard station. We got out, took to the woods and cut back to the road. Baccard was waiting. His papers and association with the Germans enabled him to go anywhere without trouble. His identity card and permission pass were from the highest command, the Commanding General of the Gestapo for the entire district.

Meanwhile, I daydreamed about the gold. Either way, I had been committed after the first few moments by not saying anything. I knew that when we went back there I could easily point out the drag marks near the river, become a real detective and walk over to the water. The only catch was the harness and parachute; Paul and I had picked them up, wrapping them around a large rock and tossing them into the water not far from the container. The swiftly moving water, though, might tear them apart and carry them downstream. There seemed little chance of the parachute and harness being discovered near the container; that is, if I decided to reveal the location of the gold. Yes, I was torn. But, then, again . . .

What about all the draft dodgers who used every angle and excuse to keep from serving, the war profiteers, the merchants who gouged G.I.s? My mind went back to a small Oregon town. A buddy, Bob Millen, and I had won an old 1937 Packard in a crap game in Rapid City, South Dakota. We were driving to our new station, Geiger Field, Spokane, Washington. We had stopped in this town, checked into the local hotel and met two girls. I recollected asking the desk clerk where we could buy a bottle of bourbon and he told us the hotel charge was $8.00 but that we could buy it for $3.50 at the liquor store. We hadn't been paid in months. Since we were combat crewmen and moved around so much, often it took months for payroll records to catch up to us, so we were low on cash. Anyway, we decided to go to the liquor store. There we were told the price was $7.00 a bottle. When we told the clerk what the man at the hotel had said about the price, he said, "Sorry, soldier, that's the price." The price had gone up in a hurry!

Events of this kind kept flashing through my mind while I remembered my career being nipped in the bud. The best years of my life! Why not?

We reached Brive where we hid in an abandoned farm house, sleeping on the ground that night. What a comedown after the luxury of a wonderful bed shared with a beautiful woman!

We went through the same routine at Brive. A much larger single plane, perhaps a Lancaster, came over. Since there was no moon, the drop came swiftly. We all kept our eyes on the parachutes as they floated down. We retrieved the equipment and supplies without trouble, though not quite as much was dropped as before. Approximately fifty members of the F.T.P.F. and the F.F.I. surrounded the area; no chances were being taken.

We returned the next night the same way, passing blockade after blockade back to an area not far from the delightful chateau. Baccard drove down the mountain and into the valley boldly, the scene of the drop. By now I was thinking a bit differently about that gold.

I remembered I was a first generation American. My parents had come to the United States as immigrants. I was a natural-born American. All our relatives, friends and people of the same heritage were so very proud of me; I had become an officer with little formal education . . . I smiled as I thought of my first leave home after I became a second lieutenant. I was treated like General McArthur. Hundreds of people came to our home to pay their respects. All of my relatives, every single one of them, and friends of my family came to visit. In the four days at home, relatives and friends of the family sent over food. The butcher didn't give a damn about any ration coupons and sent dozens of steaks. I was treated with respect and admiration. But if I kept the gold: What if I got fouled up, tripped up, somehow? Disgrace and humiliation waited at the end of the road. I didn't care about me. I was single. But what about my father and mother, my sister and my brothers? They cared; they believed in me. I made up my mind.

All the money in the world wasn't worth bringing disgrace to my family. I had grown up in the roughest, toughest section in Allentown, Pennsylvania, the Sixth Ward. Too many of my friends had gone off to reform school, some to prison.

At fourteen years old and in the ninth grade, I had run away from home to New York, working in restaurants and clubs from March until late fall when school began. I had started singing, first in a joint in Greenwich Village, in time getting a job as a page boy at Radio City Music Hall. Despite all this, I had never been in trouble once. Always I kept to the straight and narrow; I had learned to take care of myself. Now that I was an "officer and a gentleman" with a reserve commission from the President of the United States of America, Franklin Delano Roosevelt, I didn't feel like throwing it all away. Yes, I had made up my mind by the time we reached the valley . . .

We hid the car beneath the large trees. I emphasized that we had seen the first parachute come down off to our right toward the river. Since the Germans hadn't found the drop and neither had the Maquis, I asked, "What about the possibility of the drop falling into the river?"

It was like striking a match. We headed for the river.

The river water wasn't quite as muddy or deep. But the deeper areas seemed to be in eddies near the shore. I brought this to their attention. Eureka! Perhaps the container had fallen in the middle of the river!

I spotted the two large rocks. Off to one side was an area where water did not move swiftly. It was much deeper there, possibly eight to ten feet deep. As I walked by the exact spot, moss had been torn away from the large rock. I pointed this out to Marcel.

"I wonder," he said, "if something tore the moss away. It sounds logical!" He called to Baccard and Robert. They looked and couldn't see anything. Paul and I had picked the perfect hiding place; unless the water level dropped considerably, there was no way anyone was going to see anything.

Robert found a long tree limb and pulled the branches off, making a pole about ten feet long. He probed the water with it. Nothing, of course.

Another Maquis, Jame, offered to dive in, after a futile search of an hour. God, this had been the perfect place to leave the gold, if I wanted it. I said, "It has to be here. Where else could it be?"

Jame stripped down to his shorts and dived in. I wasn't about to do the same; it would've looked too obvious.

Jame came up; he had found nothing. Down he went again. Nothing. "But I felt something as I turned to come up for air!" he said. "I felt it with my foot, and it wasn't a rock." Now he tried to figure out what to do. He picked up a good sized rock and held it as he jumped into the water. The rock kept him down, and when he broke the surface, he screamed, "I found it, I found it! It's the container. But we can't lift it."

We all let out a yell of joy!

Baccard had brought along a heavy rope. Robert and Jame went into the water, weighted down by small rocks, just enough to keep them on the bottom. After three or four tries, they looped the rope around the container, we all pulled, and up it came. We dragged it to shore, after another rope had secured it, and eager hands tore off the quilted cover. There was the container, and out came the bags: ten of them, each bag heavily loaded with gold Napoleons. So much for my dreams . . . But I had made the right choice. My heart and my conscience felt lighter.

Marcel removed a handful of gold coins and showed them to me. Then, he took about twenty or thirty coins and handed them to me, evidently a mind reader. "Here," he said, "you might need these in getting to Spain. You never know what might come up. But if you do get back, they'll make a beautiful necklace for your mother or sister . . ." And, he added slyly, with a wink, "Even a girlfriend."

I wasn't bashful about accepting the coins. I loaded them into the large pockets of my jacket, running my fingers through them. I was satisfied. This was more than I had expected.

Marcel drew tight the strings of the open bag and replaced the bag in the container. Then, we loaded the container into the car.

We took off to meet the Maquis who were to go with us to Perigeuex. I felt downhearted when we passed the road which led to the Dordogne River and up to the chateau. I strained my eyes, looking up the mountain. But I couldn't see the chateau.

– 21 –

Two hours later we were outside Perigeuex. We pulled to a halt at a Maquis barricade. Heavy fighting had broken out. The Maquis were fighting German soldiers left behind; Marcel had given instructions for them to wait. But the Germans had started it and the Maquis were elated. Liberation was at hand. The last of the S.S. troops had pulled out the night before. Only about 100 Wermacht soldiers remained with several junior officers in command.

"How did it start?" Marcel demanded.

A Maquis said, "All during the night the Germans loaded trucks with paintings, objects of art, all stolen, of course." In fact, a fat German major had commandeered a moving van, his soldiers loading it with antique furniture and paintings he'd confiscated and furnished his villa with during the occupation. He had departed about two o'clock that morning with a squad of his most trusted troops. The Maquis had been waiting with an ambush. The troops were killed, but the van caught fire during the skirmish and the priceless antiques had been lost. The major had escaped with his skin and a French mistress.

Marcel turned to me and explained, "The German officers took over the finest homes and villas, the best, as well as the hotels. They lived the good life with their girlfriends and mistresses."

"But how could a French woman do this?" I said.

"Simple. For food and money, they are betrayers, all of them, and they will pay."

"How?" I wondered aloud.

"You will see!" He signaled for the car to move ahead.

Heavy firing and explosions could be heard in Perigeuex as we approached. I was eager to see and possibly join the fighting. But Marcel insisted, "You have gone through enough. I do not want to lose you . . . No, you have done enough."

We circled around the town to a point where other Maquis from St. Etienne were waiting for us. I felt my excitement growing. Soon I'd be reunited with my old buddy Richard. We had gone through hell together, and I didn't want to lose him now.

All the roadblocks, as we circled Perigeuex, were a delight. They were manned by Maquis, members of the F.T.P.F. and the F.F.I., fighting with anything they could lay hands to, shovels and pitchforks as a last resort. We heard tales of heroic fighting, of many casualties. But the French had had enough, despite the well equipped, hard core professionals of the German army who were ordered to stay and fight.

We took a short cut through Perigeuex. But as we started to turn a corner, mortar shells began hitting close to us, and we came to a stop. We were near the Perigeuex prison, and most of the German soldiers had retreated to the prison where they were killing political prisoners and captured Maquis. They were firing from behind heavy walls, and the entrance gates were barricaded with sandbags. The natural fortifications and fixed machine gun towers added to the danger.

We watched the action, Marcel insisting I stay near him. Unfortunately the Maquis weren't having much effect on the heavily fortified German positions. Meanwhile, the town itself was almost clear of Boche, with the exception of a few holdouts at the Vichy police station where some Vichy police were allied with the Germans. That was hard to swallow, the Vichy fighting with the Germans, and I said as much.

Marcel said, "They've grown accustomed to the power they have. Now they know their goose is cooked and they're marked for execution by the Resistance. We have a list of collaborators and traitors three pages long; they will be dealt with." The tone of his voice left no doubt about it.

We stayed on for almost two hours, Marcel shaking his head and saying, "The Maquis are getting nowhere."

Two German tanks were set up at both entrances to the prison; their cannons were taking a hell of a toll on the Maquis. Now, with it growing dark, matters would only worsen. Marcel made the decision to leave.

A half-hour later found us driving up a beautiful, wide, tree-lined street. As we came to a hotel, I saw a group of people standing out front, and there was a familiar face. It was Richard!

He wore the beret and jacket of a Frenchman, a machine gun slung over his shoulder. When the car came to a stop, I jumped out, and we embraced. Then, we both started talking at once. Finally, we shook our heads, promising we'd fill one another in at a later time. For now, we escaped the growing clamor in the streets by entering the hotel restaurant which had been the German officers' mess. The

German troops had been billeted next door.

Women, children, men, everyone, began filtering into the streets, shouting with jubilation, waving flags, blowing whistles, men firing weapons in the air. Except for the prison, the town was free of Germans. Just as soon as the hotel was checked for booby traps, this would be headquarters, and we'd all move in.

The restaurant was serving food as swiftly as possible. But the kitchen was too small to handle the many men who had congregated there. We were served a German soup and sandwiches. There was plenty of wine, beer, cognac; everything was being broken out. Two large wine barrels sat on the counter. The taps were turned on, and we helped ourselves.

Our meal completed, we were notified the hotel was clear. Eagerly we went along with Marcel and his men to the lobby. Baccard had gone ahead of us.

The hotel was lovely, perhaps four stories high. Through the back was a delightful courtyard with benches, shrubbery and a fountain. Rooms overlooked a courtyard. The Germans had lived first class.

Even with the years of occupation, the hotel carpeting was clean and in excellent shape. Rooms were being cleaned out. Everybody was congratulating each other. Rene shook my hand. It was like a 4th of July picnic. I was so damned weary, though, I dropped into a chair.

Rene said, "You will have the same rooms the German general staff had. They are on the third floor, the largest rooms in the hotel."

The operators of the hotel were the same people who ran the hotel during the German occupation. Finally they got everything shipshape. The city electricity came on and the world lit up like a Christmas tree. Everything was working, including the elevator!

As we started toward the elevator, Richard suggested we take food and wine to our room. We grabbed Rene and he took us to the hotel manager, Andre, and introduced us, telling him I was American and Richard was English.

Immediately Andre began apologizing, saying, "I am not a collaborator . . ." He spoke broken English, a short, fat, bald-headed bastard.

I didn't like him from the start.

Rene told him what we wanted.

"Anything you want, anything you want," he said, bowing and ingratiating.

Rene turned away from him and whispered to us, "He has been accused of collaboration. He will probably be tried." Then, he smiled coldly. "But we need him for now." Then, he called the Maquis lieutenant in charge; his name was Jean. He emphasized we were to get anything we desired or wanted.

The Maquis clicked to attention. "*Mon* Colonel Eduarde, I am at your service."

Rene called out to Andre, "Take them to their room. Don't forget they want food and drink." He and the lieutenant went off to attend to other business.

Andre led us into the kitchen, saying, "You will have the best."

We took a few bottles of wine. Then, we noticed bottles of German beer and we grabbed these. Andre removed a large cold roast from the refrigerator and said he would warm it up for us. But first he would show us to a special room off the hall. In the room were about twenty young girls, all nude, but not the least bit sexy. Some of them were crying and the others were obviously unhappy. They had been stripped of their clothing and were guarded by two Maquis who seemed oblivious to their nudity.

The girls were collaborators, the mistresses of German officers; they had thumbed their noses at the French men and women during the occupation, becoming like Nazis themselves, gloating over others when they had plenty to eat, clothes to wear, jewelry to impress. Now it was over. To Andre, I said, "What's going to happen to them?"

"You shall see. They still have a few more to round up. Already plans are being made. Tomorrow will be the day of *La Liberacion.*"

The name of the S.S. major who had occupied our room was still on the door. Hastily Andre ripped it off, apologizing for this oversight.

The room was large and lovely with twin beds. To one side was a small sitting room with a loveseat, two chairs, and desk; a window overlooked the garden in the center of the hotel. German newspapers lay on the coffee table. I glanced at them out of curiosity. Evidently the German officer was from Kiel, since these were the newspapers he read, stacked in rotation day by day. I remembered how I used to get my hometown newspapers. They'd catch up to me in packages, seven or eight at a time. I did the same thing, stacking them in rotation by date.

Stationery, letters he had received and photographs of the officer's family were piled on the desk. I smiled to myself. The bastard had departed in a hurry . . . But I did feel a twinge of pity for him as I looked at his wife and two children. Shaking my head, I began opening drawers. Well, I'll be damned!

The drawers were filled with clean shirts, shorts, socks . . . I even found a heavy German wristwatch, a German ring with a swastika blazing on top. But the item that caught my eye was a beautiful German short dress sword with belt and inscribed buckle. The inscription read *Gott Mit Uns.* Even I could figure that out: God With Us!

After what the Germans had done at Oradour-sur-glane, how could they even use the word God? They were mother-fucking murderers . . . I turned away and concentrated on the sword, trying not to think.

The sword was magnificent, the blade engraved with swastika

markings and German inscriptions. I dug down further into the drawer and hit another jackpot: a beautiful, shiny black leather holster. I opened it eagerly and there it was: a handsome Luger, not the ordinary Luger made for junior officers, but a well-made Luger which hadn't been mass produced. I held the gun up.

Andre acted flustered.

I glared at him.

"Anything you find," he muttered, "is yours. Anything. It is yours."

"You are damn, fucking well right. Anything we find is ours. You better believe it," I said harshly. "Especially since you've been kissing ass to these Krauts all the years of occupation."

His lips began to tremble, his body too. Then, of all the goddamn things, he dropped to his knees, clenched his hands, as if in prayer, and begged, "Please, colonel, please, colonel, have mercy. I only did what I had to do, Colonel Eduarde."

I felt like kicking the bastard in the face. He had kissed ass just like the rest of them.

The beds were messy, and I was feeling cocky. "I want these rooms cleaned immediately," I snapped. "Fresh linens, pillows and blankets. Do you understand? I will not sleep in the bed of some dirty, fucking Kraut. And," I paused for effect, "if it isn't done within thirty minutes, I'll shoot you myself. I have no use for anyone who associated with the Nazis!"

"Yes, *mon colonel*. Yes, *mon colonel Americain*. Please have mercy."

Word had gotten around that I was *le Premier Americain*. But he had no idea who I was or from where I came. As the gossip spread, it had built to the point where I was now a high-ranking officer. Me, of all people! But Andre believed every word I said, and I enjoyed seeing him crawl.

The poor bastard disappeared. He was back in fifteen minutes with two men in aprons. Politely he said, "We will install new box springs and mattresses from a room not occupied by Germans." He swore up and down, "By my mother's grave this is so," and continued to apologize for the inconvenience, while adding, "Anything you want is yours."

"We want more cold beer, cheese or cold cuts, until the roast is ready," I said sternly. "Oh, and coffee served with the roast beef!"

Richard was lounging in a chair, his feet propped on the window sill, laughing his head off. Now he said, "Boy, I've heard everything, Ed. You must have really made an impression. All I've heard is Colonel Eduarde . . . Goddamn, you've had one hell of a promotion . . . Maybe it'll stand up when we get back to England and we'll collect your back pay!"

We were like a couple of kids, laughing and joking, as the bedding was changed. Then, a short, dumpy woman (it seemed all of them were short and dumpy) entered the room. She too apologized, going

222

down on her knees, taking my hand and kissing it like she might be kissing the ring of the Pope. I couldn't believe it!

This sent Richard into a fit of hysterical laughter. "What the fuck did you do, Ed? I heard you got yourself involved and helped blow up a tunnel — a big hero. But what else did you do?"

Colonel Marcel walked in and embraced me. "I am so happy that you are reunited with your friend Richard. It makes me happy, happy for you both." He turned to Richard. "Your friend Eduarde has distinguished himself with much bravery. For this, I can assure you, he will be awarded our *Croix de Guerre* with the Silver Star. I, for one, would honor him with the French Legion of Honor, but it can only be bestowed upon a Frenchman. The *Croix de Guerre* is our nation's highest award for one who is not French. And this pleases me greatly." Then, he turned to me, and I'll be damned if he didn't say, "Eduarde, did you tell Richard about the girl in Ussel and your marathon session?" He laughed; he had a great sense of humor. "Oh," he continued, as he moved to leave the room, "I heard about your delightful conquest at the chateau." He clucked his tongue. "*Mon ami*, you outdo me as a lover without doubt. But, of course, you have the advantage. You are a much younger and stronger man." He returned to embrace me as if I might be his son.

Like the good son I was, I showed him the sword, Luger and holster. "What about these? Can we keep them?"

"They are yours. Anything you wish to take from the Germans is yours. If you want any of their mistresses, they are downstairs. Go and take your choice."

"Are you serious?" Richard asked.

"They are all going to be tried tomorrow in the square. If you want any of them for the night, you are welcome. They are pigs. But my orders are that you are to have anything you want in this hotel, in this city, anything. I repeat, anything within our power to grant." Now his glance was for me. "Eduarde, I mean this with all my heart." He shook my hand and departed.

Richard had stood when Marcel entered. Now he fell back into his chair. "Ed, what in hell did you do? I don't believe it. What in the fuck did you do? It must have been a bloody good show to be lauded like this by the head Maquis. C'mon, tell me."

"Later," I said.

Another woman came into the room. While the little, short, fat, dumpy woman changed the linens and put on fresh blankets, the second woman scrubbed the bathroom. I walked into the bathroom and told her sternly, "Do a good job."

"*Oui, mon colonel, oui, mon colonel*, do not worry, *oui, oui*." She understood every word I had said. She scrubbed harder.

By now, the other woman had finished the linens and was cleaning the floor. It was like hell's a-poppin'.

Richard sat back in his chair, laughing and drinking his beer.

Then, he reached down and felt something along the cushion pad. He brought out a wallet, the German officer's wallet. It contained French and German money, his cards, photos . . . Richard counted the money, thinking he had hit the jackpot.

I brought out a half-dozen gold pieces from my sagging jacket pocket. "Here, do you want some *real* money?"

His eyes widened. "My god! Gold pieces!"

"Yep. Napoleons." I gave them to him.

He shook his head. "No . . ."

I showed him I had more.

Now he didn't hesitate. "These will make a hell of a souvenir . . ."

"I'm thinking of having mine made into a bracelet for my sister," I said, "and another bracelet for a girlfriend of mine."

Meanwhile, everything was happening in that room. The bathroom had been scrubbed, and that woman was brushing down the draperies. Andre arrived, pushing a large serving cart covered with a white tablecloth upon which were plates covered with silver warming covers. This was class!

He had brought along a large chunk of roast beef, boiled potatoes, a salad, hot loaves of bread with butter and a dozen bottles of various wines. He arranged two chairs on either side of the cart and sliced the roast beef. Here he paused to don an apron, becoming our waiter and hustling off to return in minutes with a bucket of ice cubes. I hadn't seen ice cubes since London.

The wine wasn't chilled, so I instructed him to put ice cubes in the large glasses and pour the wine over the ice cubes. Still and all, I'd just about had my fill of wine. "Anymore beer around?"

"But, of course, *mon colonel*. There is plenty of beer. It is all German. But it is good, I assure you."

"Get it," I barked.

He rushed off, returning with a dozen bottles of beer in a large water bucket filled with chipped ice. I pulled out a bottle and read the label. It was Lowenbrau, a dark German beer. I hate to admit it, but the beer was good.

Andre uncovered a large tray filled with sliced cheese, salami, and assorted German cold cuts. He stood back, ready to serve us.

I said, "Get your ass to hell out of here!"

"Would you like to have me clean out the clothing?"

"We will do that!" I yelled.

Then, Richard and I went through the rest of the drawers, hoping to find something of interest. There was nothing. I had an idea. I grabbed up the phone and got the manager on the line. "Come up here!" I yelled at him. He arrived flushed and gasping for breath; I thought he was going to have a heart attack. "Find us another room which was occupied by a high-ranking German officer; one that's not been searched."

Andre thought a minute. "Yes, yes," he said, "there is one on the fourth floor. Come this way."

We followed him, locking our room behind us, to hit the jackpot in the other room. We found a Luger with holster and belt, not unlike the one I prized. We also found a beautiful, double-barreled German shotgun, hand engraved; accompanying it was a hunting jacket and a special shooting vest. The officer had obviously loved to hunt birds. Mounted pheasants were in the room, as were shooting trophies. We were souvenir hunters now, and we were having a ball.

On our return to our own room, we found another room. But it was empty. So, we had to settle for enjoying the food and wine.

We didn't stop to wash. We just started eating, making pigs of ourselves. We tried everything, mixing wine and beer in the process. The only thing we didn't touch was the cognac. Then, we washed up in a bathroom that wasn't bad at all. It had a shower, straight from Germany, engraved: *fabriken Germany.* It had probably been installed especially for the German officer. Oh well, it was my first good shower since I left the states. It had a fully adjustable head and was very well engineered. That was one thing about these damn Germans, they were good at engineering things.

After I finished showering, I shaved; then it was Richard's turn. He was delighted; he hadn't had a bath since we were both scalped, cleaned and bathed in St. Etienne. He stayed in there until the hot water ran out. Then I picked up the phone and called our dear friend Andre, screaming at him, "No hot water!"

Andre promised immediate reformation on the hot water front, while huffing and puffing, the prelude to a heart attack.

Richard didn't care. He was finished with his bathing. So, now we set to work trying on the clothes. We had grabbed a bunch of shirts, socks, etc., from the room we had visited on our souvenir hunt. With those in our room we figured to end up looking spiffy. We did. We wore gray shirts with shoulder epaulets, the insignia removed from the shoulders. We were clean and neat from the skin out.

In the streets the excitement was mounting, attended by yelling and screaming. "Let's join in," I suggested.

"Righto!" said Richard.

I donned my beret with the American and French flag sewn on; and we went down to the lobby to step into pandemonium.

The bar was wide open, filled with Maquis elite. Marcel had gone, but Captain Jacques was there to tell us Marcel was taking charge of the prison. The Boche had run out of cannon shells for the two tanks, and the mortar fire had stopped. Things were looking better. Then, he told us, "Over 100 Maquis have been killed. Now, with the exception of the prison, every Boche in town has been killed or captured."

Good news, bad news, and good news . . .

"Come, Eduarde," he said. "I want to show you something." He led us to the room off the rear corridor, the room where we had seen the

225

nude girls earlier.

Records had been kept on these girls for the past three or four years. They had accounted for all the girls on the list except for two who had escaped with the Germans and one who had committed suicide by taking poison with her German lover.

"These last days have been a riot with the German officers trying to leave with everything they could carry. They loaded up cars, trucks, motorcycles, trying to steal everything." He paused in thought. "The Maquis stopped most of them. But it is sad. Many brave Maquis were killed. The bodies are all at the morgue or hospital for identification by their families and relatives. Today is the day of liberation. Tomorrow will be the mass burial. We do not have facilities for preparing the dead. Many wooden coffins are being readied hurriedly."

It was amazing to see how well organized the F.T.P.F. Maquis were. They didn't miss a trick. Many former members of the military and city bands were polishing their instruments for the funeral procession.

Meanwhile, the Germans had destroyed much. They had blown up most of the telephone system, the banks and warehouses. The main airfield outside town, for all practical purposes, had been destroyed and was booby-trapped. We asked Jacques if by chance any planes had been saved.

"Not a single one. Everything blown away. Everything. The runways are so badly torn up it will take weeks to repair them."

Richard was enjoying the sight of all the naked woman. "What are you going to do with them?" he asked.

"Tomorrow morning," Jacques said, "before the funeral in the afternoon, they will go on trial in the public square. Have you seen our public square? It is one of the most beautiful in all of France. Come, I will show you."

Jacques led the way to his car out front.French flags flew from both front fenders of the car. He even had a chauffeur he had commandeered. We rode in style, driving to the square and all around. The town was beautiful and picturesque, an old town. It was much prettier than the area around Brest and Paris which I saw later.

We stopped at a public park with magnificent old trees. Graves were being prepared for those who had fallen fighting for the liberation. We talked with some groups of Maquis and heard unbelievable tales of bravery and tales of foolish mistakes which caused needless deaths. But that was war.

After an hour's sightseeing, we returned to the hotel. Richard wanted to go back and see the girls again. Jacques saw the lustful look in Richard's eyes and said, "If you want any of them you may have as many as you like. But you must be responsible." Then, as if to discourage, he added, "They fucked for the Germans." He shrugged.

226

"But at least the Germans were strict about diseases. They were very careful. The girls had to keep themselves clean." He spat. "That's the only part of their bodies which are clean, the filthy bitches!"

Richard sighed. "It's so long since I made love to a woman . . ." He looked me squarely in the eyes. "Well, I'll be a son of a bitch. You damn, bloody Yank. I knew it! You've had yourself a ball. Tell me about it."

"Later," I replied smugly.

Richard's eyes swung back to the naked girls. He selected a very cute, well-built blond, probably about twenty-two or -three years old. She was pleased as punch to get out of that mass of bodies. The girls had begun fighting among themselves.

"Get her some clothes," Jacques said to a guard.

The guard went off to come back with a light coat. He threw the coat over her.

"Now," said Jacques, "you must either guarantee she will not escape, or allow us to post a guard outside the door."

"Place a guard on the door," I told him, not wanting to take chances.

On the way to the room Richard was going out of his mind. He kept saying, "It's been at least eighteen months since I had a lay, and I don't care who she is or what she's done, as long as she's female."

We took the girl into our room. She hadn't said a word.

"Can you speak English?" I asked.

She shook her head. She couldn't speak English. But she added, *"Ich spreichen deutsch."* She spoke German. But her mind was on the serving cart, eyeing the leftovers.

For some peculiar reason, I felt sorry for her. What the hell! We could afford to be generous. "Are you hungry?"

She blurted out, *"Oui,"* and started crying.

In French I said, "Help yourself."

She took off her coat and sat on the edge of the bed, nude. She began eating like mad. I poured her a glass of wine. She gulped it down.

Poor Richard stood in front of her, his eyes feasting on her. He began touching her. She didn't mind. He sat on the bed beside her, placing his arms around her, grabbing her breasts as if he planned to eat her. While she cleaned up the food from the serving cart, he became bolder. She said to me in French, "It has been two days since I have eaten. I was trapped in a villa without food. When the Germans made a break, I was grabbed by the Maquis and herded into the hotel with the other girls." She downed a cold boiled potato neat.

She was a beautiful girl, well proportioned, not a mark on her body except the marks on her arms where she had been grabbed by the Maquis.

Richard was mumbling and moaning, a tiger at bay. "Look," I said, "as soon as she's ready, I'll leave the room."

"Hell," he groaned, "you can stay and watch. I don't care."

She kept on eating, cleaning up the cold cuts, oblivious to our conversation, the expression of a frightened, hungry child upon her face. "She looks scared," I said. "Take it easy with her. You'll probably enjoy yourself a hell of a lot better. She probably thinks she can fuck her way out of this fix and will cooperate."

"Don't worry," Richard sighed. He got off the bed and sat on the floor directly in front of the girl.

The poor thing could see the hunger in his eyes and face. She spread her legs wide apart. Then, she took his hand and placed it right on her pussy. There was nothing bashful about this little girl; she was grateful for the food and wine. Then, she asked me in French, "Will you have your friend wait a little? I want to freshen up. I am more than willing, but I must wash. I am ashamed to make love without doing it."

"Go ahead," I told her, "and don't forget to wash the dirty Boche stench from your body!"

"What's she saying?" Richard demanded.

I told him.

He followed her into the bathroom. She filled the tub with water, washing herself all over as well as between her legs. Richard was mad with desire, feeling her big tits.

"Why don't you take a bath with her?" I asked. "She'd love it."

He laughed, glancing at me shyly. "Do you really mean it, Ed?"

"Hell, yes. I've done it twice myself already."

Richard ripped off his clothes as if I might not be there, and hopped into the tub. He had an erection that was about to burst.

The girl smiled her first smile.

I told her, "We are both former prisoners of war. This is his first woman in well over a year."

She smiled again. "I will make him most happy. But please," she pleaded, "try and help me. I have three sisters and a small brother. My father was killed in the war. It was the only way I could help my mother get food and clothing for them. I had to take up with the Boche. What else could I do? I hated the pigs!"

I felt a twinge of pity. "I don't know what I can do. But we will discuss it later. Take good care of my friend."

She promised.

Richard was thrashing around in the tub. He was all over her. Then, she began washing and massaging him. Richard yelled, "Hey, Ed, Ed, she's washing my bloody cock. This is a dream from the Arabian Nights. Don't wake me. Don't do it. Did you hear me? Let me be!"

It was hilarious. I stayed on for a few more minutes. She pushed him to one end of the tub, bent over, and started to suck him off. Poor Richard was going out of his mind. I was too embarrassed for the poor son of a bitch to stay on. I said, "You goddamn Aussies are crazy!" and went through the bathroom door.

"Thank you, Ed, old buddy," Richard yelled after me. "You're a super good chap to leave all this for me. Thank you, old buddy . . ."

I closed the door behind me, then went to the hotel room door. A guard stood outside, an old man in his late sixties or seventies, hunched under the weight of a German Mauser rifle. I nodded to him and said, "Take good care and see no one disturbs my friend."

He snapped a French salute and told me he had served in the French army in "the first war," fighting at Argonne with the Americans. "I am glad *les Americains* have arrived."

I couldn't help laughing. Hell, I was the only American.

He saluted again. Instinctively, I returned his salute, walking down the stairs, rather than taking the elevator. I couldn't get over how well appointed this little hotel was. What a way to fight a war, I thought; I could imagine how the goddamn Krauts had lived it up here.

On my way down the stairs I stopped off to look over the different floors. On the second floor I ran into my friend Andre. On sight, he came running to me, saying feverishly, "What can I do for you? Anything. Just name it."

"Did you find any other rooms the German officers occupied which haven't been searched?" I wanted more Kraut souvenirs to take home.

"Yes, yes, colonel," he admitted. "Follow me."

He led me down the hall; taking out his pass key he opened another room. Up to now we were the only ones to occupy a room. I was sure the bastard was grabbing loot for himself.

Inside the room I searched the drawers and closets. The room had belonged to a German oberleutnant; the special markings on his uniform, though, told me was something more too. I said, "What do these markings mean?"

Andre said, "He was the executive aide to the general. He rated the room to be near the general. He . . ."

I spotted a camera on the shelf. "Get that for me," I ordered. I was afraid it might be booby-trapped. The camera didn't explode. "Are there other unsearched rooms?"

He swore on his mother's grave that he didn't know.

I wore the 7.65 automatic at my side. I pulled a "Nazi Special" on him, holding the automatic to his head. "I know fucking well you were a collaborator, and I'm going to blow your goddamn brains out right now, if you don't tell me."

"Please," he pleaded in a sweat, "I'll show you." He took me down to the opposite end of the corridor to a setback entryway.

This was a large suite of three big rooms, two bedrooms, a living room and a big bathroom. Hell, this bathroom even had a bidet in it! "Whose room was this?"

His eyes sought my feet. "Field Colonel Rudolph Friedrick's. He only used it for his mistress when he came to town."

"Why didn't you tell us about this room before?" I shot back.

"I just discovered the special key to this room. I thought it had been searched. We are going to prepare this suite for Colonel Marcel. I haven't touched a thing. I swear . . ."

"I know," I snapped. "On your mother's grave!" I began to search the room: a colonel's dress blouse and coat with all his decorations hung in a closet; the decorations included the Iron Cross with the Iron Cross ribbon. Here was the kind of stuff I wanted. I was just another American souvenir hunter at heart . . . Why I even found another fine Luger and took it to make sure Colonel Marcel received it. I also came upon another dress belt. Hell, the colonel had about five uniforms and a beautiful long, black leather coat with a belt and full insignia on the shoulders. I thought of taking it, but . . . What in the hell was I going to do with a coat? For laughs, though, I tried it on for size. It wouldn't go over my shoulders. The colonel had been one skinny bastard; the coat was half my size.

Meanwhile, the two pairs of boots in the closet were very small. So much for that. I searched the drawers, finding the usual crap, photos, French change . . . Then, I spotted a locked attache case. I tried to open it and failed. It had been stashed under some clothing and carried the colonel's name, rank and insignia on top. I picked it up and handed it to the manager. "Make sure Colonel Marcel gets this . . . Or I blow your goddamn head off."

"*Oui, mon* colonel, *oui, mon* colonel . . ."

The only other stuff I found of interest was a beautiful silver cigarette case with Nazi insignia emblazoned on top and the colonel's name engraved with his rank and insignia, half a dozen red and black arm bands with Nazi insignia and, as luck would have it, a Nazi flag!

I took all the loot back to our room. The little guard at the door gave me a big smile as I approached. He wanted to open the door. "No," I said, "just guard this stuff and put it in the room when my friend is finished."

He smiled. "Your friend is having a good time. I can hear them. Ah . . . it brings back memories of my youth. I have not done that with my wife for many years." A wistful look crossed his face.

"Why don't you help yourself to the girl after my friend is through," I said, kidding him.

He was stricken. "I could not do that, *mon* colonel. There are orders that none of the Maquis is allowed to touch them."

"What are they going to do to them?"

He shook his head. "I do not know. Their trial is tomorrow in the public square."

Temptation reared its ugly head. I placed my ear against the door. Grunting and groaning ran rampant inside the room.

The old man laughed, enjoying a vicarious thrill. He held up two fingers. "Twice already they have done it!" He shrugged sadly. "I have not done it twice since I was a youth, a handsome youth. You would not believe it, but I was very handsome in my uniform when I was a sergeant in the first war. I earned my insignias. I was a good soldier."

I liked the old gent, and I felt sorry for him. He couldn't keep his ill-fitting false teeth in his mouth. I patted him on the shoulder. "You are a good soldier now," I said.

He straightened and snapped me a salute. He was enjoying playing soldier.

I went down to the lobby then and sat around until I got tired of getting up and shaking hands as I was introduced to others a dozen times. Each time my rank grew. I was now *le General Americain!*"

My manager friend Andre spotted me. He came bustling over. "Is there anything you would like?" He had brought me a bottle of cognac and a large glass.

I sipped the cognac and approved it.

"I am going to bring you something very special."

"What is it?"

"A surprise!"

Boy, was he buttering me up!

When he returned, well, I'll be a son of a gun, he carried two tins of Camel cigarettes, manufactured before the war, the yellow Camel insignia on top. Though I didn't smoke, a wave of homesickness almost overwhelmed me. I opened one and took out a cigarette. I thought of my father who smoked three packs of these every day of his life. It was like a touch of home.

Everyone gathered around now, thinking I had brought the cigarettes from America. I passed them around. They all thanked me. Many other people had crowded into the lobby. Some were Maquis with wives or girlfriends; some of them even had children up late. They all wanted to see *"le Premiere Americain."* It was like sitting in a display window. I made my apologies and escaped upstairs.

The old man was sitting on the floor by the door as I got off the elevator. A look of fright filled his face as he struggled to his feet. "No, no," I told him. Please sit. Don't worry. You are a good soldier."

He apologized. "My legs were wounded during the first war and I can't stand too long."

I patted his shoulder. "Don't worry. Stay as you are."

"Your friend came to the door and I gave him the souvenirs," he said.

"Very good," I told him and opened the door to our room.

Richard was stretched out on the bed, happily contented. The poor girl was lying there exhausted, but she rallied to start rattling at me in French. I finally got her to slow down. The gist of it: Richard was formidable, and he had made her much happier than when she made love with a German officer. She swore up and down that when she slept with German officers that she faked everything. "They were beasts, animals!" She spit on the floor.

I didn't believe her, but I let her rave on. I was tired. "Look, all I want to do is stretch out on my bed."

She begged forgiveness for lying on my bed. She had been careful not to mess it up; she had taken off the bedspread and covered the pillow. Then, she was spouting the same old crap, begging me to help her.

I dropped into a chair without replying.

Finally, she excused herself and went to the bathroom. Water ran. In about ten minutes she came out to say, "I have washed thoroughly," and now she wanted to take care of me. "I will please you."

I looked at her. I didn't want any part of her. Of course, I didn't tell her this. But after the day and night with Danielle, anyone else was pale in comparison.

She continued to plead. Richard came to life long enough to say, "She was a hell of a good piece of ass!"

"I'm not interested," I said.

"Is it because you are married?" the girl asked.

Excellent excuse! "Yes, I am faithful to my wife."

Now she gave me the bullshit about how wonderful it was for an American officer to be so faithful. German officers were beasts. "My German officer was married. He had a wife and four children in Germany." He was, in a few words, a sexual pervert.

"Is my friend thoroughly satisfied?" I asked her.

Richard was half asleep. But he rallied and said, "My good old Yank buddy, I am completely satisfied. I've more than made up for the last eighteen months."

"How many times?" I joked.

"Three. A total of three," he blurted out with pride.

"You're a champ!" I proclaimed.

"Aw, no. Colonel Marcel told me about your six time marathon in Ussel. Is it really true?"

"Don't believe everything you hear . . ." He was in a contented mood now. "Look, Richard, Captain Jacques asked the girl be returned as soon as possible."

"Hell, I don't care if you throw her out the bloody god-damn window!"

Reassured, I stepped into the corridor and told our good and faithful soldier he should go downstairs and get another Maquis to help him return the girl. I was afraid she might knock him down and get away. I promised to guard the door until he returned.

Shortly he returned with another man, but this one was as bad as he was. This guy had served in "that great first war" as a sergeant. I shook his hand. "Now be sure you get her back down to the room," I cautioned.

They gave me a snappy salute. "Do not fear, we will stake our lives on it!"

I went back into the room and told the girl to put on her coat. She began pleading and begging again. I said, "I'll speak to the colonel about you personally."

She dropped to her knees, grabbed my hand and tried to kiss it.

"Put on your coat and get going."

She picked up the coat and started to leave the room. Then: "May I please have a little more cheese and bologna?"

I groaned; I was really tired of her. "Help yourself."

She filled the pockets of her coat, and I took her arm and steered her to the door. The two old soldiers each took an arm of her and escorted her away.

The phone rang. I answered. It was our manager friend. He invited us down to the dining room for a late dinner with officers of the Maquis. Upon questioning, I learned that Colonel Marcel was still at the prison. Since he wasn't there, I declined and asked that our late dinner be served in our room. He was pleased to do anything I requested. "And," I said, "while you are at it, send up more German beer and clean up this mess!"

Within twenty minutes, he appeared at our door with two young boys to help. They wheeled in another serving cart with a beautiful dinner. Included in the dinner was something I hadn't eaten for two years: real Italian spaghetti, only French style with the sauce mixed in. The meat in the spaghetti was veal; extra slices of veal were on a plate. We also had rolls, butter, jelly and another bucket of a dozen bottles of beer. One of the boys — they were no more than thirteen years old — hustled off to return with more wine and another large bottle of brandy. It looked like we were in business. But I couldn't stand that bastard Andre. Jacques had told me they hadn't rounded up all collaborators as yet; they were leaving some of them alone, like Andre, until everything was settled. First things first. And Andre was subservient as hell.

I shooed him out the door with his helpers; then, Richard and I sat down and enjoyed a late supper.

The spaghetti was in a large casserole. It was enough for four men. But Richard and I ate about half of it along with the veal, washing it down with the beer. We covered the remaining food in case we grew hungry later.

The phone rang. It was Andre. He wanted to know if we needed anything else. "Yes, we do," I snapped. "I want the bathroom cleaned up and fresh towels sent along in a hurry!"

The sniveling little bastard came himself with fresh towels, the two boys trailing in his wake. He apologized; the maids had gone home. However, he claimed he and the boys wanted to clean the bathroom personally.

I felt sorry for the kids. "No, you clean the bathroom yourself!"

He went off to clean the bathroom, and Richard said, "My, aren't we getting fussy! I remember you when we were both back there in that goddamn swamp . . ."

I laughed. "I just want to harass that goddamn collaborator!"

Andre heard me. He bounced in from the bathroom to plead, "I was *not* a collaborator. I had to take care of the Germans. They would have killed me. Have mercy on me, *mon* colonel."

I waved him away to the bathroom. He finished up, collected the two boys and left us in peace.

When I checked the bathroom, I discovered he had brought along a dozen towels of all sizes, washcloths, soap, plus shaving tools, tooth paste and a toothbrush. I had told him earlier that Richard had nothing with which to shave or brush his teeth.

Outside the celebration was still going on. We closed the window to shut out the clamor. The phone rang once more. It was Andre. "Anything else?"

I yelled at him, "Do not disturb us until Colonel Marcel returns. Understand?"

I was becoming one hard-nosed son of a bitch, and I didn't care. The little weasel deserved everything I could dish out.

About 1:00 a.m. the phone rang and it was Marcel. He was in good spirits. He was calling from the prison. "The dirty Boche have surrendered!" he proclaimed triumphantly.

I was as thrilled as he was. Then, I heard the other side of the coin. Over forty Maquis had been shot down in cold blood in their prison cells by the Nazis before it was over.

"What about outside the prison?" I said.

"Many men, even some women and children, were killed. They used their cannon fire and mortar shells around the area, not caring who or what they hit."

He sounded very tired. "Are you all right?"

"Oh, yes. How is everything at the hotel?"

"We have been treated royally."

Then, he asked, "Eduarde, if you like, you can come for the execution tomorrow."

"That soon?"

"Yes, tomorrow morning. There will be a quick military trial tonight. The sentence will be carried out at dawn. Would you both like to come?"

"Yes," I replied. "Yes, of course, Richard and I will be there." I hung up the phone and related the conversation to Richard.

Richard was aghast when he heard about the Maquis in the prison and the civilians killed and wounded. He had had a hard time believing the story of Oradour-sur-glane. But he was here and he had seen what was happening. He became incensed. He definitely wanted to go with me in the morning.

I called the desk and left a wake-up call for five o'clock in the morning with the Maquis officer in charge; the Maquis had taken charge of the hotel completely now.

Richard and I crawled into bed. Richard sighed and said, "Well, Ed, old buddy, this will be my first night of rest with complete satisfaction."

I laughed. I knew exactly how he felt.

– 22 –

An apologetic Maquis soldier awakened us. The Maquis didn't know how to work the switchboard yet. Nevertheless, a car was waiting to take us to the prison.

"Is the hotel manager around, or is the kitchen open?" I asked.

"Oh, yes, colonel, everything is in full operation and has been all night. What do you wish?"

"Breakfast. Anything will do. Probably just some coffee, bread and butter or pastry. Something we can eat in a hurry."

He snapped a salute and hurried out.

Richard and I were dressed in minutes. He was surprised to see me strap on my gunbelt with the holster and gun. Likewise, I picked up my light folding stock machine gun and my beret with the newly-sewn American and French flag insignias.

"Why are you getting armed to the teeth?" he demanded. "I thought everything was over."

"Only in this town. While you were with your little French whore, Captain Jacques told me that only isolated spots have been liberated. There are still thousands of German troops in Toulouse, Montpellier, Beziers. Libourne, not far away, still has several thousand storm troopers. There have been rumors of their moving north, but a courier arrived from that area; only about half the division left, the rest are being held in reserve in the event of an invasion in the Gironde peninsula sector. Libourne is only eighty kilometers to the east. The German occupation troops who had been in Tarbes, Bayonne and Marmand have moved north to Angouleme. Angouleme is heavily fortified. There's no chance of liberating it." I pulled out the map Marcel had given me and showed it to Richard.

He looked it over and realized how far away we were from the invasion in Normandy and Cherbourg, at least 500 to 600 miles, it was obvious. The Allies weren't going to head south toward us. They were planning to encircle Paris, if possible, a great psychological advantage, since Paris was the jewel of France.

"No," I said, "the Germans are a long way from being licked. There's still a lot of blood to be shed. Within a few days in many towns now liberated by the Maquis, a large German unit heading north will stop in those towns and fighting will come again. Meanwhile, all the main forces of the Maquis are going to concentrate on Limoges, about ninety kilometers to the north; it's one of the largest cities in France."

Resigned to more of the same, Richard dressed and we went downstairs to the small dining room where we had coffee, a large tray of sausage, eggs and rolls with butter and jam. I wondered where they were getting the food; I asked one of the men.

"All taken from the Nazis. They had stored tremendous amounts of supplies!"

We relished our breakfast even more.

Richard had turned quiet since our little talk about the war and how it wasn't over. As we walked out to our waiting car, I asked him, "What's wrong?"

"Why in bloody hell are we getting involved in all this so-called liberation? I'm an Australian. You're an American. Our only duty is to get the hell out of here. You know that, Ed. That's what it's all about, and that's why you and I have been going through hell. Frankly, I was surprised you volunteered to go to that Oradour place, or whatever it is. Our main duty is to escape so we can fight again in our own way, not get killed on the ground, fighting with some bloody French in out of the way places. Our best bet is to head south across the Pyrenees Mountains."

"The Pyrenees," I reminded him, "are almost 300 kilometers to the south of us. That's an area heavily occupied by the Nazis. Meanwhile, the coastal areas of Beziers, Sete, Montpellier and Arlese are heavily fortified. Marcel told me it was out of the question to liberate these areas. The Germans have prepared fortifications, since they expect the next invasion from the south in the *Golf du Lion*.

We were outside now, the car waiting. We stood in front of the hotel, Richard saying, "You're beginning to sound like a bloody French general. You're really gung ho for these frogs, though I guess you make sense. I know they want to help us, but all this liberation crap is taking time. I'm anxious to get back to merry old England.

"You're right in some respects, Richard. But I had this conversation with Baccard, after I found the gold." I explained about Baccard, who he was and how powerful he was in the Resistance. Baccard had said there were civilian planes at some of the small airports in the south of France. These planes had been partially dismantled and hidden from the Krauts when the war broke out. If we could locate a civilian plane and find some petrol, we might be able to fly it out.

Richard's face lit up like a 200-watt bulb. "Now that's what I call a bloody good idea!"

"I feel close to Marcel," I pointed out. "All of them have taken a liking to me. I think they'll help us."

"Where do you think these airports are?"

I pulled out the map again; I had circled potential spots on the map. Angouleme was one of them, though out of the question. Perigeux was another, but it had been destroyed. The others were Limoges to the north and Bergerac, a short forty kilometers to the south. "Baccard told me Bergerac was the hometown of Maurice Chevalier and that he knew him quite well. Except for patrols which passed through Bergerac now and then, the Germans have steered clear of it. Now that Perigeux is liberated, I surmise there probably aren't any Germans in Bergerac." I smiled. "Baccard said there was a small airport to the north of there, only about thirty kilometers from here. He's going to contact certain people to find out if there's anything around."

Richard rubbed his hands together in anticipation. "I'm with you," he said.

We stepped into the car, of one mind now, and arrived at the prison well before dawn. What a difference a day had made!

The walls of the prison were torn open in several places from heavy shelling on both sides. The gates were intact, though, and Maquis soldiers manned them.

Many of the Maquis had donned uniforms, and it warmed my heart. The uniforms had come from an air drop by the British; they wore brown OD pantaloons, jackets and berets with the French insignia. They gave us a snappy salute as we entered, leading us directly to Colonel Marcel's office.

Marcel appeared tired. "Did you get any rest?" I asked.

"Not even for a moment. The Germans have been tried. They will be executed at sunrise, approximately thirty minutes from now."

Marcel took us through some areas of the prison, and it was sickening. A very old civilian prison, it smelled dark and musty, especially the lower levels. We saw the mutilated and bloody bodies of the Maquis as they were being carried out for burial. Then, we returned to his office which overlooked a courtyard.

They had prepared the firing squad. We watched as the German soldiers were led to the wall. They were blindfolded, their hands tied behind their backs. Richard muttered, "The poor bastards . . ." I couldn't agree with him. I, for one, would have been happy to pull the trigger on the Nazi bastards.

Finally, they were lined up against the wall. A deputy of Colonel Marcel's read the orders in French. I understood some of the words. It had been officially decreed by the Military Command of the F.T.P.F. that these soldiers were to be executed for crimes they had committed during the occupation and against the civilians of France.

Two drummers stood next to the firing squad. They started the roll of their drums. The command was given: "Ready. Aim. Fire!" The sharp crack of rifles followed. Again: "Ready. Aim. Fire!" The rifles cracked again.

It was nothing like the movies. Nazi soldiers screamed, yelled, begged for mercy up to the last second. No, I didn't have a bit of pity for these cold blooded murderers!

After three groups were executed, an officer executed the *coups de grace*; then, a doctor went to each man and pronounced him dead.

I glanced at Richard. His expression was one of almost utter disbelief. While he said nothing, I could tell he was upset. The sight was ghastly, no doubt about it . . . And it was over.

We requested transportation back to the hotel. Marcel said, "I will join you later, probably before noon. Do you know if they have quarters for me?"

"Yes," and I told him about the suite they'd prepared.

At the hotel, the girls who had shacked up with German officers were being led from the hotel and loaded into trucks. It was a real circus. They were screaming, crying, carrying on. But at least they wore clothes, though they were all barefoot. I was surprised to see they were handcuffed, or had their hands tied behind their backs. Richard's girl called out to us to help her. But the trucks pulled away, and that was over too.

Inside the hotel, Captain Jacques was just leaving. "How did the executions go?" he asked.

We described what we saw.

"Then, you and your friend must come with us. There is going to be a rare sight in the main square in town. All the girls will be stripped naked to their waists and their hair shaved off. This is the mark of disgrace. They will have to leave here. This you must see."

We followed Jacques into his car and drove to the square, a short distance away. When we arrived, the girls were lined up, all of them tied to a guard railing, their hands still tied behind their backs. Meanwhile, I'll be damned, if a uniformed band hadn't been assembled. They were an old band unit of soldiers who were in the army in Algiers.

The band stood on a reviewing stand and a small stage had been built. The former mayor and other officials of the town were on the platform. The mayor read a proclamation: These women had committed a crime against the citizens of France by their personal acts. It was decreed their heads be shaved and they be banished from the region. Then, the band struck up the French national anthem. The crowd of several thousand people sang along lustily; it was a stirring time . . . I looked into the faces of these people. As they sang tears ran down their cheeks. Men, women and children, it made no difference. I wondered if Americans were as patriotic as this. I joined in with them, singing what words I knew.

Once the anthem was over, the mayor delivered a short speech. Then, a priest appeared on the platform to follow with a prayer. A woman standing a few feet from us had shaken my hand and told me she spoke English and was glad I was here. She said, "The priest asked God to forgive these wretched women for the sins they committed."

One by one the girls were stripped to the waist. With hand clippers, their hair was cut to the scalp. Then, they were shaved. Each of the girls screamed and cried to no avail. The change was sudden and dramatic. Without hair, they were ugly.

It only took about twenty minutes for a dozen or so men to complete the job. Throughout, the crowd had remained grim. But once it was over, they broke into applause and jeers as the women were led away.

Said Captain Jacques, "They will be taken to the edge of town and dumped out on their own."

I, for one, thought it was fair. They could have been put in prison or even executed, and I said as much.

Richard reminded me about the sweet little girl he'd had: "Hell, it wasn't her fault. She had to do it for her family!"

I wasn't about to argue with Richard. "Yep, she had to do it for her family."

"You know bloody well right she had to, Ed."

I just nodded my head. It was sad, but war is not a happy affair.

Back at the hotel, Marcel had arrived. We joined him in his room and sat drinking wine, while he bathed and shaved. That done, he donned a uniform similar to what the Maquis now wore, except many decorations and insignias were on his uniform, along with the cords of the *fouragiere* and other honors. He looked regal in his uniform.

Now Marcel said, "I have a surprise for you both. It should arrive shortly . . ." Then, one of his men came into the room, bringing two jackets, handing one to Richard and the other to me.

They were short jackets, just like the one he had on, except mine had an American flag sewn on one shoulder and a French flag sewn on the other. Richard's jacket had a British flag on one shoulder, a French flag on the other. We were delighted.

"Where," said the colonel to his man, "are the rank insignias on Eduarde's jacket?"

The aide mumbled an apology.

"Forget it," I said. "I'm tired of the colonel bit. The jacket is fine the way it is!"

"No! I insist! You are officially Colonel Eduarde! You must join me for lunch in a short while."

"But first," I said, "we will return to our room, bathe and shave, and look presentable."

We met later in the dining room. By now, about half the men were in uniform and the atmosphere was different. Somehow those uniforms made it all official. These magnificent, brave, loyal, patriotic Frenchmen had laid their lives on the line for their country. They deserved any recognition they could get.

After a delightful lunch, many speeches and toasts followed. Then, a sombre announcement was made. A mass funeral of the Maquis comrades who had fallen would be held in the afternoon, after the funeral parade, which would begin within an hour.

Just as we were leaving, Baccard arrived in front of the hotel in a beautiful old Mercedes; it looked like a sports car with wire wheels and extra wheels mounted on each side of the front fenders. A convertible, the top was down. The driver was uniformed, evidently an aide. Baccard was something special. What, I couldn't exactly figure out. I sensed he was very high in the Maquis ranks as an undercover agent. But there was more. I just couldn't put my finger on it.

He greeted all of us, placing his arm over my shoulder, telling us fierce fighting had broken out in Limoges the day before; like Perigeuex, it was unavoidable. The Germans had begun to plunder and steal. Then, with a sly smile, he said, "I have heard of an airplane in Bergerac." We were to go there directly from the funeral. There were several hundred soldiers of the Resistance in and around Limoges; they had been given orders to take the airport first to prevent the Germans from leaving. Meanwhile, if there were any aircraft they could salvage, they were to do so.

Richard's face broke into a big, wide grin. "I see what you mean, Ed, old chap." He shook Baccard's hand heartily.

"Bloody good show, old chap. Bloody good show."

Said Baccard, in his broken English, "What does he mean by dat, good show bloody?" He cast inquiring eyes at me.

I tried to explain.

He laughed.

When we arrived at the square, it was filled with people, perhaps 20,000 to 30,000 of them, jamming the streets, hanging from windows. The stand in the square was decorated with French flags and bunting. Even American, British and Russian flags were hung. The Russian flag bothered me; what in the hell had the Russians ever done for the French?

The parade had started and it was a solemn ceremony. The band had grown to well over fifty pieces; it led the procession, playing a funeral dirge march. It was eerie with a very slow measured beat, dum, dum de dum. At least 300 uniformed Maquis marched behind the band in slow shuffling steps to the drum beat, fully armed and impressive to see. Then came the hastily built coffins. They were in trucks, piled high, one after the other, finally arriving at the burial sites in the square.

First the mayor, in a most impassioned speech, cried, ranted, raved and pounded his chest as he blamed the Nazis. There wasn't a dry eye to be seen. His speech was followed by more speeches, lasting an hour or more. Then, four priests went from coffin to coffin, giving the last rites. Where in the world they had gotten so many flags to cover the coffins was beyond me. Then, these brave men were lowered into their graves with the sound of drums and the firing squad. Taps, similar to our own, sounded, and it was over. Here Baccard signaled us, and we departed. We were off to see an airplane.

– 23 –

As we rode along in Baccard's car, Richard showed me his identity card which the Maquis had gotten him. It was similar to mine. We both laughed at our well dressed photos in suits and ties.

The road we traveled was hilly. We were stopped by several men who appeared to be Maquis. Then, they recognized Rene Baccard and rattled on at him in French. It seemed there had been several squads of S.S. Waffen troopers pass through the town coming from Libourne in the last few hours. They had stopped to eat at an inn; the Germans were on their way to Canors. The Nazis had had two large moving vans and a couple of trucks with them. I laughed along with Rene. We knew what they were doing. But unfortunately there was only a handful, probably less than a dozen men of the Resistance in Bergerac, and they were mostly old men. They weren't combat fighters; they didn't have arms or equipment. But there was more. While Rene would have no problem getting through with his high command German pass and his reputation, we were in a difficult position. Did we still have our identity cards?

Yes, of course, we did. We had just talked about them.

Very good. We should temporarily trade jackets with some of these men. Our arms would be hidden somewhere off the road where the men could take care of them. Then, Richard and I could drive into town with him. If we were stopped or anything happened, he would say we were working for him on one of the farms of his suppliers. It sounded okay. But Rene kept a Sten machine gun under the seat, wrapped in a towel, as well as a couple of grenades.

Quickly we changed jackets, while Baccard told us we'd have dinner at this lovely inn he'd stopped at many times; Maurice Chevalier was part owner of the inn.

The men described the airport as being about six kilometers

south of town. It was actually on a farm and had a grass runway. They understood there were two planes stored there. My heart beat with excitement. I glanced at Richard. He was primed and waiting. We exchanged grins. Then, we returned to the car with Rene, and we were off.

In town, we went directly to the inn, stopping only for a Vichy police check. Most of the Vichy had turned color. They knew their goose was cooked; and it was just a matter of hours or days. In fact, they were nice and polite as they went through the motions, returning our identity cards with some indifference. Then, they said something to Baccard. He laughed, saying, *"Muet."*

They stared at me and said something I didn't understand. My response was a mumble, a motion with my hand, pointing to my mouth and ears, while shaking my head. They laughed and directed us to the inn.

As we walked away, I asked Baccard, "What did they say?"

They had complimented him on picking strong-backed workers who were *muet*. We couldn't talk back to him or talk about his many amorous escapades and affairs. In fact, they were most cordial and jovial. What a relief!

The inn, *Villa de Franche*, was a beautiful place. Inside, we were well greeted. Everyone knew Rene, and Rene knew everyone. We were seated in a combination dining room and bar with perhaps thirty or so other people. Rene asked the innkeeper where all the people had come from today.

The innkeeper's response: "Only a few a night came in the last years. But everyone is out to celebrate. They have heard the news of liberation and activity."

Now Rene asked about the Germans. Had they stopped in?

They had; but they weren't their usual insolent selves. "Ha! The dirty Boche even paid for their lunch for a change!"

We each had an aperitif and the usual wine. But Baccard's innkeeping friend wasn't satisfied. He had rare wine hidden in the courtyard.

I told Richard, "Practically every Frenchman buried his good wine in the backyard. All you have to do is dig up their yards and you'll find it."

The innkeeper brought along four bottles of *St. Croix du Mont*, a very rare white wine. The bottles, labels and corks were ten to twelve years old. Rene opened a bottle with a great fanfare, and well he should have. It was the finest white wine I had tasted in France. We polished off two of the bottles before dinner.

Dinner was a disappointment. It was all they had, though: vegetable stew, a large salad, bread and butter.

Richard said, "You've grown bloody rich in your tastes, old buddy. Don't you remember the cold potatoes, the raw frog legs, the rhubarb?"

We laughed and it felt good to laugh. It was almost as if worry had been banished.

Always before Rene had seemed something of a cold fish to me. But he was relaxed and happy, putting away his pipe and enjoying a cigarette in a holder. He complimented the innkeeper on the fine meal. And he was right. The stew and salad were fine. I had become spoiled. Digestion was encouraged by an old man on a small stage playing an accordion. Everyone was in a jovial mood. One thing for sure, there was no shortage of wine. I thought they must pump the stuff from the ground!

Rene now surprised me. "Danielle has told me you have done some singing, Eduarde. Is that not so?"

"Yes, before the war . . ."

"Do you know any French songs?"

I had learned a popular song, "Maria." I had heard it several times and had looked at the words and sheet music at Ussel. "Yes," I admitted. "Maria."

Rene instructed the old man to play the song. He did, and most of the people began singing along. Rene joined in and so did I. Then, much to my surprise, the people stopped singing and began listening to me. I finished the song, and the sweet sound of applause engulfed me.

The innkeeper came over and said, "*Mon Ami*, would you like for our musician to play American songs?"

My jaw dropped. How in the hell did he know? I nodded.

Rene said, "Most people here know who you are; they know you are not two Frenchmen."

The accordion player began playing "Paper Doll" with a corny French beat. Rene, feeling no pain, said, "Do you know it?"

I nodded.

"Then, sing it."

I stepped up on the stage, gave the accordion player a nod and began singing "Papier Dolle" in French. I completed one verse. The room grew very quiet. I looked up. Everyone was watching the door. The accordion player and I stopped at the same time. Four German officers were standing at the doorway of the dining room!

I glanced at Rene. He nodded to me, saying, "*Mon ami*, keep singing in French. Make it up. The musician will help."

The Germans, two oberleutants and two captains, sat at a table near ours. They wore the dreaded black uniforms of the S.S. Waffen. A captain said, in horrible French, much worse than mine, "Do you know any German songs?"

He had taken me for a musician. So far, so good. The accordionist said, "I know 'Lili Marlene,'" and started to play it.

The captain asked me politely, "Please try to sing it. I am very sad. Please, *mon ami*. I will help you."

The fucker calling me his friend just about tore it. But my heart pounded madly and, yes, I was scared to death. What else could I do? Perhaps, in the meantime, someone would call the Maquis to help us. The accordion player started "Lili Marlene" again . . .

The captain came over, and of all the goddamn things, he put his arm around my shoulder, mouthing the words to me, asking in broken French, "Sing it again. You have a good voice."

And, hell, sing it again I did!

The accordion player and I finished with a flourish, the German officers rose to their feet and applauded. I felt perspiration trickling down my spine in a cold even track. I'd gotten away with it.

Now the captain patted me on the back and said, "I heard you singing an *Amerikaner* song."

The old accordion player was swift on his feet. "Someone requested it," he said politely.

"Ah, I recognized the song. It was "Paper Doll," I have a record of this song by the Eenk Spoots." I gathered he meant the Ink Spots. "It was once very popular in Germany. Would you do it again?"

Rene nodded to me very slowly. The expression on Richard's face was absolutely frozen.

Talk about acting. This was the most superb of performances. I sang it as though I was singing in very broken English, flubbing words thither and yon, substituting French where I could, as if I didn't know English worth a tinker's dam.

The accordion player was perfect. He played away with the calmest of elan, though he wasn't loose like he had been when he began.

Once again, the Krauts applauded, only this time all the French joined in.

"Now sing for us in French," the German captain said almost sadly.

I sang, *"Maria, quand je vous tes yieux,"* meaning, "Maria, I love your eyes," more or less. I remembered most of the French words and faked my way through the rest of it.

The applause was triumphant, the French people joining in to applaud a true French performance. They were helping me as best they could.

The captain stood up, frowning, as if trying to place the title of another request. Sweat trickled down my spine. Rene saved the day. "Come, Eduarde," he called out, "come and finish your dinner. It is growing cold."

Somehow, I don't know how, I made it to the table and sat down. The captain came right along to the table, shaking my hand, thanking me sincerely. Then, he shook Rene's and Richard's hands. Fortunately it ended there. I don't think I could have taken much more. He returned to his table.

I sipped my coffee nervously. At one point I almost forgot to keep my fork in my left hand and knife in the right hand. But I pulled myself together, remembered, and finished dinner.

When we departed the inn, Rene patted me on the shoulder. "You handled yourself beautifully. You would make a very good intelligence agent." Richard had nothing to say. He was white as a sheet, no doubt on the verge of a falling down fit. I wasn't far behind him.

As we drove along toward the airport, gradually our spirits returned. We began complimenting one another on how we had gotten away with a miracle. That was the only way one could describe such a narrow escape!

At the airport, well, there was a grass strip with wind sock, markers and a small hangar next to a large barn, and one of Baccard's men was waiting. He took us around back to the barn, and here was the airplane: a high-winged French monoplane without wheels or prop, canvas covered. Mice had eaten holes in the canvas. Furthermore, the wheels and prop had been salvaged by someone years earlier. Replacements were not to be had, not on this model. It seemed doubtful if anyone would be able to get the plane off the ground ever.

Well, that was that. But when Baccard's man told us he'd heard more German troops were coming through, ransacking and pillaging, we knew what we had to do. We got the hell out of there!

On our return to Perigeux, we were stopped once by Vichy police. But our act went well, so we moved on without difficulty, hurrying back to our Maquis friends who were hiding a short distance off the road. We exchanged jackets, picked up our arms and felt better.

Baccard had asked the men to acquire petrol. They produced three large tins of petrol for the car. They had syphoned the petrol from a moving van which had been parked unattended; they'd gotten away with five tinsful about the size of five-gallon cans. Refueled, we arrived in Perigeuex a short time later.

Captain Jacques greeted us in the hotel lobby. Jacques was excited. Marcel had departed for Limoges where all hell was breaking loose. Jacques was to follow immediately with a car and driver the moment we returned. The main highway from Perigeux to the north was clear, Maquis soldiers all along the way. We didn't have a worry in the world. Then, he dropped the bomb: "Marcel said to tell you he will make immediate arrangements to get you both on your way to England. All is settled in Limoges."

Richard and I slapped one another on the back. We were going home!

Then, Jacques added, "Colonel Marcel said to tell you, Eduarde, he will have a surprise for you there. It is a mademoiselle that will test your mettle."

Rene laughed. "Ah, the colonel knows you well. But I am anxious to get to Limoges. We will all go together." Baccard had become very solicitous of our welfare.

I hadn't cared for him at first. But I had grown fond of him, despite the fact he had been living with that magnificent Danielle all those years.

We hurried off to our rooms, coming upon our manager friend. He greeted us cheerfully. Since we were still hungry, I barked at him, "We want some food and we want it quickly. We have to leave. Do you understand?"

"But, of course, *mon ami.*" He scurried away to do his duty, but not before saying, "I have saved something very special for you. You shall see!"

At the door of our room, the old soldier was standing guard. How nice of him . . . He gave us a snappy salute. I shook his hand and thanked him. Then, I asked if he knew where we could find a valise to carry our things in. He did, so off he went.

We took our time cleaning up and getting our loot together. I had the extra Luger. When I'd asked Marcel if he wanted it, he declined the offer. Unlike us, the French weren't eager for German souvenirs. I couldn't blame them.

Richard wanted to know what I intended to do with the Luger. I hoped to get both Lugers back home. I intended to keep the real collector's item for myself as well as the automatic pistol I had gotten in our escape. The other Luger I planned to give to my closest friend, Lou Dubnow; I had grown up with him in Pennsylvania, and he was now stationed at Bungay, England, as a flight control officer.

"How in the world did you know he was stationed there?"

It had been just luck.

We had been on a bombing raid of the submarine pens at Kiel. Our group was hit hard by flak. Though we didn't see a German fighter, our plane was in bad shape. Our oxygen system had been shot out, several holes were in the ship, plus one we didn't know about, a big hole in the stabilizer. We had feathered one of our engines and dropped altitude, straggling alone across the North Sea.

Here we encountered a heavy front; when we dropped through the clouds the turbulence was fearsome. We broke out at a few hundred feet above the water, limping back across the channel. Meanwhile, our tail gunner was wounded badly. So, we broke radio silence as we approached the English coast, calling, "May Day," indicating we were in trouble and had to get down fast.

We were instructed to head for the nearest base, Bungay, and make a straight in approach. We fired our red flares and Bill Trimble greased her in, one tire blowing and skidding the plane across the grass out of control.

By now our number three engine was on fire. When the plane came to a crunching stop we piled out the exits. The meat wagon was heading in our direction along with crash crews and other vehicles. I looked up to see a familiar figure standing in a jeep, barking instructions to the emergency crews. I couldn't believe my eyes. There was my old buddy, Lou Dubnow, and he was a 2nd lieutenant.

"Eddie!" he yelled.

It was an unbelievable reunion. After we attended to our wounds and our tail gunner was hospitalized, we sat around Lou's office, drinking our "medicinal scotch" and reminiscing, until we were practically loaded. We stayed that way until one of our group planes picked us up to return to our base.

After that, whenever I had leave, Lou met me in London. We'd had some hell-raising sessions and made up for lost time. Yes, Lou would get the other Luger.

A knock came at the door of our room. It was our old soldier. He carried two canvas bags, similar to the military bags we carried our air equipment in. They had German markings. We didn't mind. They were well made with a zipper top. We packed our loot in these bags. Then, the phone rang.

It was our manager friend. "*Mon* colonel, your dinner is ready. I have a big surprise for you!"

We went downstairs, the old soldier carrying our bags. I was embarrassed. But what were we to do? The old guy insisted and insisted; he looked like he was dragging, though the bags weighed only about fifteen pounds each.

In the dining room, the collaborator manager Andre had out done himself. He had prepared brook trout in a special sauce with almonds and mushrooms. Delicious. Dessert was a caramel pudding, followed by American style coffee. Rene hurried us along. It was a good eighty kilometers to the north, a two-hour journey at least, even with the roads clear.

At the car, the old soldier had secured the bags in the detached trunk. I couldn't get over that car. It was a beauty, its fine detail and workmanship masterful. When we'd stopped for gas outside Bergerac, Richard had opened the hood. Even the goddamn bolts that held the cylinder head were nickle-plated. Meanwhile, the paint appeared to be brand new. Now, as we tooled along, I asked Rene, "Where did you get this baby?"

"I stole it from the Germans," was his reply. It was a 1935 Mercedes Sport Sedan with all original equipment, except for the tires. The tires were Pirelli racing tires and gripped the road beautifully. We had to admit that the damn Krauts had the best craftsmanship in the world. Their cars, war planes, especially the ME-109s, guns, tanks and anti-aircraft cannons were superior to ours.

"But," said Rene, "no matter how good their craftsmaship, they are an arrogant, stubborn, inhuman race without a heart." He fell silent. Then: "Have you ever heard of a German who was a great singer, artist or lover? Or who could ever cry at a funeral or wedding?"

It was something to think about; he was right.

We drove through town after town; everything seemed to have returned to normal. There were hardly any signs of fighting. It was only when we came to a river that we saw damage to a bridge that had been blown up. But already makeshift wooden planks covered the gaping holes.

Maquis soldiers were on both sides of the bridge, perhaps twenty of them. We stopped and greeted them. At the end of the bridge, the men snapped a fancy military French salute.

The trip north was without incident, the road open all the way, eventually paralleling a main railroad. It was a north-south line, and it looked familiar, even in the dark. We came to a hill and I remarked to Rene on my feelings.

"You should know this place. The tunnel you and Marcel blew up is just on the other side of the hill."

For almost an hour we drove parallel to the railroad, seeing no trains at all. "Where are the trains?" I asked.

"You did your work well. That is one less way for the Germans to go north, hauling their stolen loot."

We stopped at a main crossroads. French Resistance soldiers manned a roadblock there. They wanted to see our identification, but once they learned Rene's name, they waved us on, saying the road was clear, and that all night and the day before, there had been heavy fighting. When the fellows learned I was an American, they made over me in the usual way, wondering when the rest of the Americans would arrive.

"Soon," I told them. "Soon." Meanwhile, I was harboring a desire to drive Rene's car. I asked him now, and he was pleased to oblige me, explaining the clutch pedal and the gearshift which were different.

The car drove and handled beautifully. It was the first car I had driven in a long time, and it was a thrill. I might have been a civilian rolling down the highway on a pleasure trip. I wished for the gang back at the base to see me, especially our next door Nissen hut neighbors, the Dempsey crew. Old Bill Dolan and his crew had always remarked, "If Ed Cury gets shot down, he'll probably drive out with a French broad," and he wasn't far off.

The instrumentation on the car was all in German. Rene interpreted for me: "You are now up to 120 kilometers," or about ninety miles per hour. Would I have loved to have that car back in the states!

We were approaching a main cross highway and Rene told me to ease up. I went over a small rise, and a roadblock loomed ahead with many Maquis. These guys weren't taking any chances. They fired a couple of machine gun bursts in front of us. I stopped in a hurry.

Rene identified us all; they had expected us. But the German Mercedes had made them think we were Boche fleeing north with French loot.

One of the Maquis at this stop was perfect for the role of a soldier in the French Foreign Legion. He was a big strapping fellow with a moustache and a Van Dyke beard. Richard and I stood by while Rene talked with him and the others.

Suddenly a look of horror crossed Rene's face and he stopped cold. I had heard the word, "*morte*," then, "Colonel Marcel! Oh, God, no!" I asked Rene. He nodded, bending over the hood of the car and burying his head in his arm. He sobbed, pounding the hood with his other fist. "Why? Why Marcel? Oh, God!"

I couldn't hold back; I cried too.

The tall Frenchman asked, "You knew Marcel?"

"Yes, Colonel Marcel was my dear friend. I was very fond of him."

"Ah, yes. You are the American who went with him to Oradour, are you not?"

I nodded.

He threw his arms around me, kissing me on both cheeks, crying with me.

The war seemed very real to me now.

It had been an unlucky accident. Marcel and his men were coming into Limoges, less than two kilometers away. They crossed a small bridge over a gully. There had been a German checkpoint there with guardhouse and gates. The Germans had fled and no one had bothered to check the bridge. The Boche had booby-trapped it with high-powered explosives.

Colonel Marcel reached the bridge, driving his Citroen in the lead, with his three men, and two more cars full of men behind him, followed by a truck loaded with many more Perigeuex Maquis. His car hit a trip wire, setting off the trap; the high-powered explosives had blown the car apart and everyone in it. He had gone up in a ball of fire; all that remained were bits and pieces of metal, some of it fifty yards away.

I was stunned, heart broken. I didn't know what to say as we climbed back into the car. Then, Richard brought me back to reality. "What will happen to us now, Ed? I guess we better turn around and head south for the Pyrenees."

Rene said, "No, *mes comrades*, I know what Colonel Marcel had in mind. I will take care of you. You are my charges, my responsibility."

We reached Limoges, having stopped at three barricades. At the third one, we talked with some of the men. Everyone was saddened by the death of Marcel and his men. Meanwhile, Limoges was clear, except for a few pockets of Germans here and there. The command post had been set up at Le Grande Hotel; the hotel had been taken from the Germans a few hours earlier.

At the hotel, shelling and the stacatto of machine gun fire could be heard north of us. We were met by a handsome young man, about my height with blondish, light hair and a fair complexion. He embraced Rene, then turned to me, saying in perfect English, "You

251

must be Eduarde, Colonel Marcel's American friend, are you not?" He embraced me as if I might be a member of his family, kissing me on both cheeks, telling me how sorry he was to hear of the death of our good friend and noble patriot, one of the great leaders of the Resistance. He introduced himself as Robert De Havilland.

"Colonel Marcel told me about you," he said.

The hotel was quite old, but very beautiful. I remarked on this.

"You have a good eye. It is one of the showplaces of our town. Limoges is one of the most beautiful cities in all of France, with the possible exception of Paris. Fortunately, we were able to get the Nazis out without their doing too much damage."

"There aren't many people on the streets," I noted.

"Civilians have been ordered to stay in their homes until we give the all-clear signal. Some collaborated with the Nazis, of course, and they tried to flee with them with whatever they could salvage. But very few made it, except the big operators who fled quite early to Switzerland and Spain. Most of the high-ranking Nazis fled early, taking their troops with them. That's why we were able to defeat them." He went on to delineate one unusual incident during the looting. A Gestapo major had gone out to the De Havilland plant and tried to take several sets of rare china. But they'd hidden all the fine china in their kilns.

"Is this the famous De Havilland Limoges china plant?"

"You have heard of us?" He seemed delighted.

"I certainly have."

"Would you like to see the place?"

"I would. Indeed, I would!"

"We can go tomorrow if everything is clear. I would like for you to meet some of my family."

Right now, demolition men were checking the floors of the hotel, working from the bottom up. They wanted to be sure everything was safe. The Germans had blown up their command communications prior to leaving. "We rounded up many experts who had worked for the Nazi high command to do this work. They have been working around the clock. They deserved this honor."

I liked De Havilland's style. He was more like an American than a Frenchman.

Rene inquired about the airport. The Maquis had their hands full in town. They hadn't tried to go out there yet. For weeks German transports had been flying in, loading up and flying out, his people reported. Meanwhile, trucks went to the airport fully loaded, then returned empty, repeating the process many times. It was mass thievery. The Germans were more concerned with stealing than fighting. Very high-ranking Germans had plundered museums, jewelry shops, antique shops, silver shops, even churches.

France had been rich in history, tradition and art, as well as famous museums, libraries, churches, castles, chateaus and fine ancestral homes with valued items. The saddest part: The German officers had given orders to destroy what they could not take. Tears filled De Havilland's eyes as he told about it.

Every Frenchman, from the lowest peasant to the highest official, felt as De Havilland. They treasured their art, artists and traditions. "I have been told," he said, "by one of the bishops of the Catholic church that the same Gestapo major who came to our plant had gone to a famous cathedral with his men and stolen priceless artifacts." He shook his head. "Nothing is sacred to these pawns of the devil, the filthy Boche," and he spat on the floor. "I only hope and pray that this time they will be defeated for good. With our fine allies, the Russians from the east, advancing on all fronts, and our other allies from the west, the Americans and the English, Germany will be crushed to the ground."

"Amen," I said.

While we had talked, officials of the Resistance milled around the lobby. Guards were posted at all exits. Yes, the Resistance was in business.

De Havilland patted me on the back. "You must be very tired. Come, I will see that you and your good friend Richard, and Rene Baccard are assigned suitable accommodations with food and drink for your well-being." He barked the command to an aide, and within minutes we were escorted to the second floor to the first rooms clear of booby traps. Our room overlooked the street, nice and airy.

Maids were still cleaning up. The word spread quickly through the hotel that I was an American, and the maids began to whisper about *"le premier Americain."* It was the same thing all over again.

Richard said, "You bloody Yanks get all the fucking credit!"

I knew he was joking. Then, I received a real shocker, when Rene added, "Yes, and even my most delightful mistress, Danielle. How about that, Eduarde?"

Blood rushed to my head. I was thoroughly ashamed. I didn't know what to say.

He patted my shoulder. "I am not saying this in anger or jealousy. I am most happy for Madame Danielle. Perhaps I should not have said anything to embarrass you. But she told me of the delightful afternoon and night she spent with you and of her complete satisfaction. You, my friend, are a young man. I envy you. But this is what she needed, something I could not give her."

I had thought all Frenchmen were great lovers. Anyway, he wasn't really old. But it made me realize how much more open, more advanced and level-headed the French were about sex. This was *savois faire.*

The maids finished their work, and Richard and I made a mad dash for the drawers and closets. "What are you doing?" Rene asked.

"Looking for souvenirs!"

He laughed. Then, he went into his room, next to ours.

We found an assortment of extra uniforms, shoes, stockings, caps and the usual full-length black leather overcoat. The only thing which appealed to me, though, was a black leather riding crop with a hand-engraved silver handle; it was stuck in a boot in the closet. Then, Rene began pounding on the wall. We could hear him yelling, "Eduarde, Richard, come!"

As we walked into the room, Rene said, "You'll like these." He handed me a case with binoculars in it. He gave Richard a large case which contained a very expensive German camera; he knew I already had a camera, and Richard was delighted. The camera was loaded with extras, telephoto, regular, wide angle lenses, and other accessories. It was a Leica, one of their best models.

I examined my binoculars: a small officer's model manufactured by Zeiss, *fabriken* Germany, and they were the best in every fine detail, even to small covers which fitted over the lenses. "Are you sure you don't want these?" I said to Rene.

"I am sure. We French have no use for Boche things. It would only bring us memories of hate. It is different with you. Your country has never been occupied or suffered. I know to you these will bring fond memories that I hope you will long remember."

His room was like ours only larger. There were two chests of drawers and two closets. He had looked in one closet. Now he asked, "Would you like to search the rest of the room?"

We jumped at the task. Richard screamed immediately; he had found a small black leather suitcase with a special lock and straps around it. He started to open it; Rene stopped him. "Do not touch it until I look at it."

Carefully, he carried the suitcase to the windowsill and placed it there. He listened carefully. Then, he said, "One of you go down to the lobby and bring a man who is checking the rooms."

I hurried off to find a demolition expert. It was odd that such a fine suitcase had been overlooked.

De Havilland was still in the lobby. He called to a man carrying special equipment and a tool bag to go up to the room with me. We ran back upstairs.

Here the expert took out a stethoscope, just like a doctor, and used it to check out the bag. "Out," he said. "Everybody out."

We retreated to the doorway, feeling we could jump to the side if anything happened. Not good sense, but we were filled with curiosity.

The expert removed a small pair of needle-nosed pliers and screwdriver from his kit. He dismantled the lock very carefully, section by section. Then, he took out what looked like a chrome-plated retractable clothes rod. He pulled this out until it was almost the length of the room. He attached a special tool to one end, then crouching down behind the bed, he pried the case open . . . And nothing happened.

The case was about eight inches wide, about twenty-four inches in length and nineteen inches high. He lifted the lid, and we all gasped. It was money, French money, in all denominations! Richard lifted out bundle after bundle of the money, amazed.

Said Rene, "The Nazis printed this like they were the French treasury. You may keep all of it, if you want it."

"We don't want it," I said.

"Please take it for souvenirs. I am sure all money will be changed after the war. There's so much of this paper money in circulation, it will have to be done." He smiled at Richard. "Even you English have been printing this as fast as the Germans."

"What would we do with it?" Richard asked.

"Spend it, of course," said Rene.

Richard and I exchanged glances. "But how?" I asked delicately.

"All shops and services will be open tomorrow, after a grand celebration. This money will still be used."

We took it back to our room, deciding to count it. We counted for at least a half-hour. We estimated over a million francs. Richard was in a daze. "If we get this back to England, we're rich!" he said.

"This stuff isn't worth ten cents outside of France. Probably most of the merchants won't accept it for merchandise."

"What do they use?"

I patted my pocket. "They take gold, hard cash." I hated to discourage him.

"Look. We'll give it a go anyway, huh, Ed? Tomorrow, old chap."

"I'm with you!"

We had grown pretty cocky and spoiled by now. I remarked on the room, how it wasn't as nice as the room in Perigeuex. The hotel was old; though the linens were fresh, they were patched.

"Hey," said Richard, "why don't you try some of that Yank influence and complain to the management about poor service?"

"Beats the swamp," I laughed.

We stowed the souvenirs in our bag, cleaned up and went looking for something to eat. The electricity was on, the entire hotel lighted; though it was late the dining room was in full swing. Soup, sandwiches, wine and German beer were being served. We joined the festivities, eating our fill, and hit the sack, emotionally drained.

The sound of band music and people yelling and cheering awakened us. I glanced at my watch. It was nine o'clock. I jumped from bed and went to the window. A parade was going down the street with a uniformed Maquis band, cars and trucks of all kinds loaded with people waving French flags. We even spotted American, English and Russian flags. Not wanting to miss anything, we bathed, shaved, dressed, and went down into the lobby.

There we came upon a Maquis leader, Colonel Andre. One of his trusted aides was Robert De Havilland. Colonel Andre didn't speak much English, but enough to tell us that Richard and I were their "honored" guests. We were to do what we liked and their humble facilities were at our service. In fact, he was placing a car and driver at our disposal with guards to accompany us everywhere.

Rene came up then. He had to leave; he had important business. He would see us later in the day. Yes, he was a very important man. Even Colonel Andre took orders from him. Rene departed with a lieutenant and four other men, all fully armed Maquis soldiers, in his car. I wondered where they were going. But it wasn't my business to ask. Meanwhile, I was delighted to have time in which to spend our money.

Soup and sandwiches were still being served in the dining room. We settled for coffee. A captain came over. He rattled French so fast and his English was so bad, we couldn't understand him. Finally, he called over a distinguished older man sitting at a table with uniformed officers. The gentleman, owner of the hotel, was in civilian clothes, and he could speak English. "Not very much, *une petite*," he said. It seemed that Colonel Andre had told the captain to ask if we'd like a host to interpret for us. The colonel had to leave and he wanted to be sure we were taken care of.

We didn't care. Frankly, we both wanted to be on our own for the day.

"The colonel, *mon ami*, was not speaking of a male interpreter, but of a female," the gentleman said. It seemed the colonel knew two lovely sisters, and both of them spoke English. They had attended school in England and were the daughters of a former high-ranking French officer who had been killed early in the war. These girls were well bred; they had never once collaborated or associated with German officers.

"Did you have the same problems here as they had in Perigeuex?" I asked.

He nodded his head. "Yes, it is a way of human nature. Food was very scarce. What we are eating here in this hotel are German supplies left behind. During the occupation the people who ate well were in rural areas." He chuckled. "*Mes amis*, the captain is waiting for your answer. Take my word for it, even from an old boulevardier like me. I know these two girls and I knew their father, God rest his soul. They are beautiful young ladies, well built and very personable, although very poor because of the war. When their father was killed, everything he had was confiscated and his beautiful villa in the country leveled to the ground by the Boche. The daughters escaped and live with a cousin here in town. They barely get by. But I'm sure you will find them most accommodating." His smile was whimsical.

Richard embarrassed the hell out of me then. "Let's go, old boy. Let's go get the girls and see if they fuck."

"Please, Richard, take it easy. Let's act like gentlemen."

The old gentleman went to speak to the captain.

That damn Richard asked now, "Ed, you forgot to ask him the

important question."

Like a sucker, I bit. "What's that?"

"Hell, you forgot to ask if they both fuck!"

The captain came to our table with the driver of the car assigned to us. "Some of the restaurants are open. I just heard. There's a good one not far from the hotel. They received supplies from farms down south and are open." He handed us an official pass, plainly stamped: HEADQUARTERS OF THE F.T.P.F., THE FRENCH RESISTANCE FORCES BY ORDER OF COLONEL DE SIMONE. This pass would grant us every courtesy; anything we wanted, food, drink or entertainment, would be gratis and all charges submitted to the headquarters of the F.T.P.F.

"Hell, you can't beat that!" I told Richard.

Again he said, "Just tell them to hurry up with the bloody fucking girls!"

Goddamn that Richard . . . I felt we must show some class and said as much. "Didn't you get enough the day before?"

"Hell, no. I'll never get enough pussy, not until the day I die. Besides that, old boy, I had gone eighteen bloody months without a piece of ass. How do you like that, old chap? Anyway, all the time we were apart you were screwing your ass off."

I laughed, understanding perfectly.

Robert De Havilland wouldn't return until lunch time. He would be at our disposal the rest of the afternoon. It was now about eleven o'clock. I wanted to take off, look the town over with the two sisters. I threw a little gloom over Richard's happy anticipation. I made him a bet, since Australians were big bettors. I gave him five to one odds that the sisters would be ugly as hell.

Richard looked at me balefully. "Ed, old chap, you really don't think so, do you?"

I rubbed it in. "Hell, yeah. Don't you remember how he emphasized the well-bred, intelligent and well-educated? They're probably short, fat and ugly. But what the hell! Why not? They can interpret for us."

By now we had moved to a sofa just off the entrance. A commotion commenced. We looked up quickly. Ooh, la, la, we had hit the jackpot in spades.

Two lovely young ladies, in their early twenties, entered the lobby. One was a strawberry blond; the other had dark brown hair. They were tall, wearing the typical homemade platform shoes we'd seen which were made from old tires cut up for shoe soles and braided with rope; but they were very smart looking. The shoes made the girls an inch or two taller, helping us to admire their long, lovely legs. They both wore frilly summer dresses; and they wore them above their knees as the French women did. I couldn't believe our luck.

They smiled as they approached us. I made up my mind to grab the strawberry blond, if possible. She must've had mental telepathy;

she came directly to me, took my hand and said, "I am Lucienne," while her sister told Richard, "I am Pierette," and I'll be go to hell, they embraced and kissed us.

Their English was perfect with a pronounced English accent. Richard ate it up; he was going a bit crazy. Meanwhile, Lucienne took to me like a fish to water. Now, "Where would you like to go? We understand you have a car and driver," said Lucienne.

"Let's get the hell out of here," I said joyfully. "We want to find a nice place to eat."

It was like a Sunday picnic, come to think of it. This was the Liberation holiday and a real cause for rejoicing. Flags were flying, and thousands of people had taken to the streets. We flashed our pass to the girls, and they were dutifully impressed. Then, I grabbed one of the four bundles of thousand-franc notes in my pocket and displayed it. We were on our way in high spirits.

The restaurant was jammed with people. The girls were excited. This was the first time in four years that the civilian population could go to restaurants; everything had been rationed. Of course, word had gotten out about the little restaurant and its fresh meat and vegetables.

The girls knew the family who ran the restaurant. They were smart entrepreneurs. Previously, only German officers and their mistresses were allowed there. I asked Lucienne, "Did many French girls who collaborate with the Germans get caught?"

"Only about six," she said.

I told her what had happened in Perigeuex, a town much smaller than Limoges.

"Most escaped with their lovers," she said. "They have no future in France."

The few caught suffered the same punishment as those in Perigeuex.

"Well, they had to eat," I said, trying to excuse them.

"So did we," said Lucienne. "Look how thin we are." She placed her hand around her beautiful tiny waist. Above, they were both well titted!

Lucienne carried a white sweater. It had been patched and repaired in a few spots. This made me sad. But I was encouraged by their suntans and complimented them.

"Oh, we sunbathe nude in the small courtyard of our cousin's house. We'll take you there later."

We received preferred treatment at the restaurant. They emptied a table as word spread that we were Americans. After we were seated, many people came over and congratulated us to the point where the proprietor politely asked them not to bother us while we ate.

They didn't have a menu yet. We were offered, "Anything you want." The girls ordered eggs Benedict.

I didn't mention my experience at the chateau. Instead, I said casually, "Oh, hell, we have that in the United States all the time!" So, we had eggs Benedict.

The food was damn good; nothing like at the chateau, but damn good. The girls were appreciative in the extreme.

After lunch, we allowed our young soldier chauffeur to drive us around town. The girls thought Richard and I were cultured, so they directed the chauffeur to all the historical places, the cathedral, the museum, and so forth, the girls explaining everything we saw. Then, they took us to their cousin's house, a neat three-storied row house, just like all the others. It was shuttered against the sun and the temperature, which was in the high eighties. Inside, though, it was very comfortable, since they opened the shutters during the night to allow cool air to flow through.

The cousin was a much older woman, probably in her sixties. The girls explained how difficult it was for them to get by during the occupation, since the Gestapo looked for the daughters of the general, so they could punish them for their father's deeds.

Next on the agenda was a tour of the delightful courtyard. A ten-foot wooden privacy fence surrounded it with a small passageway in back to the alley; the girls had torn out all of the flowers and shrubs and planted every foot with food. They plucked a few tomatoes from a vine to show us. Very good. But I wanted to be out and about.

I apologized to the cousin for not staying longer, and upon our departure I slipped a pack of thousand-franc notes into the cousin's hand. I thought her eyes would pop out of her head. "This," I said in my broken French, "is for taking care of the girls during the occupation." Richard and the girls were on their way to the car.

We were just starting to pull away in the car when the cousin came running out, though I had told her not to say a word. She rattled something in French to the girls.

Lucienne turned to me and said, "Why did you do that?"

"I wanted to."

She embraced me and kissed me like she planned to remove my tonsils, awakening desires which had been quiet these last few days. A few more hours of sightseeing and we returned to the hotel.

De Havilland was there. He wanted to take us out to his plant. We decided to go. It was a chance of a lifetime. He showed us through the entire operation, the kilns, how they had hidden people and inventory from the Germans, etc. Then, he took us into the finishing plant, an old wooden building. Two or three old men worked there. One worked on an antique machine, pedaling the small pump with his foot which operated a belt that turned a small round turntable. He was applying real gold leaf to a piece of china. As he pumped his pedal, the top turned and he applied the brush softly to the china. It was fascinating.

Robert said, "We're just getting back into operation. Before the war I had as many as sixty people working in the finishing room where the decorations were applied." Unfortunately his mother wasn't there. But he took me aside, "Eduarde, I know you are single. But I want you to select a pattern you would like, then write me after the war and tell me where to send it. That will be your wedding present when you decide to marry. Will you do that for me?"

Picking out a china pattern was the last thing I had on my mind. But, hell, I obliged him. I selected a beautiful scalloped edge dish with a lovely gold pattern and all the matching pieces. He made notations and told the woman in the office what I had selected. I thanked him very much, and we departed. Over the years I forgot and never wrote him.

The next two days were heaven. We did everything! Needless to say, the girls stayed with us night and day, slept with us, never left our sides. It was like being in a harem. Richard was going out of his mind. We even got around to switching partners that first night.

There was Richard in bed with his Pierette in that small twin bed and me with Lucienne. I recovered from making love in front of someone else. As Lucienne and I were at it, Richard and Pierette were finished. We took turns watching each other. It was a riot.

The movie theatre had opened, and we attended. The girls were extremely passionate and couldn't keep their hands off us, not even in the movies. But that was France. We were even able to spend some of that money. We bought clothes for the girls. I tried to buy jewelry, but the paper money was unacceptable, except on small items. I purchased a white gold ring with small diamonds for about 150,000 francs. Our suitcase was plenty full, but hell, I didn't give a damn.

Baccard had been gone for two days. I was beginning to worry. Then, a messenger came to our door in the wee hours of the morning. I awakened Richard quietly and told him. Before we departed, I awakened Lucienne and told her we would be back. She was upset, but she understood. "If anything happens to us," I said in parting, "you may have everything in the room." She stared at me in fright as we went through the door.

The messenger had a car outside. We rode with him for about thirty minutes, until we reached an airport. Rene was waiting. "Eduarde," he said, "I think I have found something. We have taken over the airport. Everything is gone. But we found an old farmer adjacent to the airport. The old sly one had towed away a German twin engine plane. It is in his large barn." But first Rene wanted us to see the airport.

The runway had holes blown in it, but repairs were being made. The Maquis had captured three Germans, one a young leutnant engineering officer, who spoke perfect English. He was in his twenties and terrified. When he found out I was an American, everything was "Sir, this, sir, that." They planned to return the

Germans to town, lock them in prison, then execute them.

The young leutnant, whose name was Erik, begged to stay with me. He was a nice looking young man; he pleaded for me to take him prisoner. I couldn't. Were American troops nearby? I shook my head. Then, he said, "Sir, I have never touched a gun. I wouldn't know how to fire a gun. I was in the university when the war broke out and was assigned to aircraft maintenance as a sergeant. Only recently I qualified to become a leutnant." He pulled out all kinds of identification cards to show me.

Rene said, "We checked him out. It is true. He was stationed here for the last two years. He never mistreated any of the French slave workers. I have been told that he didn't act like a soldier; in fact, he never carried a gun."

Directing myself to the leutnant, I said, "Do you know about that aircraft in the farmer's barn?"

"Yes, sir. One was stolen some weeks back. It landed several hundred yards short of the runway out of fuel. Before we could take fuel out, we were attacked by American planes. They shot up and strafed the entire airfield." So, they had left the downed plane where it was, far beyond the perimeters of the fence, and it had disappeared. Since things were so hectic, no one had taken time to look for it. "You have no idea what the 8th Air Force did to us," he went on. "The war is over for Germany. Germany is defeated. I just hope and pray that I can get back to help my parents on their farm in Desau."

"I know the place," I said. "I bombed near there — Desau-Sorreau."

"Yes, I know where you bombed." He shook his head. "I haven't been home in two years. I have no idea what has gone on."

"What kind of plane was that which turned up missing?"

"A Heinkel-III."

I motioned for him to come along with us.

We found the farm and the aircraft. The farmer apologized for having stolen it, but he was taking it from the Germans. As far as we were concerned, he was a hero.

Both tires on the plane were flat. Several holes were in the plane. Some of the instruments and the machine guns had been cannibalized. One of his sons was in the Maquis; he had taken them a few weeks back to barter for food. He didn't have any idea where they were now.

I turned to the young German. "Erik, can you make this plane fly?"

He looked it over carefully. "Yes, but it will take a few days." He outlined what would be required.

Rene said, "These things can be had." Then, Rene granted him complete protection; if he could repair the plane, they would not harm him. Rene would see that he was kept as a prisoner.

261

The young man was jubilant and thanked us over and over again. "I had always heard you Americans were wonderful people. Now I believe it. I have an uncle living in Milwaukee. Do you know where that is?"

I smiled. "Yep, I know where that is . . ."

"He works in a brewery that manufactures beer!"

The plane was towed back to the airdrome and locked in a hangar which had remained intact. Rene had guards posted. The German leutnant was given *carte blanche*. He prepared a list; of course, at the top of the list was petrol. The Germans had blown up the fuel tanks at the airport before they departed.

Rene asked him, "Can the plane be flown on regular gasoline?"

"Yes, but not efficiently. It needs a mixture of aviation fuel."

The only petrol salvaged was a drum full of aviation fuel which was put under guard along with the plane. Then Rene, said, "I heard about sixty or so buses stored in a large warehouse north of Limoges. They will have gasoline there." He dispatched men with empty drums and siphon hoses in a captured German truck to acquire the fuel.

Our spirits soared.

$-$ 24 $-$

We had made up our minds that we would leave the moment the plane was ready. Richard and I were convinced we could fly the plane between us. He would fly left seat and I would fly right seat. I had flown co-pilot many times. Hell, at our age, we could handle anything!

Meanwhile, we had been warned by Rene not to tell anyone about the plane, not even members of the Maquis. So, we said nothing to the girls, spending our last night with them. But I couldn't get my mind on sex. Neither could Richard. We were thinking about that airplane.

Finally, about nine o'clock on the morning of the third day a messenger arrived and handed me a note. It was from Rene and had two words: "Ready. Come."

We were sitting in the dining room with the girls. Immediately we returned to our rooms and packed, telling the girls we'd only be gone a few days. Of course, they began crying. So, Richard and I decided we'd take them to the airdrome, rather than leave them behind and arouse suspicion. We all went out to the waiting car and sped to the airport. There was one thing I'd asked Rene to make sure we had: a quart of white paint and a two-inch brush. I hoped he had not forgotten.

They had been able to salvage eight drums of regular gas. They'd mixed it with the drum of aviation fuel. We had enough fuel for about five to six hours of flying time. Erik pointed out he had reset the firing to adjust to the lower octane. So, we were ready to learn how this plane operated.

Erik took us to the aircraft and explained the starter, the controls, fuel mixture, switching fuel tanks, on and on. Then, he took out a German operational manual, in German, of course. But he had written in English, a complete checklist on take off, cruising and landing. He had listed most everything, even to switching the fuel tanks to maintain the balance of the plane and conserve fuel.

We climbed out of the plane to talk to Rene. Immediately the girls started badgering us with questions. Angrily I said, "We brought you here against my better judgment. Hush!" Rene was not happy with us. "Now please sit down until we're ready to go."

We didn't dare take the plane out to practice taxiing or to test the runway; there were still agents around, even disguised Nazis and collaborating Frenchmen. It was too much of a chance to take.

Erik went to work again, patiently explaining what RPM we had to maintain, how many inches of mercury we would have to pull and how we could determine air speed. I found a piece of cardboard and jotted down the information, writing in heavy black crayon. Inside the hangar, he started the engines without any trouble. He'd revved them up to about 2800 RPM and they pulled enough pressure. Personally he felt the gas mixture was fine. Meanwhile, he had repaired the damaged control cables. His only concern was the vertical stabilizer. It had been badly shot up. But he had patched it with hunks of canvas and glue, then, with typical German thoroughness, he had gotten black paint and painted it along with the Nazi markings. Further, he had cleaned and polished the Plexiglas® in the aircraft; we would have good visibility. For better range, he had removed the two Plexiglas® gun turrets, one on top and another on the bottom. These holes he had patched with metal. "Less drag on the aircraft and more range will result," he explained.

Now Erik addressed the flying characteristics of the aircraft. The stall speed was very low. When it stalled, the plane yawed a bit and shuddered; but all one had to do was nose it down slightly to pick up speed. As for the plane itself, we shouldn't subject it to stress. It was not in good condition. But one thing he promised, "You can get it off the ground, fly it straight and level, and get it down."

Oh, one last thing . . . The wheels had to be handcranked up and down; the gear's motor had been damaged and he couldn't repair it. He explained how to operate the gear by hand.

We were so goddamn eager to go, I don't think Richard or I heard half the stuff he said. We just wanted to get the hell out of there and go home. As far as we were concerned, though the French had been wonderful to us, England was home. Once I was in England I'd be shipped to the states; under the Geneva Convention I could no longer fly combat since I was an escaped prisoner of war.

Erik gave us two sets of helmets with goggles, regular Luftwaffe issue.

I shook my head. "We won't need them."

"There is still much air leakage, though I tried to patch it up as much as possible. One other thing. Be careful of your airspeed. Without an airspeed indicator you'll have to guess or feel your speed.

When you have obtained sufficient airspeed to take off, the tail will lift first. You will feel it. Then, you may begin your climb."

Richard yelled, "Hell, we can do it! The Wright brothers flew without instruments. We can too!"

"I'm with you!"

We were both so jubilant there was no containing us. We'd completely forgotten the girls; they were the last things on our minds. We threw our packed canvas bags aboard the aircraft. Rene came over to me. "I would like a moment alone with you, Eduarde."

I could have cut off my arm. After all he had done for us. "Sorry . . ."

"I must ask you to tell the girls to leave. The car will take them to their home. Is that satisfactory?"

"Of course." Before I did, I went to the aircraft and removed the small valise with the French money. I took several packs, threw a few to Richard and snapped the bag closed. Then, I took it over to the girls. I handed it to Lucienne. "I want you to have this. It is for you and your sister, to help you get started again. Use it with Richard's and my best wishes."

"What is it?"

I told her.

She hesitated.

"I'll only have to throw it away. Take it."

"Where are you going?"

I shook my head. Then, I lost my patience. "You must leave right now. Immediately!" I practically threw the case at her, and with that, ushered them to the hangar door. The Maquis soldier was waiting with the car. Richard didn't bother to say goodbye. He just waved from the cockpit. They were shocked and upset. But I had to get rid of them. I sent them off and hurried back to the plane.

Erik handed me two aeronautical maps. He had stayed up all night, after repairing the plane, charting our course to England, penciling the route, marking checkpoints along the way. I told Richard, "All we have to do is get in the air and follow a heading of 290 degrees to 300 degrees. When we reach the ocean we bear slightly to the north."

"What if we miss England?" he demanded. "We'll go down in the ocean!"

"No way. We won't be in the air five minutes before we're picked up."

"You're kidding, old chap. You mean we've got to fight the Germans?"

"No, I mean the Americans. They'll pick us up so fast it'll make your head spin. The trick will be to identify ourselves quickly, before they shoot us down." Now for the white paint and the brush Rene had gotten for me. On each side of the plane's fuselage I painted: USA DON'T SHOOT! The letters were almost the height of the fuselage; I repeated the markings on the wings.

Rene and Richard laughed. "Hell, there's no radio! I don't want to be shot down by our own people!" To insure success, in small letters I painted, Good Luck!

I checked my watch. It was exactly 12:45. We went over our pre-flight list. We would start the engines before the hangar doors were opened. Our plan was to taxi directly to the remaining usable runway. We had seen the windsock and would be taking off against the wind coming in from the west. Here was another break. We would be heading directly for England. The good Lord was watching over us.

"Well," said Richard, "what do you say, old buddy. Are you ready?"

Of course, I was ready.

Then: "We can't go, old chap."

"What the hell are you talking about?"

"Regulations, old chap. R.A.F. regulations. We can't fly this bloody aircraft without a parachute," he joked.

I nearly hit him right then and there.

Rene tapped my shoulder. He embraced me, wished me good luck and looked into my eyes. "I say, old chap," he said with a distinct Cockney accent, "it's been rather good being with you, you know. I hated like the devil not to let you know I was English. But I think you may have guessed that I am British Secret Service. An agent. There was no way I could tell you."

I thought my teeth would fall from my mouth. I had suspected something, but not this!

He handed me an envelope. "I say, old chap, I am going to ask one favor of you. I have done all I could for you here . . ."

"Anything. I'd consider it an honor . . ."

"Post this letter for me, old boy."

"Post it?"

"Mail it. Or if you can take the time, deliver it in person."

"To whom?"

"My parents. I haven't seen them or heard from them in eight years. All I know is that they're well."

"Eight years?"

"I was here long before the war, getting set up. Oh, and one other thing, old chap. I want you to know that I greatly admire you, your courage, your loyalty and most of all, your patriotism. You are a real American and a credit to your country. I know what you did, much more than you think I know."

I wondered about the gold . . .

He shook my hand, a real man-to-man English handshake, and said, "God speed, and God be with you both. Make a good show of it. Show those bloody Krauts what you are made of!"

"Rene, you can rest assured I'll see that this is personally delivered." I tucked the envelope in my jacket. "Where do your folks live?"

"Knightsbridge. The address is on the envelope. If you do see them, tell them I'm well and think of them often." Then, typically British: "And, of course, I love them very much."

I shook my head, amazed by the man. Now I knew why "there'd always be an England." I turned around and thanked Erik. Shaking his hand, I said, "Baccard has assured me you'll be his prisoner and return to Germany safely."

Erik smiled his thanks.

I climbed into the cockpit. Richard had adjusted the seat to fit him. I didn't bother. I just pulled back the window and gave the signal.

The hangar doors were opened. We started engine number one, which fired quickly. Then Richard hit the button and pushed the second throttle and fuel control, starting engine number two. To hell with synchronizing the engines. We'd worry about that as we taxied. "Let's go!" I shouted.

We taxied out of the hangar so fast, it's a wonder we didn't ground loop the plane. We taxied directly across the grass. It was firm enough . . . and right out to the runway, then, down to the edge, hitting the one brake and spinning around a full 180 degrees. We were ready to take off.

Quickly we checked the mags and revved the engines. Then, we pushed everything forward, the plane responded beautifully and we were sailing faster and faster down the runway.

I glanced at Richard. He was handling the plane nicely. I put my hands on the wheel and I felt it starting to take hold. The tail began coming up. Slowly, then, it was up, and we were airborne. I got busy cranking up those goddamn wheels by hand as if my life depended on it. Hell, it did!

We climbed slowly. "Remember," I reminded Richard, "Erik said our worst time would be take off. Be careful not to stall. Just a long, slow gradual climb."

Richard nodded.

For the first five or ten minutes, we didn't look around. We didn't look back at Limoges. Nothing. We were busy, concentrating on the controls. We began to get the feel of things. The plane handled nicely . . . And I caught a glimpse of something shiny in the sky. It was in the distance at about one o'clock high. As it drew closer, I realized it was a fighter. Then, I saw them, a flight of three a few thousand feet above us. They were coming straight in, diving on us!

As they closed in, the flight leader swung around in a shallow turn to his right, then, a left turn, coming in on us from eleven o'clock high. I prayed to God they wouldn't shoot. The flight leader was closing. I didn't wait for Richard to respond. I grabbed that wheel and started rocking the plane, to call attention to our markings.

They were long range P-51s with the unmistakable markings of the United States Army Air Corps, and they were coming in for the kill. Tears welled in my eyes; so close to home, yet, so far away. Then, the P-51 swung around, the two wing men picking up on the sweeping turn to cover him as they came in for the kill. We rocked the aircraft like crazy: side to side, up and down. I didn't know why the damn thing didn't stall.

I cocked my head out the side window, looking back. The P-51s were at four o'clock, then, three, then two, then, out in front of us, and all three planes flew around us, a 360-degree circle. The flight leader must've sensed something wrong. He came alongside us. We were traveling so slowly he had to put his flaps and wheels down to match our speed. I yanked back the window, put my arm out and waved frantically. The pilot pulled back his canopy and pushed his goggles up. He slapped his forehead, shaking his head from side to side. He must've thought we were a couple of nuts; at that distance, I was almost positive he could read our U.S.A. markings. Finally, he rocked his wings to let us know he had read us, retracted his wheels and flaps, and shot forward, picking up his men far ahead. Now all three planes covered us. Then, suddenly P-51s came from everywhere. They were above us, to the side of us, behind us, all around us. It was a beautiful sight, those four flights of P-51s!

I could imagine the chatter on their VHF radios. Undoubtedly they had broken radio silence to talk it over. Having done so, they became cowboys, protecting the wagon train crossing the western prairie. Two flew along beside us, wheels and flaps down, to look us over. Then, they pulled up again.

I glanced at the fuel gauges. We had to keep the left and right tanks in balance. Okay. We felt more at ease now, able to concentrate on flying the aircraft. But compared to the P-51s, we might have been standing still. Nevertheless, we were making progress as we picked up one checkpoint after another. I ticked off the town of Melle, then Fontenay, and finally, there it was, the Atlantic Ocean. And I picked up our third checkpoint, Sables. We had it made now, with the fighters circling, hovering, protecting us.

A P-51 came in close again, rocking its wings, signaling us to turn north. Our compass swung about ten degrees, following him. He rocked his wings again to let us know we were on course. We flew over water for about an hour, then, something entered my youthful 20/20 vision. It was far off on the horizon. Yes, it was a good old U.S.A. Lockheed Hudson with its camouflage paint and the circled markings of the Royal Air Force. They were coming to help us.

The Lockheed passed high above. Moments later, it flew along our left side and slowed down. Then we saw a flash of light, a signal gun. In Morse code, they sent the message: DO YOU READ US? CONFIRM. NOD HEAD IF YOU READ. SHAKE HEAD IF NEGATIVE.

Richard and I nodded our heads, having yelled out each letter. Then WHO ARE YOU? We both let out a howl. How could we tell them?

The window was still open. I put both hands out and clasped them in a fighter's acknowledgment of victory. The response: ARE YOU U.S.? I waved my hand and nodded my head.

They were reading us, looking us over with binoculars from perhaps a hundred yards away. ARE YOU R.A.F.?

Richard nodded his head.

GOOD SHOW! God bless the R.A.F. Then, our conversation became rather brisk. DO YOU HAVE SUFFICIENT FUEL? I laughed at them having spelled out "sufficient." We both threw up our hands; we didn't know. But I was secretly thankful I had paid attention to Morse code as a cadet aircraft student at Keesler Field, Mississippi. ALMOST THERE. DO NOT WORRY. IF HAVE TO DITCH SHIPS WAITING. DO YOU READ? We nodded. Again: GOOD SHOW! Now: FOLLOW US. STRAIGHT IN APPROACH TO FIRST RUNWAY. GOOD LUCK!

And here it was, the English coast ahead. That old German Heinkel-III had hung together. I said to Richard, "We've got to write the Heinkel Company. Thank them for this wonderful airplane."

As we approached the coast, we had to climb; we weren't more than 800 feet above the water. And climb we did.

We reached the coast, clearing the cliffs, and we were home. Hell, we didn't care if we had to crash this thing in the middle of a field . . . But there in front of us was an airfield and our nose was pointing directly at the runway. We threw in one-third flaps. I cranked the wheels down. I couldn't tell if they were locked into place. But what the hell! We were home!

Now Richard hit the lever for full flaps. We slowed down a little. Before we had hardly been moving. Now we were crawling and closer to the ground, the ground coming up to meet us. We passed the threshold, both of us with our hands on the wheel. Steady, steady as she goes. Finally, we were over the runway, the ground just below us . . . Only one thing was wrong. The wheels weren't touching the runway. Evidently the wheels had not gone down. We floated, floated . . . Then came the crunching sound of metal on concrete. We careened along the runway, the props stopped, and we were down, if we ever came to a stop . . . Finally, we skidded off to the left into the grass; all the screeching and noise ceased. We had stopped.

We were in England, and we were alive. Richard and I grabbed each other, embraced, yelling and screaming, "We made it, we made it!"

We couldn't climb through the small window. We had to go back through the fuselage and out the small door. We didn't waste time getting there, grabbing only our bags.

The ambulance and crash truck plus another vehicle with a machine gun mounted on it had arrived. Someone yelled through a bullhorn, "Stay where you are until you are properly identified. Are any of you injured?"

We yelled, "No!" I couldn't contain myself. "I am an American, 8th

Air Force." Richard yelled, "I am an Aussie R.A.A.F."

"All right, Yank, identify yourself first. Name, rank and serial number."

I did my duty.

"What is your station?"

"401st Bomb Group Deenthorpe Station 128."

"What squadron?"

"615th Bomb Squadron," I yelled.

"The name of your squadron commander?"

"Major William Seawell!"

"Your commanding officer?"

"Colonel Harold Bowman." That seemed to satisfy them. The questioning moved on to Richard.

Finally: "Stand fast for a few moments, old chaps."

We both kissed the ground; we were jubilant. It was a circus!

The machine guns were trained on us. An officer talked on his walkie-talkie. The atmosphere was tense. Then, finally and at long last, "Welcome to the U.K. That was one hell of a bloody good show you put on!"

We all ran toward each other . . . Such shaking of hands, such questions right and left, such congratulations, such good old-fashioned solid handshakes and pats on the back. Then, the group commander cleared the way.

Said he, "Where in bloody hell did you chaps come from? And what were you doing?"

I grinned, shaking his hand. "We just took a little time out for war!"

ABOUT ED CURY

Prior to being shot down, Ed Cury was one of the most decorated officers in his group, having been awarded two Distinguished Flying Crosses, six Air Medals, two Purple Hearts, two Presidential citations, the European Theatre of Operations ribbon with three Bronze Stars. He later received the French Croix de Guerre and Silver Star for his combat with the French Resistance Forces in Southern France along with the Silver Caterpillar for having bailed out in combat and the famed Silver Flying Boot, the British emblem for escaped flyers. He was released from active duty in December 1945 but remained in the Air Force Reserve.

Cury in civilian life had been a singer with name bands, beginning his career singing with Patti Page. For a brief period after World War II, he returned to show business, later to enter the furniture business where he became a successful entrepreneur of furniture and interior design. He married and raised a family of five children.

Cury has appeared on the Merv Griffin television show and Sixty Minutes television show with Morley Safer on two occasions. Today he lives a successful and happy life in Boca Raton, Florida.